# Contents

# Author's Note

Although I am an MP and a Metro Mayor, this is not a book about politics. It is about service and family – specifically my time in the Army, and the death of my late wife Caroline. I used to be a soldier, and although soldiering provides the backdrop to some of the book, what it is really about is love, life and death – and all the stuff in between. It is about making decisions when under extreme pressure, about keeping calm, keeping going and keeping a smile on your face – well, most of the time, anyway. It is about the two biggest challenges I've faced and the way I tried to cope with them, and what I think I learned from those experiences.

My service in the Army required me to lead soldiers under the most demanding conditions. I have used the time since I returned from the most testing part of my Army service, in southern Afghanistan, to think about what happened in Helmand province – to try and make some sense of it all. They were the best and the worst of times, and hard as those experiences undoubtedly were, in one respect I was well prepared for them by years of training at Sandhurst and with my Regiment, and by other deployments overseas. But it came at a very tough time for my family and me. Caroline had been treated for cancer and a set of circumstances dictated that I arrived in Afghanistan woefully underprepared for the challenges I was to face.

Caroline's death meant that I was forced to try and cope with the trauma and pain of bereavement. Based on my experiences I have reflected on how grief can consume you when a loved one is tragically lost, but also on how you have to come to terms with that loss and try to get on with living your life.

I met and fell in love with Caroline in February 2000. We swiftly married and had two children. Six years later she was diagnosed with cancer, and in July 2010 she died, leaving a gaping hole at the heart of our family. Caroline's illness and death was a tragedy; one that I had never imagined having to face. It simply wasn't something my life to that point had equipped me to cope with. My professional life had involved a series of tough challenges but none of them had really prepared me for losing my wife and having to bring up our children without her.

Since then, in different places and in different ways, many people have asked me essentially the same two questions. What was it like at the sharp end of the Army? How did you cope with losing your wife? These were not unreasonable questions, just ones that I didn't particularly want to answer, and as a consequence I developed numerous nifty blocking manoeuvres and ways of shifting the conversation on and away from them.

It's time to stop doing that.

For years I did not feel ready, willing or able to talk about these things, even with best friends and close family. I took the view that it was bad enough going through it all the first time without having to relive it. Also, because of the sensitive nature of my service in Afghanistan I felt I should give it a decade or so before talking about it in detail. It's been twelve long years, so I choose to do so now for the first time.

In this book I talk about my early years in the Army, about meeting and falling in love with Caroline and about our life together, and I describe what happened to us as a family when she was diagnosed with cancer. I talk about the horrors my soldiers and I faced in Afghanistan and the extremely testing operational decisions and moral judgements I had to make on a daily basis. This is followed by the aching grief and pain of bereavement and then how, somehow, along with my kids, we made it through to the other side.

I'm relieved to have been able to get it all off my chest, and heartened at the thought that it will be of some value to others. The account I have given is just how it was. No fluff. No varnish. It's the good, the bad and the very ugly. Some of it has been quite uncomfortable for me, some of it very painful, but all of it is just as it was. Describing my most private moments and emotions has been difficult, made more so because I know it will be seen not just by friends and those who might not be quite so friendly, but also, having remarried, by my wife Rachel, and in time by my children (though not till they're older). But I felt I owed it to them, and to myself, to be unflinchingly honest. It's the only way.

I decided at the outset that to protect the privacy of my three children, who are all under eighteen, I wouldn't refer to them by their first names. In order to protect the security of those people who are still serving in the Armed Forces or who have left but do not wish to be identified, a few of the names have been changed. On occasion I refer to people by their job description rather than by name, and I refer to those Afghan soldiers with whom I served by their first name only. Other than that, it's how I remember it.

It is an understatement to say that this book has not come easily. I have slowly pieced it together over several years, amid the daily demands of a family and a challenging political life over a particularly tumultuous period. There have been moments when I wondered whether I would ever finish it, but I was determined to do so, because I want to share what I've learned about the power of the human spirit, about fortitude, resilience, endurance and survival. About finding ways to cope with pressure and never ever giving up, however tough things get and whatever comes your way. And also what I have learned about taking nothing for granted; remembering to appreciate and cherish those around you, and above all learning to make the most out of this precious life.

It has been hard to write, but I hope it is easy to read.

Dan
Barnsley, Yorkshire, December 2019

# 1

# Serve to Lead

## September 1996

—

It was with a sense of foreboding that, on a Sunday morning in early September 1996, I arrived at the Royal Military Academy Sandhurst and parked my battered old Metro in the car park, among the shiny new Golfs and Audis.

I took my kit out of the boot and headed towards the guard room, struggling under the weight of my bags and attempting to balance my ironing board under my arm. The joining instructions had been very clear about the need to bring an iron – 'good quality' – and an ironing board. I suspected that both would come in for a lot of use.

The guard room was stuffed with other nervous-looking new arrivals. Most seemed to be immaculately dressed, either in expensive City-type made-to-measure pin-stripe suits or aristocratic-looking tweed jackets and brown brogues. I began to feel a bit self-conscious about my off-the-peg suit, which I'd just bought in Marks & Spencer, and my Clarks shoes. No part of my upbringing had prepared me for a place like this. Good though my comprehensive school in Nottingham was, to my knowledge it hadn't sent anyone to Sandhurst for generations, if ever.

Though supportive, my parents were bemused by the path I'd chosen and I felt, standing in that guard room, in the impressive grounds, as if this might not be a place for someone like me. That I was an outsider, maybe even an imposter. That I didn't belong – and that as a result I was at a disadvantage. If that was true, it was a disadvantage I was determined to overcome.

I had grown up reading tales of adventure and derring-do, and was fascinated by great explorers and adventurers such as mountaineers George Mallory and Eric Shipton, and travellers like T. E. Lawrence and Wilfred Thesiger. I had been stirred by the sacrifice and dedication of climbers like Alison Hargreaves and Joe Simpson, and closer to home had been inspired by two formidable grandmothers. When I was fourteen my parents had – purposefully – stranded my twelve-year-old brother and me on an uninhabited island off the coast of Mull for the night. They thought it would be character-building (which it certainly was). We were dropped off by a little boat on the island with an old orange Vango tent, some food and water and a white bed sheet. The sheet was to be placed on the rocks if we needed to signal for help, though we never worked out how it could be seen all the way from the mainland, or at night. We watched the little boat chug away, and with it went the sun, soon to be followed by a storm. We pitched our tent on the tiny stretch of beach but had to frantically relocate when the tide rushed in. On higher ground we shivered in our sleeping bags, ate nuts and raisins, and listened to the shipping forecast on a battery-powered transistor radio. Though not exactly Health and Safety compliant by modern-day standards, it was an amazing adventure that helped foster independence and resilience, something my parents were keen to instil in my brother Rob and me.

While at school, I had done a paper round, worked as a cleaner and then as a shop assistant to earn enough money to travel to Asia. I did a bungee jump and joined the Territorial Army. I thrived on challenging experiences, the more extreme the better.

Despite seeking adventure, and in part probably because of my parents' jobs – a college lecturer and a probation officer – I also believed in the importance and value of public service. I wanted to do something worthwhile with my life that gave me the opportunity to make a constructive contribution to the country. Soldiering seemed to me to be the ultimate form of public service, and offered that chance – but it was not an undertaking I'd entered into lightly. I had spent some time considering the risks and drawbacks before finally committing to it.

However, at that moment in the guard room at Sandhurst, I was humbled and intimidated by my unfamiliar surroundings and basically 'bricking it' about what the coming months would bring – as, I imagine, was pretty much everyone else.

After quite some time, Colour Sergeant Boyle of The Scots Guards arrived to take me to join my platoon. Wearing his immaculate No. 1 Blues dress uniform and with the shiniest black parade boots I had ever seen, he half greeted me, in his thick Scottish accent, with the words 'Ah, Mr Jarvis. I've been particularly looking forward to meeting you. Come with me.'

I wasn't sure what he meant by this, or if he said it to everyone, but it turned out to be the only vaguely civil thing he would ever say to me.

We walked, too quickly, through the grand, imposing

rooms and corridors of the Old College, past huge paintings depicting battles won and lost, and statues and busts
of great military commanders. I think the route had been
chosen to inflict maximum intimidation and I struggled to
keep up with him as he strode purposefully along with drill
pace-stick in hand, while I fumbled with my heavy bags and
ironing board. For a fleeting moment I considered asking
him to give me a hand but quickly thought better of it.

When we arrived at the 22 Platoon accommodation (or
'lines' in Army speak) which would be home for the next
few months, some of the other cadets were already stood
waiting nervously in the corridor. Not a familiar face in
sight. Colour Sergeant Boyle showed me the room I'd be
sleeping in and told me to go and stand with the others. We
all stood there sizing one another up and making small talk,
until eventually everyone had arrived and we were lined up
along the corridor.

The Colour Sergeant explained in his brusque way that
we would soon be hearing from our Platoon Commander,
Captain Cleave of The Devon and Dorset Regiment. We
were told to stand to attention, which some of us knew how
to do, and wait for him to arrive.

There was a pause – I suspect for dramatic effect, or for us
to learn about waiting – and then Captain Cleave appeared,
dressed in pristine green barrack dress and accompanied by
a bouncing young black Labrador. Though his attempt to
channel gravitas was somewhat undermined by the dog yap-
ping and jumping about, he spoke briefly about the history
and traditions of Sandhurst. He said that we were following
in the footsteps of many who had gone before us, that 'Serve
to Lead' was Sandhurst's motto, that we were privileged to
have the opportunity to serve and that we should make the
most of it.

He and the dog departed and we were left alone with Colour Sergeant Boyle, who walked menacingly down the line of us stood in the corridor, saying nothing. He then walked back up the line before dramatically spinning around to face us.

'Right, you lot, let's get one thing crystal clear from the beginning: I run this platoon. What I say goes. Do I make myself clear?'

'Yes, Colour Sergeant,' we all instinctively shouted.

'If I say jump, you say how high. Get it?'

'Yes, Colour Sergeant.'

'I can't hear you!'

'YES, COLOUR SERGEANT!'

What have I let myself in for, I thought to myself – a sentiment that I suspect was shared by most of the others stood to attention in that corridor.

'Right. Get outside now, and line up in a straight line,' the Colour Sergeant bellowed. 'Tallest on the right, shortest on the left. You ugly lot are getting haircuts.'

I had just graduated from Aberystwyth University, on the mid-Wales coast, where I'd enjoyed a phenomenal three years. Many nights had ended in one of the local pubs, and big nights with skinny-dipping in the freezing Irish Sea. I had thrown myself into all that university had to offer and relished the freedoms and the relaxed atmosphere. Like most, I'd made some mistakes and the occasional prat of myself, though mercifully all before a time when people had cameras on their mobile phones.

After my A levels I'd spent time in Nepal and India, and was deeply affected by the appalling poverty I witnessed in Bangladesh. While at university I had an epic adventure trying to climb K2 in Pakistan with my brother Rob and three friends. In the summer of 1994 we travelled on the Karakoram Highway from Rawalpindi to Skardu before setting out on the long walk to K2 with our diminutive but phenomenally strong guide, Manzoor. We endured blistering heat during the day and freezing temperatures at night. We battled the unpleasant effects of giardiasis (infection of the intestine with the *Giardia* parasite) and kept walking, through the mountain amphitheatre of Concordia (described by Shipton as 'the ultimate manifestation of mountain grandeur'). By the time we eventually reached K2 base camp we had virtually run out of food and run out of friends – they were now scattered along the route with injuries and ailments, to be collected on the way back down. Amid the carnage of snow drifts and avalanches, a group of professional Italian mountaineers bemused by the presence of 'two crazy Brit kid amateurs' adopted Rob and me, and in an act of entirely unprovoked kindness let us gorge on their magnificent Italian rations. Replenished, we advanced up the mountain, taking it in turns to wear our grandfather's ancient Barbour coat for warmth. We went as far as we could, but at the point at which we would have likely died if we had continued, we stood to enjoy the extraordinary vistas before climbing back down and walking all the way back to Skardu, where we bathed our battered bodies in the cool, healing waters of the Indus river.

This was all in stark contrast to life at Sandhurst. It was a truly austere regime: a frenetic period of training, with no personal time and none of us even allowed out of the academy until those five weeks had been successfully completed. Our first few days were a whirlwind of activities: the issuing of clothing, stores and equipment, the filling-in of forms, physical training and the teaching of basic military skills. As we tried to adapt to our strange surroundings a number of the new joiners decided it wasn't for them and upped and left.

The days were very long and consisted of endless washing and ironing of different uniforms (the iron and ironing board did indeed come in for a lot of use). Many of us slept on the floor to avoid the extra work of ensuring our beds were immaculately made for the early morning inspection: our pillow cases and sheets had to be arranged into what were termed 'bed blocks' and our lockers had to have all our different uniforms perfectly presented and folded to the correct dimensions (rulers were required). We were up well before 6 a.m. for 'block jobs' (cleaning the toilets and showers, or 'ablutions' as they were referred to) and we usually didn't get to sleep until around 1 a.m. Some of us developed near OCD-like tidiness tendencies – because life was made easier if our rooms and communal areas were kept spotlessly clean and immaculately tidy. It's a habit I've never shaken off.

The inspections, the discipline, the standards, the demands were unrelenting. It was a knock-you-down then build-you-up approach, designed to banish what the Army saw as previous bad habits and force us to work together as part of a team. Above all we learned the rules. At times it could be brutal, and it certainly was not for the faint-hearted.

We were being trained to be commissioned as young officers in the British Army. It was a fiendishly well-organised training programme, designed to give us the skills we would need to hold our own. There were no short cuts and it was damn hard work. More than two decades on I can just about crack a smile thinking about it, but I wasn't smiling then. From day one of the first term it was a strict, highly structured environment where we lived in fear of the Colour Sergeant instructors, who ruled the place with a rod of iron.

One of the great Sandhurst institutions – some would say obsessions – was marching, or 'drill' in Sandhurst speak. Marching up and down the parade ground in front of the Old College, perfectly (or very nearly) turned out in ceremonial dress uniform, instils discipline – reaction to words of command, which basically means doing what you are told – and forces you to work together as part of a team. Even though I had some limited previous experience of drill from the Territorial Army I was useless at it and, worse, believed it to be a waste of time. I thought there were better ways of instilling team spirit. All of which did not go undetected and did not go down well. This was made all the more difficult because of my profound misfortune in sharing a surname with one of the leading exponents of drill at Sandhurst, Colour Sergeant Jarvis of The Coldstream Guards. He decided to educate me in the value of his calling. He made my life a misery.

Our first meeting was when Colour Sergeant Boyle dispatched me to see Colour Sergeant Jarvis to ask for the keys to the 'indoor mortar range'. This was the Army's equivalent of tartan paint (a prank played on new employees). Mortar bombs are fired very high up into the air, so I was pretty certain there was no such thing as an 'indoor mortar range', but Colour Sergeant Boyle was not in the mood to argue about it. I went and found Colour Sergeant Jarvis and despite knowing I would likely be ridiculed I dutifully went through the motions of respectfully asking him for the keys to the indoor mortar range.

Colour Sergeant Jarvis had clearly been expecting me and completely blanked my question, choosing instead to tell me that he was not impressed by my lack of effort with drill and furthermore that he didn't like the shape of my beret. Ominously, he said that he was going to help me, as he put it, 'sort it out'. He instructed me to place my head on the ironing board that he was stood behind (hot iron in hand) so that he could iron my beret. While it was still on my head.

I initially thought that he was joking. But he wasn't. I politely and reasonably calmly tried to suggest that while I was grateful for his help I didn't think that was, as I put it, 'a terribly good idea'. But he persisted. It started to feel as if this was some kind of weird initiation ritual. Colour Sergeant Jarvis was a figure of authority and disobeying him would likely bring severe consequences, but what he was suggesting was obviously a mad idea. We had an awkward Mexican stand-off, him insisting he was going to iron my beret, me insisting that he wasn't. I think he was testing me. Seeing how I would react. Probing for weakness. Seeing what I was made of. I felt very uncomfortable but I just about held my ground until in the end he relented and dismissed me.

A couple of weeks later he attempted to test me in a more public way. In front of a large group of other officer cadets he instructed me to run head-first into a brick wall as punishment for (a) being useless at drill and (b) having the temerity to share the same name as him. Again, I wasn't going to do it, but he was persistent. There was another awkward stand-off, until again he relented.

Though some would describe this as banter, others would say it was bullying. Whatever it was, I don't believe it should or would be tolerated today, but it was part of the culture at that time. I don't bear any grudge towards Colour Sergeant Jarvis; the Army is an extremely tough environment and as a young officer you do need to be tested and put under pressure. I hope that what he was doing was seeking to simulate the pressure I would no doubt experience in the future. It can be a very fine line between getting that right and getting it wrong. But while Colour Sergeant Jarvis walked that line, others pole-vaulted over it in a way that was utterly unacceptable.

Seven miles down the road from Sandhurst is the now infamous Army barracks called Deepcut. Between 1995 and 2002 there were four deaths at Deepcut of trainee soldiers undertaking recruit training. All were found dead with gunshot wounds and in each case the verdict reached by the Coroner, following investigations by both Surrey Police and the Royal Military Police, was that they had committed suicide. While it is still not clear exactly what happened, it has been alleged by some, including the families of the deceased, that the deaths were a result of bullying and intimidation by Army instructors. Subsequent inquiries have been damning about the failure of leadership and the culture of neglect that existed at Deepcut at that time. All of which reflects very poorly on those responsible for training at Deepcut over that period.

Although occasionally there would be a 'bad apple' at Sandhurst, I do not believe that the same systemic culture could have existed there, because those two establishments were so different. Sandhurst was fortunate in the sense that it attracted the very best instructors from across the Army; standards were high and rigorously adhered to. Deepcut did not recruit the same calibre of instructor and while some were no doubt highly professional, others were clearly unsuited to the particular challenges associated with training new recruits. Nor was Deepcut subjected to the same level of scrutiny as the higher-profile Sandhurst.

So it is not a coincidence that these abuses occurred at Deepcut but not at Sandhurst.

Sandhurst trained officer cadets and Deepcut trained recruit soldiers. The intake at Sandhurst came overwhelmingly from a well-educated, well-connected demographic. The young recruits at Deepcut would have been, by and large, from working-class families, often in poorer parts of the country. The kind of young people who had neither the connections nor in some cases the wherewithal to stand against the abuse that some of them shamefully received. The Army let down those young people, and what happened at Deepcut stands as a stain on its reputation.

The military is a unique environment and that necessitates doing some things differently, but there can never be any excuse for humiliating people or taking unnecessary risks with their health and safety in the workplace – not in the Army, not anywhere. The whole point of training new joiners, be they officer cadets or recruit soldiers, should be to inspire those young people to achieve great things, to get the best out of them so that they can fulfil their potential and go on to serve the country. Yes, the training must be demanding, it must test people to their limits and beyond, in order to prepare them for the rigours that conflict undoubtedly brings, but there is never a place or an excuse for the kind of behaviour that occurred at Deepcut over that period. It may not have been his intention, but Colour Sergeant Jarvis taught me that.

# 2

# Skive to Survive

## *October 1996*

—

Colour Sergeant Jarvis was to teach me something else as well.

Each day there would be formal drill lessons on the parade square, and additionally we would march around the academy formed up as a squad to give us extra drill practice. Despite this I struggled to reach the required standard. The first five weeks of training culminated with a drill test, which involved both individual and collective marching. Those who successfully complete this test are deemed to have 'passed off the square' and are allowed a highly prized weekend of leave. Those who fail run the risk of having the weekend taken off them. After five weeks of intensive training that weekend of leave is precious – the prospect of losing it appealed to nobody.

I knew that my chances of success were marginal but on the day I did my best. I thought it had gone reasonably well but I still feared the worst. Back in the platoon lines the long list of names who had passed was read out, the remainder were told to stay behind. My name was not read out, and along with two others from the platoon of twenty-eight I was told I had failed. Despite previous threats I would still be allowed out for the weekend, but on my return, along with the other 'drill biffs' (the failures from the other platoons), I would be placed on remedial drill: instead of playing sport on a Wednesday afternoon we would undertake remedial drill practice. I was mightily relieved to be heading out for the weekend but gloomy at the prospect of yet more drill when I returned.

The remedial drill training didn't turn out to be too bad. We were an amiable collection of drill misfits and generally the duty Colour Sergeant responsible for conducting the training would get bored after a while and send us back to the accommodation. It meant that while the sporting activities ran on right throughout the afternoon, the 'drill biffs' were back in their rooms catching up on some much-needed extra sleep – or Egyptian Physical Training (PT) as it was sarcastically called.

After a few more weeks of remedial training we were finally deemed to be ready to 're-show' on the drill square and were given another opportunity to 'pass off the square'. The Sandhurst Colour Sergeant instructors cranked up the pressure and we were told in no uncertain terms that a second failure would bring very severe consequences.

The re-test day arrived and we were formed up on the parade square, ready to go. The Old College Sergeant Major beavered about doing his best to encourage us all.

'Sirs, I am expecting great things from you today. Do not let me down, sirs. Do I make myself clear, sirs?'

'Yes, sir!' we shouted back.

It was one of the many curious traditions at Sandhurst that officer cadets called Sergeant Majors 'sir', and in return

Sergeant Majors called officer cadets 'sir'. The difference being that the officer cadets meant it as a mark of respect, while the Sergeant Majors mostly did not.

The sun shone and the band played, and as we moved off as a squad to perform a series of collective drill movements I caught Colour Sergeant Jarvis's eye. 'Eyeees fronttt, Mr Jarvisss!' he screeched. 'You should be marching with your mates in Broadmoor.'

Charming, I thought.

We were eventually brought to a halt as a squad by the Old College Sergeant Major. We were then called out individually to march up and present ourselves to the Academy Adjutant, who sat resplendent on his massive white horse.

When it was my turn to be called out I marched forward and halted in front of the horse. I saluted and stood ready to receive the interrogation that I knew was coming my way. The first question was a googly which stumped me. The Academy Adjutant, with whom I was not permitted to establish eye contact – I had to stare directly to my front – asked me in his very fine clipped accent, 'So, Officer Cadet Jarvis, tell me now ... who do *you* think is the smartest man here on parade today?'

What I was supposed to say, immediately and with total confidence, was 'Sir, *I* am the smartest man on parade, sir.' But I didn't know that. I toyed with the idea of suggesting that I was the smartest, but it seemed boastful, and frankly not true, so after what felt like far too long to consider this first question I eventually began to stammer some sort of answer. I tried to inform my response with a quick scan around to see who looked the smartest but no sooner had I done so than the Academy Sergeant Major (not to be confused with the Old College Sergeant Major) bellowed, 'Eyes front, man!'

I readied myself. 'Sir, I would say that – on balance – the smartest man on parade today is, probably ... er, er ... the Academy Sergeant Major.'

It was at least an honest response, in the sense that the Academy Sergeant Major, all six feet seven inches of him, probably was the smartest man on parade that day, but it clearly was not the answer the Adjutant was looking for. He didn't even bother to hide his contempt, though I am sure I detected a faint flicker of a smile (quickly suppressed) from the Academy Sergeant Major stood next to him. The other questions, one of which was about where I had been to school, merged into something of a blur, and when finally I was dismissed I performed a not very slick about-turn drill movement and marched forlornly back to join the rest of the squad. I was certain that I had failed again. It seems ridiculous now to have felt so downcast at such a relatively trivial thing, but in that moment I felt genuinely gutted.

Back in the squad I was told to stand 'at ease' and I did so in a way that betrayed both failure and despair as I inwardly seethed at the prospect of further disgrace. At that point, and while another officer cadet grappled with the 'Who's the smartest man?' question, Colour Sergeant Jarvis sauntered over towards me. I assumed it was to gloat. I steeled myself for his withering criticism and for the torrent of abuse that was undoubtedly coming my way. The drill god was readying himself to cast judgement on my complete and continuing inability to grasp even the very basics of his sacred religion.

Given that the parade was still in process, Colour Sergeant Jarvis did not want to disturb the Academy Sergeant Major or Adjutant so was not able to openly bawl at me; instead he moved to hover menacingly just behind me before leaning forward to whisper quietly into my ear.

Like me, he also clearly thought I had failed, but rather than take the opportunity to rub my nose in it, as I had anticipated, he just gently whispered into my ear a few simple but sincerely expressed words that have stayed with me ever since, words which came as an extraordinary surprise to me.

'Fuck it, Mr Jarvis, sir, it's only drill – it doesn't *really* matter. Don't worry about it.'

I could not believe it. Here was *Mr Drill*, who had harangued me for weeks to the point of humiliation, seemingly now quietly accepting that it didn't really matter after all. He was right of course – it *was* only drill – and he had taught me another very useful lesson, about perspective, and how you need to work out what is really important and what is not. I have never forgotten it.

Somehow I passed the drill test – although everyone else did too – and at last I was able to focus on those aspects of soldiering that I considered to be more worthwhile.

Sandhurst continued to be punishingly hard graft, but there were lighter moments – including an incident now enshrined in Sandhurst folklore when a cadet was instructed to march off the parade square and apologise for some minor infraction to a big statue of Queen Victoria at the edge of the parade ground. This was humour Sandhurst style. The cadet marched off purposefully, appeared to have a brief conversation with the statue, and then turned and ran off towards the platoon lines as fast as his little legs could carry him, with a very irate Colour Sergeant shouting, 'And where the eff do you think you are going to, sir? You, sir! Sir! Get. Back. Here. Sir! Now, sir!' The cadet turned and shouted words that have long entered into Sandhurst's history: 'But Colour Sergeant, Queen Victoria has given me the rest of the afternoon off!'

On one very cold winter morning, an overseas cadet from Qatar decided to keep his pyjamas on under his ceremonial No. 1 Blues dress uniform (many of the overseas cadets who came from predominantly warm climates understandably found the British weather particularly tough to deal with). During an inspection before an important parade his old-fashioned striped pyjama bottom somehow flapped out from the bottom of his trouser leg. In the court of Sandhurst, this was a heinous crime about which some got very excited indeed. The cadet was sent off in disgrace to change before being made to march around the square for a very, very long time.

Sandhurst is divided into three long terms. While the Junior term focuses on the bullshit of drill and the basics of learning to look after your equipment and yourself (note the order), the Intermediate and Senior terms teach you military skills and knowledge and consist of a series of long and demanding training exercises. Fortunately (at least for me), at the end of the Junior term, though the officer cadets all stay together as part of their platoon – 22 Platoon, Somme Company in our case – a new set of Directing Staff are appointed. This meant we moved from Old to New College and parted company not just with Colour Sergeant Jarvis but with Captain Cleave and Colour Sergeant Boyle who were succeeded by Captain Cummins and Colour Sergeant Gargan.

Captain Henry Cummins was an archetypal Cavalry officer from The Scots Dragoon Guards. He was posh, old-fashioned, flamboyant but fair. Colour Sergeant Frank Gargan was a down-to-earth, no-nonsense and highly respected Non Commissioned Officer (NCO) from The Parachute Regiment. (In all parts of the Army, NCOs were promoted from the ranks having passed basic recruit training, and started as Privates. Commissioned Officers had passed the commissioning course at Sandhurst and been commissioned as Second Lieutenants in their respective units.) Though like chalk and cheese, they formed a strong team and were determined to make the training as useful and operationally focused as possible. They expected total commitment from us, but wanted us to succeed and were determined that we would. It felt like a breath of fresh air after the stifling atmosphere of the Junior term in Old College.

The pace of life steadied a little which offered opportunities to get to know other cadets from other platoons. I became firm friends with Officer Cadet David Blakeley, and our shared comprehensive school background meant we soon became known as the Marks & Spencer brothers. Also in my intake was a young cadet who was destined to be commissioned into the Household Cavalry Regiment. His name then was James Blount, now better known as the singer James Blunt. In his capacity as duty officer cadet, 'Blunty' once told me off for coming back a bit late one night, which with the benefit of hindsight wasn't particularly rock 'n' roll of him, but he was good value and regularly entertained us all by playing his guitar and singing.

And then there was Briggsy – Officer Cadet Briggs, for whom the Army expression 'social hand-grenade' could have been invented. Briggsy was hard as nails and very determined. He was an exceptionally capable soldier in the field but a nightmare to manage in camp. He was no fool, but his constant misdemeanours, lateness and scruffy appearance meant he was almost permanently placed on Restrictions of Privileges (RoPs), which meant that he was required to wear a special white belt (the Sandhurst equivalent of a dunce's hat) to demonstrate to everyone that he was a 'defaulter'. This involved the bind of an additional 10 p.m. nightly parade to have offending items of kit re-inspected, and generally to be mucked about as a punishment for what was in his case a very wide variety of transgressions. On a daily basis our instructors would revel in reminding us that Sandhurst's motto was 'Serve to Lead'. On an equally regular basis, Briggsy would offer some more practical advice by helpfully reminding us that its unofficial motto was 'Skive to Survive'. The logic being that the demands of the course were relentless, so unless you protected yourself by occasionally, when out of the spotlight, swerving and skiving, you just wouldn't survive.

Briggsy had first come to prominence during an official platoon night out. As part of the process by which we were schooled as to how to behave properly at social functions, Captain Cummins had arranged for us to travel from Sandhurst for drinks at the Cavalry and Guards Club in London. Earlier that day we all had our suits inspected. We lined up in the corridor and in turn presented ourselves for him to pass judgement on our attire. When he saw me there was a sharp intake of breath from him; my Marks & Spencer suit was deemed not to be 'sufficiently officer-like'. I was firmly instructed to buy one that was. I was also told that my shoes were 'unbecoming' and they would have to go as well.

That night we stood self-consciously in the club bar sipping drinks. Most of the platoon, keenly aware of our surroundings, were on their best behaviour. Not so Briggsy. He had clearly gone well in excess of the suggested two-drink rule when he boisterously announced to the platoon and anyone else within earshot that he was going to show us all his party trick. I could see Captain Cummins tense, fearing the worst, but before either he or Colour Sergeant

Gargan could intervene, Briggsy had swung into action. In his hand was a glass of champagne. Quick as a flash he downed it in one. He then – in front of everyone – proceeded to urinate into the glass. He downed that in one too. Now on a roll, he then bit into the glass so hard that it broke, and chewed on the shards before swallowing them. All of them.

It was definitely time for us to leave. We boarded the coach in stony silence. We knew there was trouble brewing. To nobody's surprise, Officer Cadet Briggs found himself stood outside the Sandhurst Commandant's office first thing next morning. We fully expected him to be kicked out.

Briggsy eventually returned looking forlorn.

'End of the line for me – I've been chucked out,' he announced.

'You're kidding?' I said, though none of us were surprised.

Briggsy explained that the Commandant had said that his behaviour had been disgraceful and that he'd brought both Sandhurst and the Army into disrepute. The Commandant had apparently added that while he might have expected that kind of depravity from a comprehensive-schooled boy, Briggsy had been to a public school and therefore he should have known better. This annoyed me, but it wasn't the moment to make a fuss about it.

Briggsy slunk away, then spun round and shouted, 'Ha, got yah! He's not kicking me out ... but I have been placed on RoPs for the rest of the course.'

We breathed a sigh of relief – the 'social hand-grenade' had survived to explode another day.

The discipline fostered, as it was meant to, a great sense of camaraderie, and we forged lasting friendships on the training grounds, where we'd compete on ever quicker and longer endurance runs with more and more weight carried in our rucksacks, or 'bergans'.

At 6 a.m. we would form up outside our lines in our running kit. Woe betide anyone who was late. It was not sufficient just to be on time, we had to be there *five minutes before*. We were told in a very matter-of-fact way that in the Army you get there *five minutes before*. It was explained that in war, if you're part of the team providing the fire support that enables the main attack, not being in the right place at the right time would have a catastrophic effect and people would die as a consequence. It focused the mind on the importance of punctuality. Ever since I have hated being late for anything, however trivial.

We would run through the grounds of Sandhurst, out the large back gate and on to the training area, an extensive patch of open heath land named Barossa. We would head to a particular spot called Saddleback Hill which was not only used by the Ministry of Defence (MoD) but had also become an improvised BMX bike racing circuit frequented by some of the local kids.

We would race each other round a circuit, lap after lap after lap. This was taken very seriously. We would all line up on the start line, like gladiators about to enter the Colosseum. Colour Sergeant Gargan would remind us about the importance both of fitness and of the competitive spirit – 'the will to win' as he described it. As he spoke the words 'Away you go, gentlemen' we would pelt down the circuit, our lungs drawing in air as quickly as we could. I would compete to win alongside others in the platoon: Dave 'Rock 'n' Roll' Croall, Paul 'Scouse' Maguire, Jonny 'the boy' Lacken.

As well as fitness and the practical aspects of the course – tactics, weapons, signals, camouflage and concealment, navigation, Chemical, Biological, Radiological and Nuclear (CBRN) warfare – we also spent time learning and talking

about the 'values and standards' of the British Army: courage, discipline, self-commitment, integrity, respect and
loyalty. We discussed international relations and military
history. We were taught how to write official and non-
official letters. This was taken very seriously, and a real
letter I had written requesting permission to attend my
grandfather's funeral was returned to me covered in red ink
corrections. A perfect example of how, sometimes, some
Army people can't see the wood for the trees.

Many of the activities were undertaken at platoon level.
There were three platoons in each company. One of the
companies had a female platoon. The women in it were a
seriously professional and tough bunch. They needed to be,
because they had to contend with a degree of institutional
sexism. There were some unreconstructed characters who
tried to take the piss out of them and referred to them as
'lumpy jumpers'. The Army was at that time a largely male-
dominated environment. It still is, albeit not to so great an
extent; as with other professions, women have struggled to
achieve equality of opportunity. A climate of (at the very
least) everyday sexism pervaded, and there were some who
treated women as if they were living in the 1950s and not
on the cusp of the twenty-first century.

A debate raged not just about whether women could
serve on the front line (they were restricted to certain corps
and units that traditionally were in support of activities on
the front line) but whether they should. In his own imita-
ble way, Colour Sergeant Gargan described several of the
women serving on covert operations as being some of the
'scariest, meanest bastards' he had ever met, which left us
in no doubt about the ability of women to cope with the
rigours and demands of front-line soldiering.

*

As part of the training syllabus, the Colour Sergeants would talk to us about preparing ourselves mentally for what awaited us in the Army. That was when I was introduced to the concept of a 'bank account of courage', by Colour Sergeant Gargan.

The platoon were all sitting round in a circle in the common room after yet another long day of training, wearing our green overalls and polishing our black ceremonial 'George' boots. You had to dab a cloth in Kiwi black shoe polish, then dip it in water before gently applying it to the boot in tiny circular movements, over and over again. And again and again and again, until you could literally see your own face, sort of smiling back at you, from the surface of the boot.

The Platoon Commander had gone home for the evening, so things were a bit more relaxed and the Colour Sergeant was supervising and offering advice on how to make our boots even shinier. Not being the ceremonial creature that Colour Sergeant Boyle had been, he got bored of that after a while, because when one of the cadets plucked up the courage to ask him what it was really like to serve on the front line – a question we half expected him to deem impertinent, or off-limits – he started to tell us about his experiences.

In an understated way, without underlining the risks and challenges of what we knew had been a demanding and dangerous deployment, he talked us through his most recent operational tour in Northern Ireland. Still dabbing at our boots, we listened intently. He spoke of the detail and tempo of life on operations, of the camaraderie and team spirit that came with it. And then he said, 'But it takes its toll. However tough you might think you are, in the end it all catches up with you.'

'What do you mean, Colour Sergeant?' someone asked.

'There's only so many times you can put your head into the lion's mouth before it bites you.'

He paused for a moment, took a seat.

'I can best describe it in this way: it's a bit like a bank account. A bank account of courage. When you deploy on an operation, you are fit, ready and able, your account is well in the black. The longer you're there, the more risk, danger and hardship you experience, the more you're worn down and the more you draw from that account – and the more you go into the red. In the end, if you're not careful, you'll be overdrawn, spent. That's when the problems begin.

'It happened in World War One. Some men just had too much time in the trenches on the front line. They called it shell-shock back then. The tragedy of it was that many of those men, the ones that supposedly legged it, were branded as deserters. But often they were the bravest, the ones who exposed themselves to danger time and time again. The stretcher-bearers, say, who went into no-man's land each night to recover casualties. Night after night after night.'

He paused again. We had all stopped dabbing at our boots. Everyone was listening intently.

'But in the end, mark my words, it'll catch up with you, if you let it.

'Anyway, enough of all that, pack up your kit and get yourselves away to your beds.'

He stood up and started walking out of the room, at which point we all stood up, as was the custom. As he passed me, he stopped and peered intently at my face. In his camouflage combat fatigues with a maroon stable belt and with his maroon beret sticking out of his pocket, he looked every inch the archetypal paratrooper.

'You might,' he said, 'want to put some moisturiser on

your face, Mr Jarvis, sir. Your skin is looking dry' (a result of the harsh shaving regime at Sandhurst). Solemnly he added: 'Even paratroopers use moisturiser.'

'Will do, Colour Sergeant!'

Everybody fell about laughing.

# 3

# The Coping Box

## *June 1997*

—

It was also Colour Sergeant Gargan who introduced us to the concept of the coping box. In the last few weeks at Sandhurst, everybody's thoughts turn to what's coming next as the cadets prepare themselves for their first posting in the Army. For some, me included, this meant more training, but others were destined to go straight to their regiments, and some of those were already deployed on operations, either in Northern Ireland, the Balkans or Cyprus.

In many of our lessons we were encouraged to discuss leadership and how to apply it in a military context. One of the great challenges for newly commissioned officers is taking command of a platoon of soldiers nearly all of whom will have more soldiering experience than they do. While a young officer 'commands' the platoon, the reality, in the early days, is that it's the Platoon Sergeant – the senior NCO – who makes the running and ensures that things actually happen.

We were advised not to dive straight in, but to listen and learn from the Platoon Sergeant; to make the most of their experience and get the measure of things before seeking to make changes or take big decisions. A Second Lieutenant in the British Army has a difficult job, in that they carry the rank that brings responsibility without the experience needed to underpin it.

After a long session discussing the art of leadership in the Churchill Hall (nicknamed 'the largest sleeping bag in the British Army', because its stuffy, warm atmosphere makes it very hard for exhausted cadets to stay awake after a long day's training), a few of us gathered around Colour Sergeant Gargan for some less formal instruction on life after Sandhurst.

'It's going to be tough, gentlemen,' he said. 'Great challenges await. But your training here has been excellent and you should all do well and give a good account of yourselves.'

One of the cadets had just found out that he would be deploying straight out to Northern Ireland, and it was obvious that he was worried. Colour Sergeant Gargan paused, apparently considering his case.

'Gentlemen, this is why the motto is "Serve to Lead",' he told us. 'You are the leaders. When things go wrong, when the shit hits the fan, when the bullets are flying at you and your troops, when there is fear and confusion – it will be *you* that your soldiers look to for leadership. And *you* must provide it. In peacetime, the relationship is different; but in war, in that moment of chaos and fear, it will fall to *you* to try and show leadership and bring some order to the situation.

'That can be hard over longer periods of time, because you get worn down by it all. The way I've always got myself through it is by putting all my worries, my troubles, in a box – what I call a coping box. When you're in the heat of an operation, when your mates are being killed and maimed, you don't have time to grieve, don't have time to think too deeply about what's happening. You just have to get on with it. Better to store it all away in that box, and deal with it later. When you get back, maybe then you can open it up and deal with it.'

The Senior term was mostly spent on long, arduous training exercises. We spent exhausting days and nights digging trenches on Salisbury Plain. We shivered on the Sennybridge training area in South Wales, where sometimes it was so cold that to avoid hypothermia we would cuddle up to share body heat with the person next to us in the trench. We deployed on exercise to Germany where we lived in a wet forest for two weeks and went night after night without sleep. It reached the stage where all of us in the platoon were delirious, to the point that we were hallucinating, seeing weird things that simply weren't there, because we were so tired. While on sentry duty in the dead of night I was convinced I'd seen a herd of pink elephants wander through the trees in front of me.

The sleep deprivation was a deliberate ploy – to test us to breaking point and beyond. When you're exhausted, when you haven't slept properly for days, you make mistakes, and it was on those long, gruelling exercises that we really learned about and came to understand the importance of morale. We'd had lectures on morale in the classroom at Sandhurst, but there's nothing like not sleeping for three days to demonstrate the point practically.

Napoleon said: 'An army's effectiveness depends on its size, training, experience and morale, and morale is worth more than any of the other factors combined.' He was right. Morale is a state of mind. With it, you can achieve great things – even if people are dog tired. Without it, you are fighting an uphill battle. We also learned to appreciate the value of humour, about being able to lighten the mood with a quip or banter, even when you are dead on your feet. And never to forget the value of a good hot brew. However bad the moment, it was always improved with a mug of piping-hot sweet tea. It not only quenches the thirst but heals the soul.

After nearly a year, the course drew to a close. A handful of cadets were told they weren't yet ready to be commissioned and were 'back-termed' to repeat the final term and all of those exercises to give them more time to develop. A few were discharged from the Army altogether, as they were deemed not suitable for commissioning. The rest of us were commissioned as Second Lieutenants into our respective regiments and corps of the British Army.

I was to be commissioned into The Parachute Regiment. Lots of cadets wanted to join, and although I hugely admired the Gurkhas (a regiment where all the soldiers are recruited from Nepal) I had wanted to join the Paras for years. They were considered to be an elite within the Army. Their reputation for highly professional and robust physical standards was legendary and all aspiring entrants to the Regiment had to pass an arduous physical course called P-Company (the 'P' stands for Pegasus, the winged horse emblem of Airborne Forces) before being awarded their coveted red beret.

As a fall-back plan I had looked into joining one of the county regiments, The Worcestershire and Sherwood Foresters, and had gone for an interview with the crusty Regimental Colonel responsible for recruiting their officers. The feedback I eventually received was that 'in our regiment, the *officers* come from Worcestershire and the *soldiers* come from Nottingham'. My Marks & Spencer suit had struck again.

Competition to gain entry to the Paras was fierce. I underwent a very rigorous interview with a panel led by the fearsome General Sir Huw Pike, who had commanded 3 Para during the Falklands War. The General fixed his beady blue eyes on me as he and the panel analysed every single aspect of my character and forensically examined my motivations for wanting to join. Refreshingly, they seemed uninterested in where I had gone to school and were much more interested in what I could actually do. The bottom line was that they needed to satisfy themselves that I had what it takes to lead paratroopers in war. They decided that I had, and they offered me a commission in the Regiment.

On the final day the entire Sandhurst Academy forms up for the very grand sovereign's commissioning parade, which culminates with all those cadets being commissioned slow-marching up the steps of Old College and through the grand entrance door. The Academy Adjutant ends the parade by riding his horse up the same steps and following on into the Old College. That night the commissioning ball takes place. The officer cadets arrive in their new regimental mess dress uniforms with ribbons over the Second Lieutenant rank pips they are now proudly sporting. At midnight, as the fireworks go off, they officially become commissioned and the ribbons are removed. It is quite a moment. The following morning, all the newly commissioned officers get kicked out of bed with very sore heads in order to go and clear up the mess from the night before.

And that was the end. We were finished. It had been hard going, but I had learned a lot about myself in terms of strengths and weaknesses, and about command, control and communication. I had been schooled to be comfortable with complexity and had been coached to develop my own leadership style. I thought long and hard about what it would be like to lead soldiers and how to win their respect and maybe even their admiration. I had come to understand why the core values of courage, discipline, self-commitment, integrity, respect and loyalty really mattered. They weren't just words, old-fashioned notions, but concepts to live your life by. I believed it then. I believe it now. Indeed, these days, as I become more experienced in a different form of public service – that of politics – I wish that all public servants lived by such a creed. We have Nolan's 'Seven Principles of Public Life' – Selflessness, Integrity, Objectivity, Accountability, Openness, Honesty and Leadership – but from my experience in politics, they are, too often, just words, and, to our collective shame, rarely lived by. Aspects of the training had been old-fashioned, and there was an undercurrent of sexism (the women cadets were routinely patronised) and racism (overseas cadets were on occasion referred to in derogatory terms). All at a time when the Army had the relative luxury of not being tested operationally (it soon would be) and when being good at skiing seemed almost as important as being good at soldiering.

It was also a world of some institutionalised class snobbery. As much as possible, public institutions should reflect the society they recruit from and serve. They should be duty-bound to make the most of the talent the whole of society has to offer. This is the same for the Army where, given the problems it faces in both recruitment and retention, and the complexity of security issues in the twenty-first century, it has never been more important to attract the brightest and the best from every section of British society. Despite this need, recruitment into the Army officer corps remains disproportionately biased towards those who are

privately educated. In the years since I attended Sandhurst
some progress has been made in reducing this bias, but not
enough. Every intake at Sandhurst remains unrepresentative
of the society it serves, with the latest figures showing that
just under half of entrants to Sandhurst had attended a fee-
paying school from a general population where only 7 per
cent are privately educated.

Recruitment into Sandhurst is only part of the Army's
problem with class. Far too often, any improvements the
Army has made in recruiting people from state schools into
Sandhurst are lost by the time they promote to Colonel and
above, with those who received a state education less likely
to make it to the top of the tree. A recent report showed
that two thirds of the most senior officers had attended a
fee-paying school. This is a product of both conscious and
unconscious bias by the officer corps to promote the most
'clubbable' of young officers, those often closest to the self-
image of the reporting officer – the 'right sort of chap'. The
size of the problem is dependent on the regiment or corps,
but it is prevalent throughout the Army.

In recent years this cultural bias has been enabled by a lack
of objective reporting and the further diminishing of objective exams. Instead, reporting officers often make subjective
decisions on the promotability of an individual then both
cherry-pick evidence to support it and dismiss evidence to
the contrary. This is a problem aggravated by the fact that
the future 'top brass' are often selected very early in their
careers, when people from more working-class backgrounds
have had less opportunity to assimilate into the culture of the
officer corps and learn the essentially middle- to upper-class
traditions of the mess. Those who are chosen are then often
groomed for more senior ranks. After that point it is difficult
to either fall off or get on that career escalator.

We must, however, always draw a line between attacking the class bias of the institution and the senior officers who perpetuate it, and of those who choose to join and serve. Neither their background nor the snobbery inherent within the system they have volunteered into is the fault of those who choose to serve. There remains much work to be done and it is incumbent upon each new generation of leaders to tackle this problem head on.

Ultimately, though imperfect, Sandhurst was still a meritocracy, of sorts. Along with the rest of the intake, I was judged more on my ability and potential than on where I had come from. We had all learned a huge amount about the Army and a lot of new skills. We would need them all as we were posted on to take command of a platoon of soldiers in the British Army.

In my farewell interview with the Officer Commanding (OC), who was notable in that virtually every sentence he spoke included at least one swear word and often many more, he wished me luck and left me with a simple piece of advice that for once didn't include any expletives and has stayed with me ever since: 'It's a complex world, there will be tough choices, but do what you know to be right – always do the right thing.' It was sound advice.

I stuck my head into Colour Sergeant Gargan's office to thank him and to say goodbye. He gripped my hand, shook it firmly and with a beaming smile said, 'I've just been told that I'm being posted back to the Regiment, so I'll be seeing you there!' But first, to earn the right to wear my Parachute Regiment red beret and wings I had to pass P-Company and qualify as a military parachutist.

# 4

# Ready for Anything

## *September 1997*

—

'Let the hill do the work!' shouted the Paras' Physical Training Instructor (PTI). It felt to me as if *we* were doing the work, and the hill was our foe, not our friend. It was early September and the sun beat down as we marched along as part of a squad, a heavy bergan on our backs and a rifle in our hands. 'Two hands on the weapon at all times!' screamed the PTI. Up hills, down hills we went, and then back up again for good measure. The pace quickened and the sweat poured as we made our way through the undulating North Yorkshire countryside.

The recent tragic death of Princess Diana had resulted in nearly all of the Army's training being cancelled in the period leading up to her funeral. There were certain exemptions granted, and at P-Company the training stopped for nobody and nothing. As newly commissioned officers from Sandhurst, Si, Toddy, David Blakeley and I were expected to lead the aspiring paratroopers through a series of extremely physically demanding tests including long endurance route marches and shorter, sharper assault courses.

A part of P-Company that draws particular attention is the notorious 'milling' – a purposefully violent exercise in which two soldiers are pitted against each other in a make-shift boxing ring where they are required to punch each other as much as they can for one minute. As young officers we were expected to demonstrate 'spirit' and were therefore put in the ring with the opponent most likely to give us a hard time. A very hard time. The opportunity for some soldiers to smash hell out of an officer and be complimented (as opposed to disciplined) for doing so was attractive to many, and I was pitted against a particularly aggressive young soldier. He was built like a heavyweight boxer and was known to be pretty handy with his fists. We were lined up directly opposite our opponents and I could see him grinding his fist into the palm of his other hand while trying to stare me out. He was taking it very seriously indeed.

We put on boxing gloves and headguards and were directed into the ring. The rest of the course were seated around the outside of the ring and were strongly encouraged to cheer on the combatants. The noise was deafening. I looked my opponent in the face, he glared back at me. I didn't have a great feeling about how this was going to go, but there was no choice, I had to stand and fight. Milling is a test of controlled aggression, of raw courage, designed to assess whether you can stand your ground when you are under real physical pressure.

The referee gave the shrill word of command to begin – 'Mill!' – and straight away the fists started flying. After an initial flurry of mutually exchanged blows, he connected with a big upper-cut which knocked me over. I hadn't been punched since scraps in the playground at school. I was temporarily dazed, my vision blurred, and while I picked myself off the floor he hit me several times on the side of the head before I was fully up and ready – against the rules, but the referee seemed strangely slow to intervene. I smacked him on the nose, which gave him something to think about, and then dug in to try and withstand the remainder of the onslaught – which seemed curiously much longer than the scheduled minute. It was a bruising encounter, and my opponent undoubtedly got the better of me, but I had kept pushing forward, soaking up the punishment, and I hadn't given up. It is a test unique to P-Company: the rest of the Army don't do it, and while it certainly wasn't pleasant and would doubtless not be approved of by some, when you are preparing soldiers for war, it's a brutal but effective way of assessing whether someone can cope with intimidation and demanding physical adversity.

Shortly after the milling, and as we tended our battered faces and dabbed at the blood on our T-shirts, we were directed outside to the 'trainasium'. This is an aerial confidence course designed to assess a head for heights and specifically, we were told, 'reaction to the word of command'. Basically, the aim is to test whether, when you get to the door of an aircraft and are told to jump out of it, you will jump or not. I had been on it once before, and had been dreading going back up again. But I knew I was going to do it: by this stage of the course I was more frightened of the consequences of failure than I was of the consequences of falling off the trainasium. It consists of a series of extreme playground-type apparatus – scaffolding-like bars, twenty metres off the ground, which you have to shuffle all the way along. Midway through, designed to inflict maximum difficulty, are a series of small metal blocks, exactly the right (or wrong, depending on your perspective) size to ensure that you can't just shuffle along the bars, you have to lift your foot up and over the blocks. There is no safety net. If you fall off you are on your way to hospital.

'So don't fall off' was the advice.

There was a narrow aerial walkway that we had to sprint along, and then a jump across a large, gaping gap into a cargo net. An illusion jump, where from a great height and from a standing start you have to leap across a seemingly impossible distance. It is very craftily designed to appear, as you're stood there contemplating the leap, that you will never be able to make it; but the platform you are jumping towards is at a lower height so your forward momentum carries you across. Provided you can summon the courage to leap forward in the first place. I didn't stop to think about it, and trusted that I would make it and just went for it.

After more tests including endurance route marches, the stretcher race and a shorter, sharper steeplechase came perhaps the gutsiest event of all – the infamous log run. In teams of eight you carry a heavy log at breakneck speed around an undulating two-mile circuit. It is designed to test determination, aggression and leadership. What will you do when the going gets very tough? Will you dig deep and rise to the challenge or will you slink away and seek an easier path?

There is nowhere to hide, and you are screamed at by the instructors from the moment you start. 'Go faster!' 'You're not trying hard enough!' 'Start performing!' Throughout, we were also being encouraged to give up. At the point where the pain was greatest we were invited to quit, to 'jack it in'. Every attempt was made to give us the opportunity to slow down and thus fail the test. It was up to us as individuals, and collectively as a team of eight, to ignore it all and just crack on with it, however much it was hurting and however much we were tempted to give in. If you 'dropped off' the log because you simply couldn't keep up, then as an officer you would likely fail the whole course – or, worse, you would scrape a pass but carry the stigma of having failed the log run. It was gut-wrenchingly hard going. Running along carrying that log, my arm felt like it was being yanked out of its socket. I felt sick. My heart was punching its way out of my chest as I urgently gulped air into my lungs. Salty sweat ran into my eyes, snot flared right across my face. It was horrible. I wanted it to end.

But I was not letting go of that log.

At the end of P-Company there was a nervous wait while the instructors discussed your performance with the OC, before being told whether you had passed or failed. Failure might mean that you would be allowed the opportunity to do it all again to try and pass a second time, but it might mean that you would have to join another regiment alto-gether. In typical Parachute Regiment fashion this was done without great ceremony. We were all lined up and our names read out one by one, and after each name came the word 'pass' or 'fail'. I was reasonably confident that I would be fine, but you never knew for sure.

'Second Lieutenant Jarvis.'

I stood to attention and replied, 'Staff.'

There was then a long pause, designed to keep me waiting and to wind me up, before, 'Fail.'

'What?'

'Only joking, sir – pass!'

Hilarious.

Those who have passed then get handed the coveted red Parachute Regiment beret (it's actually maroon). Again, this is done without great ceremony or fuss: the OC simply hands it over and says 'well done'. That's it. Time for a pint.

We had now earned the right to serve in the Regiment, and, in the words of the regimental motto, 'Utrinque Paratus' – we were 'Ready for Anything'.

But we still needed to pass the parachuting course. There was not much point being in The Parachute Regiment if you couldn't parachute – the clue was in the name. The parachuting course didn't start for a number of weeks, and a few of us naively expected that we would get some leave, but no, we were going to be trained some more.

Our Sergeant instructor told us that while our training at Sandhurst had been 'fine, to a point, it was now time to learn how to do things *our* way'. So we spent hours practising basic weapon-handling skills. On one memorable occasion this included a very early morning session firing the general purpose machine gun (GPMG), or 'Jimpy' as it was known. Si, Toddy, David and I all had massive hangovers from a big night out in Newcastle and our Corporal instructor despaired at our collective inability to master the art of firing the noisy weapon as we nursed our very sore heads. We worked to improve our knowledge of tactics. We did more signals training, we learned about regimental history, and the runs just got longer, and quicker, and with more weight being carried. It was hard work, but we were also expected to play hard as well.

The culture in the officers' mess at that time was a very hard-drinking one. On a regular basis we would be expected to join the other officers for drinks after dinner. This would often degenerate into naked mess rugby – which is basically exactly what it sounds like: it's rugby that is played in the mess, while naked. It had become something of a tradition, and teams would be agreed and rugby would be played. It was ferocious. People would often be injured, and there would be punch-ups, though very quickly everything would be forgiven. It was expected that we would participate. After all, why wouldn't we want to play naked mess rugby? It was also expected that whatever time it finished – 3 a.m., 4 a.m., 5 a.m. or whenever – at first parade, often at 6.30 a.m., without fail, we would all be there in our PT kit ready to go for physical training.

Often the mess would end up resembling a conflict zone. Sometimes furniture would be broken, in which case the offending officer would be billed and it was expected that he would pay up immediately. The basic rule, though unwritten, was that if it was in the mess (i.e. behind closed doors) pretty much anything went. If you broke it, you paid for it. If you punched someone, you apologised and shook hands. However, should any of this kind of behaviour take place *outside* the privacy of the mess, all hell would break loose. It was the job of the Battalion Adjutant to ensure discipline and 'good order' among the officers who, when it came to conduct, were supposed to set an example to the soldiers.

It was then decided that in order to demonstrate that we had learned our new skills we would deploy on an endurance march. This would be the culmination of our training before heading down to Royal Air Force (RAF) Brize Norton for the parachute course. So we spent days manoeuvring around the Yorkshire countryside, grabbing the odd hour of rest when we could. We eventually received orders over the radio that we were to return to base, but that to do so we would need to rendezvous with an 'agent' who would assist us. The plan was that we would covertly get ourselves to a remote car park where we would lay up for a number of hours before making contact with the agent who would secretly repatriate us back to base. We were given a time when the agent would arrive in a car.

We lay in the icy cold rain for hours, sodden and frozen. I could feel the rain dripping down the back of my neck and could barely feel my toes. Two hours after nightfall, and at the appointed time, a car quietly drove into the car park. I was tasked to go forward and make contact with the agent to confirm it was clear to bring in a van that would recover us all back to base. I moved out of the thick undergrowth as stealthily as I could manage, my frozen limbs struggling to work, shattered from the effects of the cold and the wet and the nights without sleep. My hair was matted with foliage and my face was a grungy mixture of deeply engrained black camouflage cream and icy rainwater. Rather than go straight to the driver's window, and despite my drenched, mud-soaked clothing, and the machine gun I was carrying, I opened the car door and jumped straight into the passenger seat. It was deliciously warm and I thought I would at least enjoy a brief moment of respite from the elements. Despite my dulled senses I immediately saw the horror on the face of the woman sitting behind the wheel in the driver's seat.

It was the wrong car.

In my most polite but clearly flustered voice I could only think to stammer, 'Oh, I'm terribly sorry, I think I'm in, er, the wrong car.' There was no reply. She, not unreasonably, just stared at me, aghast, so I got out of the car as quickly as I'd got into it. The car sped off. I legged it back into the undergrowth, and less than a minute later the correct car pulled in.

'Look before you leap, Jarv!' cracked a voice from the undergrowth.

'Knowledge dispels fear.' Apparently. The Chief Instructor of the parachute school very calmly explained that the more we understood about how military parachuting actually worked, the less likely we would be to fear it. I imagined I would need to absorb quite a lot of information before my terror of it receded. There was an inconvenient truth, that despite having been commissioned into The Parachute Regiment and having earned the right to wear the beret, the prospect of actually having to parachute was one that petrified me. Military parachuting is not like civilian parachuting. Civilian parachuting, though still requiring the bottle to actually jump, was something that people did for fun. Virtually nobody did military parachuting for fun. I turned up at RAF Brize Norton just wanting to get it done and out of the way as quickly as possible. Little did I know that when it comes to parachuting, not much happens quickly.

We began with an upbeat pep talk about the traditions of military parachuting. This was quickly followed by an information film about the course. As I would come to learn, military parachuting usually involves being in the C-130 Hercules aircraft for hours, often flying at low level with the pilot throwing the aircraft all over the place to simulate avoiding hostile fire from the ground. This feels a bit like being on a theme park ride for hours on end. It is hot and cramped. Nearly always someone is badly sick. The vomit usually ends up on the floor and reeks in the confined space. Once the first person is sick, others nearly always follow suit.

Eventually, the parachutists are instructed by the Parachute Jump Instructors (PJIs) to stand up and 'fit equipment' – usually an extremely heavy bergan container pack, often well over 100lb in weight, which is clipped to the chest. They then line up in a pre-determined order and in a very closely controlled sequence, and at a precisely coordinated moment move (through the sick) towards the side door before leaping out of it. Often this takes place in the dark.

The information film, helpfully, and in minute detail, outlined some of the pitfalls. One that particularly stood out as a scenario to avoid was your parachute rigging lines (which connect the parachute to the harness strapped around your body) getting tangled on the underside of the aircraft. For a moment I genuinely thought this was a joke, but no, this had on numerous occasions resulted in the stranded parachutist being dragged along, often for a lengthy period, underneath the aircraft. However, 'Not to worry,' we were told (I was pretty certain that if this happened to me I probably would start worrying fairly quickly), 'eventually you will be cut free.' The word 'eventually' reverberated around my head. Obviously the cutting of the rigging lines would render your parachute completely unusable. However, again, 'Not to worry', because under those circumstances all you have to do is open your reserve chute while plummeting towards the ground. Simple. The Chief Instructor lightened the mood by explaining the tradition that if this did happen to you, head directly to the nearest pub, where you were guaranteed to get free drinks all night. That's all right then, I thought.

Although nothing happens quickly, it didn't seem long – in fact after just a bit of rolling about on mats practising our landing techniques – before we were walking into the back of a Skyvan aircraft to conduct our first jump. Unlike the much larger C-130, this was the trainer aircraft, basically a white Transit van with wings. Rather than go out of the side you just walk off the back ramp into ... well, into nothing. As officers we were of course expected to lead from the front and therefore expected to be 'number one in the door', so we would jump first and the soldiers would follow on behind us. Prior to 'emplaning', as the RAF described it, or 'getting on the aircraft', as the rest of us described it, we were carefully lined up into what are called 'chalks', where everyone is positioned in the right order, as per a carefully worked-out flight manifest. I was No. 1 at the front. Just as we were about to start to walk on to the aircraft the soldier who was due to follow me, No. 2, decided that this was, after all, not for him and took himself off to see the instructors. We never saw him again. The soldier who was directly behind him (No. 3) was clearly not that keen either and asked if he could swap places with me.

'Why's that?' I enquired.

'Basically, boss, I'm going to need you to shove me out.'

I wasn't wild about swapping places, or 'shoving him out', or having anyone think I had bottled going out the door first, but he looked desperate so I reluctantly agreed.

We took off in the Skyvan and quickly climbed to about 1200 feet, and it was time to go. The soldier who had been behind me but was now in front of me looked genuinely petrified, and I didn't feel too good myself. Standing waiting to go, he developed what's known as 'disco leg'. It was shaking like Elvis Presley. When the moment came to jump, he hesitated, and it looked like he wasn't going to go, so, as requested, I assisted his departure from the aircraft, and then jumped out myself.

Once I had cleared the rear slipstream of the aircraft and entered clear air space, I looked up and checked that my parachute canopy had opened properly. It looked all right. 'Hallelujah!' I shouted, or words to that effect. For a second I tried to enjoy the view, but straight away the PJIs positioned on the ground were shouting instructions via a loudspeaker. I couldn't really hear what they were saying, and the process was made even more confusing because, naturally, they thought the No. 1 was me, so I could hear them screaming instructions to Second Lieutenant Jarvis, but realised they were referring to soldier No. 3 who had taken my place.

'Steer right, more yet.' Then more shrill: 'Steer right! More. More. More. MORE!'

I didn't hear anything else, and as the ground rushed up to meet me there were apparently further cries to the effect that I needed to 'keep my effin elbows in'. I hit the deck like a sack of potatoes and attempted to do a parachute roll, as we had been taught, but it wasn't a pretty sight. Lying on the ground, with the wind knocked out of my sails, I took a moment to assess whether my body had been smashed to bits, but after dusting myself down it appeared that all was fine. I packed up the parachute and skipped off the drop zone with the soldier I'd swapped places with for a celebratory hot brew.

After another go in the Skyvan, this time from a thousand feet, we quickly progressed on to the C-130, first without, then with equipment strapped to our body. We exited through the side door from 800 feet and when in clear air space felt for the release clips and released them, so the equipment trailed beneath us attached by rope.

Then it was time for the night descent. All parachuting is dependent on wind speeds; the higher the wind speed the greater the risk of injuries on the ground. For the next few days a storm blew in and we were grounded, hanging around drinking tea (and occasionally something stronger), waiting for the weather to improve. Eventually it did.

It was just dark as we took off and we were soon getting ready to go. I was first out. The aircraft side door opened and I could feel the wind blow into my face. As No. 1 you are moved into the doorway with your static line attached. I stood there for several minutes waiting before the red light came on, knowing that when it turned green it was my moment to go. Immediately. No hesitation. Green on, then go. I stood in the door. My heart pumping.

Then, 'Green on – GO, GO, GO!' shouted the PJI.

I stepped forward into a black wall of darkness. I couldn't see anything at all. There was no sound but I could feel the freshness of the air on my face. The going out was easy enough, but what was more complicated was that parachutists exited out of both the port and the starboard side. This has to be incredibly carefully sequenced otherwise you banged into the parachutist who had exited from the other side door. And of course this was more chaotic in the dark, when you couldn't see anything. The advantage of being No. 1 was that I was first, so there was nobody to bang into, but for those behind there was the constant risk not only of collision but of tangled parachute rigging lines. There were only a few seconds once your chute had fully deployed before you had to adopt the landing position – feet and knees together, elbows in – to be ready for the impact that followed very quickly thereafter.

I finished the course and was presented with my parachute wings. This was the domain of the RAF so naturally there was a little more pomp and ceremony than when I had had my maroon beret chucked at me. A senior RAF officer told us how 'splendidly we had all done, and what a thoroughly decent bunch of chaps we all were'. I was pleased to depart with wings and without injuries. Through explanation, demonstration, imitation and practice, and the knowledge that brought, I had learned to overcome my initial fear – though subsequent events would prove that I had been right to be wary of this parachuting lark.

It had been decided that David Blakeley and I were to be posted together to 1 Para who were just returning from a deployment in Northern Ireland. At their New Normandy barracks in Aldershot I stood in front of the Commanding Officer (CO) who told me that 'the ruthless pursuit of excellence means that everything we do has to be to the highest possible standards'. This was an organisation that prided itself in being exceptional, in everything it did. The Adjutant told me that I would have to work hard to prove myself; apparently passing P-Company wasn't enough – I was very much on probation. The battalion was tight-knit after spending the past six months on operations and I was sent to B Company, as the Platoon Commander of 5 Platoon.

This was what all the training had been about, the opportunity to take command of a platoon of paratroopers.

# 5

# Reporting for Duty

## *November 1997*

—

**M**y platoon were a tough-looking bunch, and when I met them for the first time, standing outside B Company's offices, I could see the cynicism etched into their faces. Over a brew, 'Chips', my experienced Platoon Sergeant, cautioned against making big early decisions. 'Take a bit of time to get to know and understand the blokes, ease yourself into it,' was his advice. Concerningly, he added, 'Oh, and another thing, don't take sugar with your brew – you never know what they might put in it!'

Many of the paratroopers in my platoon were sceptical about the requirement for young officers at all; we were seen as being operationally untested (which was true). There was a widely held view that even though the young officer was at least nominally in command, it was the Platoon Sergeant and the junior NCOs – the Corporals – who were really in charge. So to begin with, it was hard going.

A couple of months in, there had been a few hiccups.

We hosted an exchange visit from some Polish paratroopers, and after a joint training exercise we were tasked to show them the sights of London. 'You're all ambassadors for our country' was my somewhat grandiose warning to my platoon ahead of the night out. Three hours and a bottle of Polish vodka later, they had to carry me down the King's Road and back to our accommodation. That they did not shave off one of my eyebrows (shaving off one was worse than shaving off two, because you then had to take the decision yourself as to whether you stuck with one, or shaved the other off – this was the fate of many an incapacitated paratrooper) indicated that I might just be growing on them.

There were moments when my authority had been tested, including in a pub when one of them poured a pint over my head, to 'see what I would do'. I decided to have a quiet word rather than make a big fuss about it. But that aside, it felt like I was making progress. I had a decent working relationship with Chips and had got to know all of the platoon. I was beginning to understand what made them tick as individuals and how we could gel together as a cohesive team.

We were informed by our OC, Major John Lorimer, that we would parachute into an airborne exercise on Salisbury Plain. This would be my first battalion exercise and a good opportunity to prove that I could actually do the nuts and bolts of the job and command my platoon in the field. Even though the battalion had only recently returned from Northern Ireland there was constant chatter about the potential for another operational deployment. Whenever something happened overseas, the rumour mill would quickly spin into overdrive that we were about to be deployed there to sort it out. This exercise was thought to be an opportunity for us to demonstrate our capabilities to the senior military officers who would subsequently decide which units might deploy on any future operations.

The orders for the exercise were given and we were bussed to RAF Lyneham to get on the C-130 aircraft we would be parachuting from. After the usual delays we were airborne and began to get ready to jump. It was done much less formally than on the parachuting course and the chalks were tactically loaded to ensure that the right people landed on the ground in the right order. Because of the high likelihood of injury, we all knew what was expected of us; if our boss was injured, we would step up and assume their role.

The now familiar red light came on. I readied myself. Then the green light. The long chalks of paratroopers moved rhythmically and purposefully towards the doors. Here we go. I exited the starboard side door, and performed the mandatory count: 'One thousand. Two thousand. Three thousand. Check canopy!' My parachute canopy had opened as normal and I was in clear air space. So far, so good.

I felt for the hooks on my parachute harness (because they were situated under the reserve chute, you couldn't see them and had to feel for them) which needed to be unclipped in order that my heavy container be released from my body, to dangle safely below me. It would be extremely hazardous to land with the full weight of the container strapped to the body. I couldn't find the hooks. I tried again, but still couldn't find them. Shit, I thought. I had another go, but I couldn't locate them. The ground was approaching fast. A Zen-like calm descended and in a flash I accepted that I was not going to be able to release my container and I would have to land with it strapped to my body. I felt reasonably relaxed about it – I thought I would be fine – but I steeled myself for a heavy landing nonetheless.

The final few seconds of descent seemed to go in slow

motion and I could see from the air that the medic on the ground had clocked that I couldn't release my container and was sprinting towards the spot where I was destined to land. I smashed down on to the ground and was catapulted over on to my right arm. For a fleeting moment I didn't know what was happening before I skidded unceremoniously to a halt in an undignified pile on Salisbury Plain.

Then the pain kicked in.

As the medic peered over my crumpled body, I could tell from the expression on her face that something was up. I was helped into the back of an Army Land Rover ambulance. As the door closed behind me, I heard someone say, 'Welcome to 1 Para!' I was driven across the bumpy plain in agony, each bump triggering a jarring, burning pain in my right arm. I arrived at Salisbury hospital A&E to find three other parachutists who had also been injured in the jump. I had dislocated my shoulder and broken my arm, and there was significant nerve damage.

A few days later I was sat in the military hospital in Aldershot feeling very sorry for myself. Going from being fit to unable to perform basic tasks such as putting socks on was sobering and frustrating. The consultant asked me to show her what movement I had in my arm. I tried to move it, but nothing much happened. I had a moment of self-indulgent pity as I was informed that the break was a bad one, that I might not be able to parachute again, and consequently my future in the Regiment was in doubt. I pulled myself out of my self-imposed gloom and assured the consultant that it would be fine.

I was told that my best chance of rehabilitation was to go to Headley Court for a long spell of physio and rehab. At that time, nobody had much heard of 'Deadley' Court (so-called because of the fearsome regime). But it would become well known as the place where seriously wounded soldiers from Iraq and Afghanistan would go to begin long recoveries from their injuries.

Headley Court was packed with dedicated health professionals who worked me hard. Every day was exhausting; in the pool, out of the pool, in the gym, out of the gym. Hours and hours of table tennis. Back into the gym. Back into the pool. I spent months trying to fix my arm. In the margins of rehab I took temporary command of the Regimental Recruiting Team (RRT) until I was hopefully fit enough to get back to B Company. The NCOs in the recruiting team had gone feral and having had little oversight for some time they were largely doing their own thing. They spent most of their time 'recruiting' on the beach in Bournemouth so I put in place a plan which ensured that, given the Regiment was supposed to be recruiting nationally, we would widen the search beyond Bournemouth's beach. This went down like a cup of cold sick and they requested that I visit Bournemouth. I did. It's a great place (and an excellent night out, which was possibly one of the reasons they were so keen to be there), but from then on the RRT travelled a bit further afield to do its recruiting.

While at Headley Court I regularly returned to Aldershot where there was, again, constant chatter about the possibility of an operational deployment. There was a hunger and a desperation to get out and do something. Other than Northern Ireland, the Parachute Regiment had not deployed on operations since the Falklands conflict in 1982. There were still a number of veterans in the Regiment who had been 'down south' to the Falklands, and there was a long-held frustration that ever since then the Regiment had been overlooked. This was felt particularly keenly in 1 Para who had seen their sister battalions, 2 and 3 Para, deploy to the Falklands without them. Though this had been more than fifteen years earlier, it still rankled.

I made decent progress with my arm and deployed to Oman on an exercise as the Second-in-Command of C Company. Again, the rumour mill went into overdrive that this exercise was a warm-up for an operational deployment. In Oman, we did some desert training. On the first day, the OC fell off his motorbike and was casevaced (evacuated as a medical casualty) back to the UK. We all knew the rules – when your boss gets taken out, you step up and take over – so all of a sudden I found myself in charge. At the end of the exercise we came back. Still no sign of an operational deployment.

Having finally returned to 5 Platoon, B Company, and in the absence of much else to do, I took my soldiers climbing in the Nepalese Himalayas. The night before we were due to take an internal flight from Kathmandu up to Lukla, the start point of the expedition, I briefed the team that I was happy for them to go out for a 'couple of quiet beers', but that they should take it easy as we were flying up to altitude the next morning and I needed them on top form. They all nodded sagely, and immediately went on a massive pub crawl. David Blakeley and I paced around the guest house like concerned parents, waiting for the kids to come home from a night out. We were due to leave at 8 a.m. for the airport. At 6 a.m., they still weren't back. They finally dribbled back in at 7.30 a.m.

I was apoplectic. I lined them up, though some of them were struggling to stand, and gave them an almighty bollocking. I couldn't believe how they had let me down. In their defence, I hadn't specified exactly what time they were to be back by (a lesson learned), but they knew they were in the wrong. We were booked on a flight that was leaving shortly and I wasn't convinced that in their current state they should be flying. However, our tickets were fixed for that flight, so I didn't have much choice, and we got on it. Some of them seemed compos mentis, but others were in no shape to begin a gentle walk never mind a Himalayan expedition.

We landed in Lukla on a dramatic landing strip carved into the hillside, and though we had been due to begin the long trek towards Mera Peak immediately, I took the decision not to proceed but instead to make camp straight away and let those who needed to rehydrate do so. We set off the next morning at a snail's pace, given the altitude, and the fact that some were still not recovered. Throughout the course of the day, one of the team, Private Bryan, found it hard to keep up. It wasn't clear whether he was struggling with the altitude or with alcohol poisoning, or both, but we slowed the pace down even more. At lunchtime we reached a stage of the day's trek which involved some exposed scrambling. I considered making camp where we were and attempting this more difficult terrain the following morning. But we were on a tight timeline and although a few of the group had struggled throughout the morning, we agreed to push on.

It proved to be a big mistake.

After a couple of hours of precarious scrambling across and up difficult mountain terrain, we arrived at the spot where we had planned to make camp for the night. The tents went up and we cooked food. Bryan couldn't stomach anything to eat and retreated into his sleeping bag. It was now dark, and the temperature had dropped dramatically. I slid into the comfort of my own sleeping bag and was nearly asleep when our medic unzipped my tent to tell me that

Bryan had been violently sick. I went to check on him. He looked terrible. The medic and our mountain guide thought he was suffering from acute mountain sickness – in other words, altitude sickness. The unequivocal advice from them both was we had to get him back down the mountain.

'Now or in the morning?' I asked.

'Now. He'll be dead by the morning.'

Everyone had gathered outside Bryan's tent, and as the medic spoke the words 'dead by the morning', instinctively they all turned to look at me. It was just as Frank Gargan had described back at Sandhurst: 'When things go wrong, when the shit hits the fan, it will be *you* that your soldiers look to for leadership.' And in that moment, that's exactly what they did. Despite the cynicism and the piss-taking, when it came down to it, with a life on the line, it fell to the young officer to make the decisions and try to get a grip on the situation.

I grabbed my map and spread it out on the ground. I focused my head torch on it, which seemed only to illuminate my warm breath in the now freezing night. Everyone crowded around. I pored over the contours of the map, hoping that a solution would jump out at me. I talked it through with David and invited everyone to contribute. Between us, we reckoned there were three viable options.

One, retrace our steps back down to Lukla – easy in that we knew the route, but tricky in that it had been very difficult going and would be a nightmare carrying Bryan down in the dark.

Two, there was another route down that looked passable, but it took us miles away from civilisation and it would be very difficult to get Bryan medical treatment when we got there.

Three, we could climb up some more, before then

descending into a neighbouring valley – bad in that we would have to go up for a while, but then the descent looked reasonably good going and there would likely be some medical support down in that valley.

It felt like one of the planning exercises I had done as part of the Army selection processes. Only now it wasn't some arbitrary test. It was very real. This wasn't the Alps, we couldn't call for a helicopter, there was no mountain rescue, we were going to have to sort it ourselves.

Nobody could identify any other options. David looked at me: 'Your call, mate.' But none of the three particularly appealed. I felt dehydrated, I was exhausted, I was shivering, and most of all I was seething that I had allowed this to happen in the first place. But it had happened, and I now had to sort it.

'Right, option three. Let's do it.'

No sooner had I spoken the words than all the training just kicked in and the team immediately set about packing away the kit and getting ready to move. Bryan was now barely conscious, and for a small man his dead-weight was surprisingly heavy. We put him on a makeshift stretcher fashioned from a bivvy bag (an outer shell that affords protection from the elements if you don't have a tent; you get into your sleeping bag, and then into the bivvy bag) and within a few minutes we were ready to go. We took turns carrying the stretcher as we edged forward into the darkness. The path was narrow in places and the next eight hours were back-breaking, painstaking work as we ever so carefully made our way up and then back down the mountain.

As dawn broke we had descended almost three thousand feet, and set up camp. Bryan looked much better and we spent the next day rehydrating, eating and sleeping before he was sufficiently recovered for us to drop him at a medical centre to await our return. What was meant to be a reasonably demanding adventurous training exercise had turned into an epic survival effort – *Saving Private Bryan*, as it inevitably became known. Though the team had let me down in Kathmandu – as soldiers sometimes do – when it really mattered, when under pressure, they had performed exceptionally, as British soldiers nearly always do.

After the exertion in the mountains, David and I took ourselves to the Chitwan National Park. We hired a jeep with a guide and drove for miles until we eventually came to a stop at a wide expanse of river surrounded by jungle. It was an incredibly peaceful spot. Away from the others and free to let our hair down, we sat on the bonnet of the jeep sipping tea from a flask. We took photos, chatted and enjoyed the tranquillity. About an hour later it was time to head back.

The driver turned the key in the ignition but nothing happened. Not a murmur. He tried again. Nothing. Dave and I started laughing, thinking it was a practical joke. It wasn't. The jeep really wouldn't start. The driver and the guide pulled up the bonnet and started to fiddle with the engine. There was clearly something wrong. After half an hour of trying to fix the problem it became clear they weren't going to be able to get it started. We didn't have a phone or a radio and it was now nearly dark. There was no point spending the night there because not only would we be at risk from predators – there were tigers, rhinos, crocs and other animals in the park – we would still then have to walk back to get help. Nobody knew where we were. There was no rescue coming. There was nothing else for it: we were going to have to walk out of the jungle there and then.

I thought the guide was going to pass out. He knew much

better than we did about the dangers of walking through that stretch of jungle at night. No local would ever have considered doing it as it was known to be very dangerous. He looked absolutely terrified, which didn't inspire much confidence. David and I followed the guide and driver and we all padded silently and methodically through the jungle. The walk back took about five hours. We only stopped once, briefly. Pretty much every step I took I thought might be my last and that at any moment something would launch itself out of the dense undergrowth to get us. We remained calm, but we were scared. We just quietly kept padding forward through the dark, each step a step closer to safety. It was a massive relief to finally make it back to the safety of the lodge and crack open a Tiger beer, or ten.

The Army posting system means that officers and NCOs regularly get moved on to the next appointment, so despite the time away for rehab I had nearly completed my allotted time as a Platoon Commander. The Regimental Headquarters was keen to push me on into the next job and bring someone else up through the system to replace me. There was a ruthless rhythm to it; through and even during operational conflicts people were often still swapped around. As I would later discover, this was not always done in the most sensible way.

In the absence of an operation to deploy on I was offered a place on an expedition led by the British explorer John Blashford-Snell to Bolivia. I was keen to go, the CO was less keen, but he offered me a deal. 'I'll let you go; but in return, you'll accept the job of the Regimental Signals Officer.' The RSO was a vital role in the battalion headquarters, but no one ever wanted to do it. It was seen as being a bit technical, and the specialised role of the signals platoon was seen, wrongly, as being away from the main effort. I agreed the deal and dutifully headed off on the long RSOs course.

Shortly after I went, David Blakeley called to tell me that it looked like the battalion were going to deploy on an operation to Kosovo. My initial reaction was 'heard it all before, doubt it'll happen'. But it began to look increasingly like this time it might happen. The level of anticipation went through the roof and the battalion started to get ready. Just in case. I was away stuck on the course in Warminster along with the senior NCO who was due to be the signals platoon Warrant Officer, known to everyone as 'Double O, Joe'. He and I commiserated with each other on an hourly basis – surely we were not going to be left behind? 'Joe', or 'Sergeant Major' as I was supposed to call him, had been tipped off that as part of the preparation the battalion were doing some Fighting in a Built-up Area (FIBUA) training at the Imber training village on Salisbury Plain. This was just down the road from where we were, less glamorously, busying ourselves learning about different frequencies and how to tune and maintain our radios. We were desperate not to miss out on the deployment so between us we hatched a plan, to knock off early from the course, drive to Imber village, find the CO and, if we had to, beg him not to leave us behind. What could possibly go wrong?

We jumped in a car and drove into the village amid the carnage of a mock battle. We parked up, feeling conspicuous among our fellow soldiers, all of whom were dressed for battle with camouflage cream smeared over faces and hands, carrying huge bergans and belts of blank ammunition and simulation grenades. Normally any contact with the CO would be strictly arranged through the Adjutant, but I assured myself that this was an emergency not requiring the usual formalities.

While the mock battle was being waged, a company of paratroopers swarmed into the village. I caught sight of David Blakeley. Amid the noise of the firing I shouted over to him to ask where the CO was. He grinned (immediately clocking what I was here to do) and gestured to a small clump of trees just outside the village before tearing off into the battle. Joe and I walked self-consciously over to find the CO. I started to wonder whether this was such a great plan after all, but we kept walking.

When we arrived at the clump of trees it was clear he was busy, directing the battle through a frenzied conversation over the radio. I could see the surprise in his eyes when he saw us.

'What the hell are you two jokers doing here?'

'Colonel, we've come to ask—'

At that precise moment there was a large simulated explosion and the CO's small tactical headquarter group got up and started to move in the direction of the village. I think the CO expected us not to follow him – we were after all on shaky ground just appearing out of the blue and interrupting him in the heat of the battle. He was clearly very busy and this was not the best moment, but something made me keep going.

'Dan, can't you see I've got a bit on here?' said the CO, showing surprising restraint, perhaps only because he knew that in my position he would have done exactly the same.

'Colonel, don't leave us behind.'

He dropped down on one knee. I could see him weighing it all up while simultaneously listening in to the battalion radio net.

'All right, you're on,' he said after a pause. 'Now get out of my way.'

'Appreciate it, sir.'

Joe and I drove back to Warminster in triumphant mood. Within an hour we had packed up our kit and headed back to Aldershot. We were going to Kosovo.

# 6

# Baptism of Fire

## June 1999

—

The battalion crammed into the cookhouse for an all-ranks briefing. Most of us didn't know much about Kosovo, a land-locked territory in the heart of the Balkans in south-eastern Europe, and what had been happening there. The Intelligence Officer (IO) began the brief by telling us that the war, which had started in February 1998, was being fought by the forces of the Federal Republic of Yugoslavia (consisting of the republics of Serbia and Montenegro), who had previously controlled Kosovo prior to the war, and a Kosovar Albanian rebel group called the Kosovo Liberation Army (KLA).

The Operations Officer took over and explained that since March 1999 the KLA had had North Atlantic Treaty Organisation (NATO) air support. In the first few months of 1998 KLA attacks targeted at the Yugoslav authorities in Kosovo had triggered a deployment of Serbian regular forces and paramilitaries who then pursued a campaign of retribution against KLA sympathisers and political opponents. The assessment at the time was that this campaign was responsible for the deaths of some 1500 to 2000 civilians and KLA fighters. Attempts to find a diplomatic solution were unsuccessful, and NATO had intervened on the basis that the deployment was a 'humanitarian war'. This provoked a big expulsion of Kosovar Albanians as the Yugoslav forces continued their military campaign throughout the aerial bombardment of Yugoslavia.

After the war ended, the remains of almost three thousand victims of all ethnicities would be recovered, and in 2001 a United Nations-administered Supreme Court, based in Kosovo, would find that there had been 'a systematic campaign of terror, including murders, rapes, arsons and severe maltreatments'. We didn't know it in 1999, but it would later be confirmed that more than 13,500 people had been killed or 'disappeared' during the brutal one-and-a-half-year conflict.

Although there was naturally some trepidation that we were deploying on an operation to Kosovo and what that might bring, my overwhelming emotion at that point was relief. Relief that I wasn't going to be left behind. Relief that I wasn't going to watch my friends head off on an operation without me.

Years earlier I had been attracted to join the Paras because of their reputation for being an elite, a part of the Army who prided themselves on maintaining the highest professional standards of soldiering. Having to pass P-Company and the parachuting course created an ethos, a camaraderie, that was second to none. While studying for my A levels I had been on a work experience visit to Browning barracks, the then home of the Regiment. At a formative stage, I had been impressed by the positive attitude, deep commitment and bond of friendship between those I had met, and saw qualities in them that I aspired to develop in myself.

That said, the Regiment had experienced more than its fair share of controversies over the years. It was soldiers from 1 Para who were investigated for their actions on 'Bloody Sunday' in Northern Ireland in 1972. There were questions asked and an investigation carried out into the conduct of a tiny minority of paratroopers during the Falklands conflict in 1982. In 1993 a paratrooper was convicted of murder for shooting dead two teenage joyriders who sped through a roadblock in Northern Ireland, though the conviction was later overturned.

What you got with The Parachute Regiment was extremely tough and aggressive soldiers. Precisely what you needed in war, but with the old clichéd caveat of never being sure of what to do with them during peacetime.

All of the different regiments and corps of the British Army and the other parts of the Armed Forces have their own distinctive identities and cultures. There is, though, something unique about the airborne soldier, and now I found myself in a parachute battalion readying itself for a potentially difficult and dangerous deployment. We collectively took pride in our regimental ethos, pride in the achievements of those who had served in the Regiment before us, and there was a steely and unwavering determination to ensure that we lived up to the standards of our predecessors and that we maintained the Regiment's reputation as an exceptional fighting force.

5 Platoon now had a new Platoon Commander so the CO told me that I would take command of the 3 Para Machine Gun Platoon who were being attached to 1 Para for the Kosovo deployment. If 5 Platoon had initially viewed me

with cynicism, the 3 Para Machine Gun Platoon raised the bar to disdain. They didn't much like officers, they didn't much like 1 Para either. I don't think they even really much liked anyone in 3 Para – unless they were in their machine gun platoon. They mostly consisted of the battalion old sweats, who had been around for donkey's years and who didn't require much in the way of direction from a young whippersnapper like me. Because they'd come in from another battalion I didn't know any of them. The Platoon Sergeant was pretty reasonable – or 'wilco' in Army speak (short for 'will comply') – which helped a lot, but some of the Corporals were a law unto themselves. It was to prove challenging keeping them in check.

We deployed from Aldershot on 6 June 1999 (that the sixth of that month was the date of the D-Day Normandy landings in World War Two – an important regimental anniversary – only added to the sense of occasion). We flew to Skopje in Macedonia, and from the airfield were bussed out into the countryside and dropped off in a large wood where we set up camp under our poncho shelters. The wood felt very similar to the many in which I had been on exercise before, but clearly this time we were not on exercise. Having said that, it was unclear precisely what we would be required to do, nor was it confirmed that we would definitely be deploying forward into Kosovo. Like soldiers throughout history, we waited for orders from those above us. While waiting we used the time wisely, and the next few days were a flurry of activity – training, packing and unpacking kit, gaming out various scenarios; just getting ready, both physically and mentally, for whatever might come our way.

1 Para were deployed as part of 5 Airborne Brigade, and the most likely option for us was a helicopter insertion into

Kosovo. At this stage the occupying Serbian forces were still pursuing a campaign of violence and terror against the indigenous Kosovo population. There was chaos in Kosovo, with murders, rapes and arsons common occurrences.

There was a real possibility that we might have to fight our way into Kosovo. Despite the obvious risks of doing this – if we had been required to fight our way in, some of us would have been killed doing so – morale was sky high. Everyone was keen to 'get in' and do the job (whatever that actually turned out to be). Although there was a surreal feel to being given orders for a real operation, unlike all the pretend ones that had gone before, it felt exactly like what we had joined and trained for. We were airborne soldiers, this is what we did.

It also felt like a bit of an adventure, and at that stage something of a lark. Sat there in the woods enjoying the balmy summer weather, cooking food and exchanging banter, we felt lucky and excited to be a part of it, and privileged to have the opportunity to serve our Regiment. Very few, if any, of us would have rather been anywhere else in the world at that moment. On a beach in the Maldives? No. This is where we belonged. I was not married, had no kids and no real responsibilities. Sat under my poncho shelter in my bivvy bag, peering up at the tree canopy, I fleetingly entertained the prospect that I might be killed, but it seemed a remote possibility. And, well, if I was killed, at least it would be while doing something I thought was worthwhile and that I believed in.

The Corporals in the machine gun platoon wanted to use the time to teach me about machine gunning and how they liked to operate. This led to several frank conversations about how things were going to work when we got into Kosovo – and who was in charge. I tried to keep them on a tight leash but worried about how controllable they would be in the midst of any serious action. As time went on, we developed an understanding, but it was obvious that some of them resented my presence and were intent on challenging my authority at every opportunity.

As we edged closer to the likely day of deployment we moved out of the woods to a corn field, and stayed busy practising the drills for getting on and off helicopters. The hot sun was beating down and there was an air of purposeful but calm activity. Then, all of a sudden, everything changed. The CO grabbed the OCs and the senior Platoon Commanders (myself included) for an urgent briefing. Completely out of the blue, a convoy of 250 Russian soldiers in thirty armoured vehicles had crossed the River Drina into Serbia. The assessment was that they were heading to Kosovo and were destined for the airfield at Pristina (Kosovo's capital and largest city) prior to the arrival of air-delivered troops from Russia. The convoy was anticipated to reach Pristina no later than 3 p.m.

In that moment, the mood dramatically shifted. We were now on a war-footing.

The CO gave us a set of Quick Battle Orders (QBOs) tasking us to race forward to the Pristina airfield in order to prevent the Russian forces from seizing control of it. If, however, the Russians got there first, then we were briefed that there would likely be a requirement for us to use 'whatever force was necessary' to take it off them.

There was a completely surreal atmosphere about the place. It was as if we had been transported back in time to the days of the Cold War. Of all the scenarios we had gamed through, this was one that had never entered the play book. I looked at the faces of the others as we received our orders to advance to the airfield. There was an air of steely determination, but the mood had dramatically altered. Nobody had been expecting this.

For a number of extremely tense hours the high drama of it played out while we sat ready to go, waiting in the corn field for the final orders to move. Into that same corn field arrived the overall NATO commander of the force we were a part of, Lieutenant General Mike Jackson, who coincidentally was also the Colonel Commandant of The Parachute Regiment (the most senior officer in the Regiment). The General would later have his famous conversation with his commander, the US General Wesley Clark. General Clark could be a tricky character and had instructed General Jackson to deploy NATO forces to resist the Russian move to Pristina airfield. General Jackson, understandably, was extremely concerned about the wider ramifications of such a move and had responded with the line, 'I'm not starting World War Three for you.' Instead, he had worked to prevent what would have been an extremely risky encounter between NATO and Russian forces which could have jeopardised the entire mission and possibly stirred up a much wider insecurity.

He pursued the ingenious approach of deploying his son, Mark, Second-in-Command of the Pathfinder platoon (the reconnaissance element of 5 Airborne Brigade), to go and link up with the Russians. This subsequently enabled General Jackson to go and meet with the senior Russian commander, General Viktor Zavarzin, to discuss how matters could be resolved. Despite some initial frostiness, the tensions were defused when rainwater got into the electrics of the Russian command vehicle they were sheltering in and they were forced to stand outside in the pouring rain. At which point General Jackson produced from his map pocket a flask of whisky (he liked to refer to it as that 'soothing brown liquid from northern Britain'), and rather than have a fight, they had a drink, which seemed a generally much more agreeable way of de-escalating what had been an extremely tense situation. By deploying an armoured convoy into Kosovo the Russians were seeking to remind NATO and the rest of the Western world that they were still a force to be reckoned with, that they maintained the capability to surprise and that as a country they needed to be shown respect.

Although things calmed down and the rest of us were no longer required to rush forward and seize the airfield, soon afterwards the operation got underway and we were loaded on to Chinook helis and flown up the Kacanik defile (valley) towards Kosovo. Our initial task was 'picketing' or securing the high ground above the main road route north out of Macedonia up to Kosovo, to provide 'over-watch' or security to enable the heavier British armoured forces to drive up the valley road. We spent the next couple of days doing this, jumping on the helis, flying on to the next location and securing it before leap-frogging forward to the next place.

Having entered southern Kosovo, we were immediately confronted with numerous challenges. The Serbian forces had retreated back to Serbia and we were left to deal with the instability that ensued. We were confronted with small armed militias attempting to assert their authority and on numerous occasions by drunk men brandishing automatic weapons at us. We had to take decisions about whether to proceed on foot through minefields or areas containing unexploded ordnance. At one point we were tasked to get to a neighbouring village as quickly as possible and ended up running through a number of fields that possibly had mines in them. The first time I took the platoon through an area we were uncertain about was agonisingly tense. I went first and tip-toed (not that this would have reduced the threat of detonating a mine) through the field with everyone following on behind. Very quickly, though, we developed a casual attitude to the dangers and were doing it almost without a second thought. Looking back, I shudder at the risks we took in those early days of the Kosovo campaign. That none of us were blown up was much more down to luck than judgement.

The next day we were dropped by helicopter into an area that had previously been occupied by Serbian forces. As the noise of the helicopters receded an eerie silence descended, and then, while we orientated ourselves prior to moving into a small village, I caught an unmistakable stench hanging in the air. There was something about the place that immediately struck me as not being right. As we patrolled cautiously towards the seemingly deserted village I just got a sense that we had arrived at somewhere that had witnessed horrors. It simply didn't feel right.

As we neared the edge of the village we saw a woman walking along the dirt track towards us. She had long dark-brown hair and looked a bit older than me, and as we passed – she heading away from the village, me going into it – we briefly established eye contact. There was a terrible sadness in her dark eyes and a haunted expression on her face. I couldn't tell if she was afraid of us or of who had been there before. Or both. I considered stopping to speak to her, but we didn't have an interpreter and it didn't appear that she wanted to engage with us.

As I was considering whether to call out to her, there was a radio message from the lead section that they had found something. We stopped, dropped down on one knee and waited, and I watched the woman disappear like a ghost into the trees. I was called forward to examine the find. It was a sizeable pit in the ground about the size of a single-decker bus on its side. It had been covered over with a large mound of earth. It looked like it might be a mass grave. I walked cautiously up to it, wondering if it might be booby-trapped, and knelt down beside it. Something smelt very bad.

I looked around nervously and scanned the area, then something caught my eye – protruding out of the mound, just a couple of metres on from where I was kneeling. I could feel my heart pumping away. I edged up close to it and looked more closely. There could be no mistake – it was a human hand sticking out of the dirt. I edged even closer towards it to be certain of what it was. My eyes fixed upon it.

'What is it, boss?' shouted the Section Commander, so loudly that it made me jump.

I gave him a wry look before focusing back on the object. On the wrist of the hand was a watch. It was still ticking.

I marked the site on my map, but before I could look at what else might be there a message came over the radio that the helicopters were coming back for us – we were needed for another task. They would be back where we had been dropped off in forty-five minutes. We headed straight to the Helicopter Landing Site (HLS), and with twenty minutes to wait and the platoon arranged in all-round defence, for protection, I took a moment to think about what I had seen. My signaller reached into his webbing and produced a little stove; within a couple of minutes he'd made us both a hot sweet brew. I was grateful for it. I've never been a smoker but when he offered me a cigarette I took it and smoked it. Sat on the ground with a gentle breeze blowing through the trees, the fag and the brew were comforting. I just needed a moment to pause and reflect on what I had

seen, and smelt. I wondered about the young woman I had
passed earlier, what horrors she might have witnessed or
had inflicted upon her.

The helis screamed in, we ran on and shifted forward to
the next location. I put out of my mind thoughts about what
might have taken place in that village. I tried not to think
about the watch, or the hand, or what was attached to it,
and what else was hidden in the mound. I tried to put out of
my mind the very distinctive stench of death and the haunted
look on the young woman's face. Into Frank Gargan's coping
box it all went, and I got on with what we were doing.

Before long we had made it out of the countryside and up
to the urban sprawl of the capital city. Pristina was a place
that had been under siege and we were greeted as liberators and heroes. Crowds thronged in the streets to cheer us
and to shout, 'NATO! NATO!' My machine gun platoon
formed part of 1 Para's support company, and we were
tasked to patrol the streets in an attempt to reassure the
local population that we were there to try and establish
and then keep the peace and prevent further killings. As
the Serbian forces had withdrawn, the place had descended
into lawlessness. Retributions were being enacted on those
who were believed to have collaborated with the occupying
forces. In addition, long-time Serbian residents of Kosovo
were being targeted and executed simply because they were
Serbs. There was no doubt that some very bad things had
taken place during the Serbian occupation. David Blakeley's
platoon discovered a torture chamber in which appalling
acts had occurred. Two British Army engineers were killed
attempting to defuse a cluster bomb. Pristina, in June 1999,
was a wild place to be.

We darted about the city putting ourselves squarely in

the middle of these confrontations, arresting offenders and doing what we could to preserve life. Typically we would deploy into a particular area of the city and occupy an empty civilian house. Some of the houses had been abandoned with pretty much everything left behind, food still in the cupboards. We would put patrols out into the surrounding area, maintaining a twenty-four-hour coverage, the tempo of activity meaning that I would go long periods without sleep. Then, just as we were getting to know our patch, we would be moved on to another location and start doing it all again. In the supremely competitive environment that a parachute battalion is, there was chatter that the OCs were competing against each other over who could impress the CO the most by sustaining the longest and most punishing patrolling routine. It seemed strange that in a challenging operational environment, when lives were being both lost and saved, anyone would be focusing on their career. But as I would come to learn, the Army could be a ruthlessly competitive place.

At my junior level we got on with it. It was hard soldiering, and however tough you think you might be, long periods without sleep wear you down. When you are constantly on the go it is exhausting and it reduces your ability for clear decision-making. The tempo of activity was relentless to the extent that there was a constant requirement for me to encourage and sometimes cajole the blokes to keep going. Some of the older sweats struggled with the pace of it, but in the end nobody let me down and fell short of what was required. The pleasant woods of Macedonia were a distant memory as we thrashed about the city trying our best to restore some sense of normality.

The platoon patrolled on, sometimes on foot, sometimes in our Land Rover vehicles with mounted machine guns which had been driven up from Macedonia to support us. On one occasion I saw some armed men dash out of a building and jump into a car before tearing away. This was not a scenario we had trained for, nor were we certain what they'd actually done, but we gave hot pursuit anyway, weaving our way through the narrow side streets at breakneck speed before finally cornering the armed men, who at gunpoint we arrested and questioned.

The company received intelligence that some locals who had been kidnapped were being held hostage and tortured in a house within our patch. We mounted a big operation in the dead of night to rescue them, with camouflage cream smeared on our faces and grenades galore, but after kicking down a lot of doors and tearing through a number of houses and buildings we found no hostages. Not the first or last time we would fall victim to inaccurate intelligence.

Before we knew it, it was, for us, job done. Other British Army units were deploying out from the UK to take on the longer commitment of supporting the rebuilding of Pristina and Kosovo. It was time for us to head back to Aldershot. A massive party was being planned and everyone was excited at the prospect of heading home. It had been a baptism of fire for me, invaluable experience, made more challenging because of the nature of the soldiers I had been commanding, but I was satisfied that we had done everything that had been asked of us to the best of our ability. We had put our heart and soul into it and were knackered.

Before heading back we managed to grab some down time by the side of an idyllic lake on the outskirts of the city. For a few precious hours we swam and sunbathed and rested. It had been an exhilarating summer and for the battalion an opportunity to get back on an operational footing after a long hiatus. We had seen the fear and desperation in the eyes of fellow Europeans, people who resembled our own family and neighbours back home. We had done our bit. First in, first out, it was time to head back home.

Like the Sierra Leone deployment that was to come the following year, the Kosovo operation is generally considered to have been very successful in achieving its objective. Some have subsequently suggested that these successful military operations were significant in persuading Prime Minister Tony Blair of the efficacy of the military – something that would have been a factor in the subsequent decision to deploy to Iraq. But the campaigns to follow were far more difficult and, in their nature, very different.

I was starting to think about what I would do with my post-tour leave when I received word from the Adjutant to report to the battalion HQ in Pristina for an interview with the CO. I assumed it would be him telling me that I'd had my fun and I now had to get back on the RSO course. Fair enough, I thought.

I walked into the CO's office and saluted.

'As you know, Dan, the battalion will soon be returning to Aldershot.'

'Yes, Colonel, I'm looking forward to getting back.'

'You're not going back, Dan. You'll be staying here.'

'Staying here? I'm not sure I follow, Colonel.'

The CO went on to explain that General Jackson's Aide-de-Camp (ADC) – his personal staff officer – was due to be promoted and posted on, and the Regiment needed to identify a replacement. I was being put forward for the job. The General was a fearsome character, famed for his stamina – he would stay at social events until the very early hours, then go straight into the office and work a normal day. One of his nicknames was the 'Prince of Darkness' and he was famed for not suffering fools gladly. His ADC was very much in the hot seat and among many other things was responsible for ensuring he was in the right place at the right time with everything he needed.

I was gutted not to be returning with the battalion, I was worn out and needed a break, but I also recognised that working for the General was a rare opportunity to see how the higher echelons of the Army functioned, and to get a glimpse of life at the strategic level where the military interacts with the political. It would be fascinating, though definitely challenging. I was told to report to the General for a ten-day trial.

I had never met him before. His first words were along the lines of 'Welcome, but be clear – you are here on a temporary basis. I'll decide in ten days whether you've got the job or not.' I spent the next two days familiarising myself with the routine. Then on my first proper day I thought I was going to be sacked.

The Prime Minister, Tony Blair, was visiting the NATO headquarters to get an update from the General on progress with the Kosovo operation. At the end of the briefing, dinner was served outside in a small canvas tent. The chefs had done a good job in preparing some decent food, and after the meal I indicated that the helicopter was in place for the Prime Minister. It was my job to lead him and his small team to the HLS and put them safely on the flight back to Macedonia.

The camp that had become the headquarters was called 'Film City' having previously been a film studio, but it was now largely a construction site, with trenches and diggers wherever you looked. Despite this it was only a relatively short distance of a few hundred metres to walk from the dinner tent to the HLS, and even though it was dark and there were no lights, I had recced the route, brought a torch, and knew exactly where I was going. I was keen that my part of the visit went smoothly. I led the Prime Minister and his team out of the tent with the General following and headed towards where the helicopter was waiting.

To get to the HLS we needed to walk through a small wooded area which was a bit muddy underfoot, but I wasn't too concerned about that. The Prime Minister understood that we were in a conflict zone and had not expected the usual VIP red carpet treatment. As we entered the wooded area, to my horror I heard the helicopter engines revving, then the helicopter took off and flew away into the night sky. Soon it returned to hover overhead before plonking down on the alternate HLS, right on the other side of the camp several hundred metres away.

I was fuming with a combination of annoyance and embarrassment, but there was nothing I could do, other than confidently tell the Prime Minister that there had been a change of plan – nothing to worry about, but we were now heading to the other HLS. We retraced our steps, and despite the darkness I caught a more than quizzical look from the General.

Then things started to get a bit awkward. To get to the other HLS from where we were we had to go through a larger wooded area which I hadn't recced and didn't know as well but I suspected to be muddy, and I understood that there might still be some barbed-wire fencing in there. This now had the potential for me to end up in seriously deep trouble. We made our way through the very dark and, as it turned out, very muddy wood. Sure enough, after a while we reached a barbed-wire fence. I put my boot on the bottom strand and held up the top strand so the party could move on. As the Prime Minister ducked and

clambered through the barbed wire I experienced a moment
of clear realisation that this was not how I had planned
my first day to go. However, the PM and his Director of
Communications Alastair Campbell seemed to be enjoying the excursion; the PM's political adviser Anji Hunter
was wearing heels, and seemed to be enjoying it less. The
General shot me a look which indicated that I was now
skating on very thin ice.

Eventually we reached the alternate HLS but worryingly
the rotor blades were still turning on the helicopter: as I
understood it, the procedures stated that VIPs should only
get on helis when the rotors weren't turning. I decided to
ignore that particular procedure and bundled the Prime
Minister and his team on to the heli. He gave me a thumbs-
up which I took to mean that he hadn't minded the detour
and in a flash the helicopter was gone.

The General and I were now stood in silence on the edge
of the HLS. This had been very embarrassing and I was
fully expecting a huge dressing down. Worse, given that
I was still very much on probation I thought this might
result in me being sacked. There was a long pause, and I
steeled myself for the worst. The General gazed at the space
recently vacated by the Prime Minister's helicopter before
looking back at me.

Here it comes, I thought to myself, get ready for the
mother of all bollockings.

'Thank God it wasn't the Queen,' said the General. And
as he walked away he casually added, 'Oh, one more thing,
Dan, you might just tell the Helicopter Commander to go
and stand outside my office. He shouldn't expect coffee.'
An interview *without* coffee was code for 'come along for
a one-way tirade', which from General Jackson was not
something anyone would relish.

The ten-day trial was a whirlwind of multi-tasking. The General, rightly, expected the highest standards, and I was constantly being tested. On another occasion our helicopter landed at the wrong grid but we didn't realise and got out anyway. We had unexpectedly turned up at the HQ of the Turkish NATO contingent, who assumed that our visit was part of a surprise inspection regime. The General was treated as some iconic god-like figure and we were served some excellent Turkish coffee. The General did well not to spit it out when briefed by the Turkish commander that his plan to improve troop morale was to have all of his soldiers circumcised.

Shortly afterwards the General was informed that he had been promoted to become Commander-in-Chief of the Army and would be moving to Wiltshire to take up the command. He asked me if I would like to finish off the tour in Kosovo before moving with him to continue as his ADC. We still had a couple of months to go in Kosovo, where the great and the good – President Bill Clinton, Secretary of State Madeleine Albright – were in and out on a regular basis. I learned a huge amount from having a ringside seat at these political-military deliberations, getting to understand the process which led to decisions being made.

Although it was always busy, things calmed down a bit and we started to plan for what was coming next and the General's move back from Kosovo to Germany (Rheindahlen, where the permanent NATO HQ was) and then onwards to Wiltshire. As ADC I was charged with making contact with the new team in England to plan a smooth transition and I called the head of the Army's official residence to speak to the staff, armed with a long list of questions. I dialled the number and asked to speak to Sergeant Mawby, the House Sergeant.

'He's not here at the moment – can I take a message?' said a friendly voice at the other end of the phone.

'That would be kind,' I replied. 'Please can I ask who I am speaking to.'

'I'm Caroline.'

# 7

# Leave is Cancelled

## *February 2000*

—

After the move back from Kosovo, via Germany, we arrived at HQ Land at Wilton, just outside Salisbury. I went round to the General's official residence for an initial team meeting. There was Caroline. Standing in the kitchen. Looking lovely. She was a civilian employee working as the General's chef. I couldn't put my finger on it at the time, but the moment I met her I got a sense that there was something wonderful about her, and that I wanted to get to know her better. Something just clicked. We shook hands and spoke only briefly. Holly, her ever faithful Jack Russell, kept a close eye on me and stood guard by the kitchen door. I walked away thinking 'Wow!' and tried to focus on the meeting I was going into.

Over the next few weeks we bumped into each other several times and began to chat more and more. We seemed to be getting on well. Getting a grip on the new job was keeping me busy; and although I wanted to ask Caroline out on a date, I knew that I would need to tread carefully. A previous ADC had got into deep trouble after having a brief fling with the General's nanny. Any relationship between Caroline and me would likely be frowned on. The Army generally did not approve of work-related relationships – they were not, so it was thought, conducive to good military order and not helpful for the smooth running of the military machine. And although Caroline was a civilian I was mindful not to put her, the General or myself in a difficult position.

A few weeks after first meeting Caroline, I took off with David Blakeley to compete for the Regiment in the Marathon des Sables, an endurance run through the Sahara desert. Each day consisted of punishingly long runs through the baking heat of the Moroccan sands before making camp and shivering through the freezing night. Increasingly my mind wandered back to Caroline. There was something very special about her, and as I plodded up, down and through the sand dunes, I decided that on my return I would ask her out.

That decision made in the desert heat took a while to be acted on, as away from the adrenalin of the marathon race and confronted by the cold realities of military discipline I continued to err on the side of caution for a while, fearing the wrath of the General. I eventually plucked up the courage to do it. Despite the embarrassingly tongue-tied way in which I asked, Caroline said yes, on the condition that Holly could come along too. Over the next few weeks we went out a number of times and quickly got to know each other. She was tremendous fun, but caring and kind too. An accomplished chef, she loved to cook, adored animals, and donated a chunk of her monthly salary to support a range of animal charities. It wasn't too long before we reached the point where we considered ourselves to be an item.

Our relationship continued to blossom and I had been meaning to come clean about it with the General for ages. He was always very busy and it was, after all, a delicate personal matter. I kept thinking about the ADC who'd had the fling with the nanny – but in truth I dithered in order to avoid the awkward personal nature of the conversation. I naively hoped that the right moment to bring it up would present itself. But it never did. Then, at a very long and very late dinner night in Warminster, out of the blue the General turned to me. It was 4 a.m.

'I understand that you're going out with Caroline,' he said.

'Ah, right,' I stuttered, the ground seeming to open up under me. 'Er, er, yes, General. How did you ... I've ... I've been ... I've been meaning to ...'

The General looked me up and down, and allowed me to squirm a while longer. He had a very serious expression on his face. It was a look I had seen many times before and it was usually a precursor to bad news being delivered in a brutally frank way. It was a look that made me feel like I was about to be turned into stone. Not for the first time under tense circumstances with the General, I steeled myself for what was coming next.

'Two points, Dan.'

Then came a further pause.

'First, you've got very good taste.'

So far so good, I thought.

'Second, you're sacked.'

Ahh.

At that moment, someone cut across the conversation to ask the General about some inconsequential matter and nothing more was said that night. I was left the next morning wondering whether amid the haze of the night before the conversation had actually taken place, or if it had, whether the General had been joking. A couple of weeks later it was confirmed to me that it had indeed taken place when the General's wife, Sarah, told me how pleased she was that Caroline and I were, as she put it, 'stepping out'. So I wasn't sacked, and the General had been joking. I was grateful and relieved to have his and Sarah's blessing. They could, and custom said they probably should, have been difficult about it, but they weren't.

I fell in love with Caroline very quickly. She could be stubborn, but then so could I. We would go for long walks with Holly over the Wiltshire downs, or along the Dorset coast. We were a good match, and it wasn't long before I decided to ask her to marry me. I suspected that she wouldn't want to rush into anything and might want to think about it, but when, on a beach in North Wales, I proposed, she accepted. We were both deliriously happy and started making plans for a wedding in just a few months' time. I asked her father for his blessing, which he very graciously gave us.

Caroline quickly got a taste of what it could be like being married to someone in the Army when soon afterwards, at very short notice, I disappeared to Sierra Leone. Following a UK military intervention in May 2000 a British Army Training Team had deployed which included soldiers from the Royal Irish Regiment. A number of them had been taken hostage by a drug-fuelled, heavily armed militia called the 'West Side Boys', and in September 2000 a daring raid by the SAS rescued them. Following much speculation in the national press about exactly what had happened to the Royal Irish soldiers, the General requested an urgent briefing on the circumstances and dispatched a Brigadier from the HQ to travel to Sierra Leone to conduct an investigation. The General told the Brigadier to depart immediately and me to source a plane to fly him there.

Camped at Concordia on the approach to K2 in the Karakoram. Brother Rob seems to be having a better time than me.

Not particularly enjoying a Tyrolean traverse crossing. Fall in the river and you will be swept away.

At the end of a long trek. Ready for a decent meal, a bath and a hot brew.

With the band playing, Officer Cadets march proudly across the parade ground in front of the Old College at Sandhurst.

At the end of the final Sandhurst exercise in Germany. This was the first time we were allowed to put on our Regimental headdress. CSgt Gargan is standing to the left, and Capt Cummins to the right.

On the Aldershot training area with my Platoon Sergeant, 'Chips'. A Polish paratrooper is in the background.

In the corn field in Macedonia preparing for a potential air assault on to the Pristina airfield.

My machine-gun platoon grabs a quick team photo while we await a decision on whether to deploy forward.

On a Chinook helicopter flying up the Kacanik defile out of Macedonia and towards Kosovo.

First stop in Kosovo. Bumped into a local militia who asked for a picture.

In Pristina with some of the weapons we had just confiscated while on patrol.

Cadging a lift with my old friend Jon Wheale in Pristina.

Keeping a close eye on the Prime Minister and Lieutenant General Jackson at the 'Film City' NATO HQ on the outskirts of Pristina.

Caroline and
Holly the dog.

In the Moroccan
desert to run the
Sahara Marathon
with David
Blakeley and Nick
Wight-Boycott.

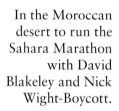

Caroline and me on
our wedding day.

The Regimental Sergeant Major, the Commanding Officer and the Adjutant (me) at 3 Para's Camp Longdon in Kuwait, ahead of deployment into Iraq.

In the desert of Iraq and delighted to have just heard on the radio that the Iraqi forces had surrendered, bringing immediate hostilities to an end.

At home with Caroline just before leaving for Afghanistan.

By this stage, I knew the General well enough to express a bit of scepticism as to how easy that would be to arrange.

'Where there's a will, there's usually a way,' came the swift and firm reply.

I phoned the RAF operations desk and after the expected sucking of teeth and expressions of doubt because of 'aircraft availability' and 'crew hours' and a host of other reasons I was able to arrange a light aircraft to fly immediately to Madeira. My experience of dealing with the RAF was that it was usually easier to secure a flight to somewhere like Madeira than to a less glamorous location. It looked like – subject to Met (weather), crew availability and a number of other factors – it might then be possible to arrange a pick-up from a C-130 aircraft to fly from there down to Sierra Leone. After a flurry of calls, during which I constantly found myself chanting the mantra of 'the General wants this to happen today', I briefed the Brigadier that it was all sorted and that he needed to leave shortly to get on the aircraft at a nearby airfield.

'Fine,' he said; then, with a broad smile, 'I need you to come with me – that OK?'

'Eh? Nobody mentioned I was going. Er, OK!'

I hadn't gone into the office that morning expecting to fly to Sierra Leone but that's what happened. A few years into Army life, like my peers I had developed a mind-set that not only expected but embraced the unexpected. I was already inoculated for a range of tropical diseases (in case there wasn't time, as in this case, to get all the required jabs). I kept a little daysack (a grab bag) in the office for emergencies such as this with some basic supplies, a change of clothes, toiletries, credit card, a passport, a good book and a stash of rhubarb and custard sweets (open only in case of emergency). I phoned Caroline to let her know that

I couldn't make dinner that night, which she accepted with typical good grace. I wondered whether she was going to ask me why I couldn't make it. She did. I explained that I needed to keep it quiet but I had to go to Sierra Leone. 'Oh ...' came the response. She understood but was worried about the risks of being there. I told her that it 'would be fine'.

We flew to Madeira, stepped off the light aircraft and, to my relief, straight on to a waiting C-130, and flew on to Sierra Leone via Senegal. We experienced a dreadful flight south over Africa during which the aircraft developed a technical fault with the navigation equipment which meant we got lost and ended up having to travel, or 'hand rail', down the west African coastline in order to actually find Sierra Leone. It was a relief to finally touch down at Freetown. We headed from the airfield to the Royal Navy ship *Sir Perceval* moored in the dock which is where the Royal Irish soldiers were, having been rescued. They had endured atrocious conditions in captivity during which time they had conducted themselves with great courage. We had many cups of tea with them, took statements about what had happened, and then headed back home.

There aren't many moments in history that are so monumental you can remember exactly where you were when you learned they had happened. Having completed my time as General Jackson's ADC, I had been posted to 3 Para and was sat at my desk in Hyderabad barracks in Colchester on 11 September 2001 when one of the clerks popped her head round the door to say that an aircraft had crashed into the Twin Towers of the World Trade Center in New York. My first thought was that it was a light aircraft and some sort of freak accident, but it was soon clear that something very much more significant was occurring. I turned on the

TV and saw footage of a passenger plane hitting the Twin Towers. Followed soon after by a second aircraft, and then by hijacked planes crashing elsewhere in the US. Although the sequencing of what was actually happening was confusing, I was certain that the world had just changed and that we as an Army, and me as an individual, would end up on the front line as a consequence of the events of 9/11. And so it proved.

3 Para's next-door neighbours, 2 Para, deployed to Afghanistan a couple of months later. Caroline and I were getting married in December in a pretty little village church in Wiltshire, so although there was a very strong view in our battalion that we were missing out on the deployment, I was mightily relieved that we didn't have to postpone our wedding, though I anticipated we would follow on sooner rather than later.

Despite the temptation of heading off on another operational tour, an ambition which the Army would happily have facilitated, I had thought that now I was to be married I should do a sensible, grown-up job, so had accepted the offer to be Adjutant of 3 Para. The Adjutant works directly to the CO and is responsible for the effective running of the battalion. It's a big and busy job, but when I had accepted the posting prior to 9/11 there had been no prospect of 3 Para going anywhere any time soon, and I'd thought it would provide a steady start to married life without the stresses of an operational tour.

But, despite the US and UK having deployed troops to Afghanistan to provide some security after the fall of the Taleban regime, the political discussions and focus quickly shifted to Saddam Hussein. In 2002, meetings took place between President Bush and Prime Minister Blair and the focus of their discussions was Iraq. Behind the scenes there was extensive military planning taking place for what became known as Operation TELIC (quickly dubbed 'Tell everyone leave is cancelled'), which would be the British military commitment to Iraq.

Throughout 2002 the momentum towards a decision on military action grew, and while 3 Para juggled a range of other non-related commitments, Iraq became our real focus and it looked increasingly likely that the battalion would be going there as part of a 16 Air Assault Brigade deployment. By Christmas it seemed certain that we would be heading out to the Middle East in the New Year, although no final decision had been taken – or if it had, we were not aware of it. Caroline was now heavily pregnant and expecting our first child in February. My workload was immense, doing what I could to ensure 3 Para were ready for war in Iraq, or whatever else was asked of us, while at the same time trying to support Caroline through her pregnancy.

On 27 December 2002 it was finally confirmed that 3 Para would be deploying out to Kuwait, to be in position for any subsequent move into Iraq from early in 2003, so we continued our preparatory training, and from mid-January the logistic elements of the battalion started to deploy forward to the desert of Kuwait. At this stage the nature of the deployment in terms of what we were actually going to do was unclear; basically we were told to get out there and get ready, but for what we didn't yet know.

I monitored the news coverage of the huge demonstration against the coming war in Iraq that took place in central London on 15 February 2003. From a distance I heard the arguments and debates play out and I was peripherally aware of the political machinations leading up to the decision to deploy military action in Iraq. It wasn't as though I didn't have views on whether we ought to be doing it or not. It was just that I didn't have the luxury of being able to choose. The reality was that my job, my life at that moment, was consumed with making sure that 3 Para were ready to undertake whatever was asked of us. As the Adjutant it was my task to work with the CO and the battalion staff to get our soldiers ready, knowing that the preparatory training we were conducting could literally make a life-or-death difference for us all.

Like everyone else in the Armed Forces, I had to accept the decisions of our political masters. When you join the Army and, as the old saying goes, 'accept the Queen's shilling' you understand – or you should understand – that you don't get to pick and choose where you go, which wars you show up for and which you don't. That's a matter for the democratically elected government of the day.

They decide, you deploy.

That said, in the rare quiet moments I did think about whether we were doing the right thing. The political decision-makers in Downing Street and Whitehall had access to intelligence and information that only a few very senior people in the Army were privy to, and certainly someone of my junior rank would never have sight of such sensitive material. I hoped that those who did have access to it were making the right decisions for the right reasons, and based on reliable intelligence – but I was so far down the decision-making chain that I was utterly powerless to shape those decisions even if I had wanted to. Whatever they decided, we in the Army would be bound by it. We had to take it on trust. And so we did.

Regardless of the rights or wrongs of the looming conflict, the Iraq deployment was terrible timing for us as a family: in early February 2003 Caroline gave birth to our first child, a boy, by emergency Caesarean section in the middle of the night. I was there and saw him lifted out. When I held him I was immediately consumed with love, but also with fear that I might not be around for him as he grew up. That I would very soon have to leave them to go off to war was an ever-present shadow.

3 Para were based in Colchester, but anticipating that I was likely to be away for some time, Caroline had sensibly concluded that she should be in Wiltshire, near to her family so that they would be close at hand to help out. Caroline's planning through the latter stages of her pregnancy had been meticulous. But just before she went into labour we found ourselves grappling with a series of domestic crises: in a bitterly cold February the central heating in our house broke down, which required significant repair, and then Caroline's car gave up the ghost. All of this added to the stress of the imminent arrival of a baby and my departure to Iraq.

I brought Caroline home with our new baby, with the heating working only intermittently and the car away being fixed. Anyone would have forgiven her for being angry and upset at the prospect of being left at this point. I know that she was worried, but she largely kept it from me to make it easier for me. Because Caroline had had a Caesarean she couldn't drive and was entirely dependent on others to ferry her around. Recovering from an operation, caring for a new baby, all with the worry of having a husband about to go away to war. It was a lot for her to cope with and is the story of Army wives throughout history.

On a bright but cold February morning we drove out into the Wiltshire countryside with baby and Holly. A last chance to enjoy some peace, and for me some green (albeit tinged with white frost) English countryside. While we sat admiring the view my mobile phone went off. It was the

CO, who needed half an hour to talk through a number of pressing issues. The calm had been disturbed and we headed home in silence, both fearing the point at which we would have to say goodbye.

My previous operational deployments hadn't carried the same level of danger or uncertainty, even if it hadn't always felt that way at the time. This was not like the woods in Macedonia where I'd had a laissez-faire approach to my own mortality; things had now changed. The risk was much greater this time. I was married, and we now had a son. It felt like real responsibility. I didn't want to die. But I was also the Adjutant, a key cog in the battalion machine, and people were depending on me. I had to get on and do my job. I tried to be stoic about it, as did Caroline. The night before I left I read though my will which served only to darken my mood further.

I had to leave the next day. With my bags by the front door we said our goodbyes. Caroline gave me a St Christopher to wear for good luck and safe travels. It was hard to walk out that door – though as it turned out this would not be our most difficult parting; that was to come. I couldn't say when I'd be back home because I didn't know. Nobody did. I hugged Caroline and kissed our newborn son and with a very heavy heart I headed off to the looming conflict in Iraq.

# 8

# Gas, Gas, Gas

## *February 2003*

—

3 Para were deploying into a deeply hostile and unfamiliar environment in which, we'd been told authoritatively by the 16 Air Assault Brigade Commander, it wasn't a case of *whether* Saddam Hussein would use chemical weapons against us, but *when*. We left for Iraq fully expecting to be gassed.

It took some time to get us all out to Kuwait, as thousands of British troops were shuttled out from RAF Brize Norton. Then we waited in a tented camp out in the desert, twenty-five kilometres north of Kuwait City, and while the politics played out and the world waited for the results of Hans Blix's Weapons of Mass Destruction (WMD) inspections, we conducted a series of training exercises to acclimatise the battalion to the scorching heat. The camp in Kuwait was made up of row on row of neatly pitched white canvas marquee tents, with desert all around as far as the eye could see. Our fleet of once-green Land Rovers and four-tonne lorries had been resprayed a sandy colour and were all parked neatly in formation. Latrine pits were dug into the sand.

The Sergeant Majors and Quartermaster and their teams who were responsible for logistics and administration beavered around the desert camp, which had been named Camp Longdon (after a battle in the Falklands War of 1982). They made sure that the place was as spick and span as possible, that all rubbish was disposed of and we kept ourselves as clean as we could. As British soldiers we used the traditional ingenuity soldiers have historically resorted to when deployed overseas – we adapted and we made do. We fashioned makeshift showers using plastic containers with tiny holes in them so the water flowed out as if out of a shower head. We made gym equipment from pretty much anything we could get our paws on. Signs were put up, showing how many miles back to Colchester, and how many miles forward to Baghdad. The sand got everywhere, and I mean everywhere. In the battalion HQ tent I tried using clingfilm (which I had brought with me) to keep it out of my laptop, which seemed to work, but only for about a day.

We established a daily routine, of which food formed an important part. The old maxim that 'an army marches on its stomach' was as true as ever before and we piled into the marquee cookhouse to consume quantities of the scoff that had been skilfully cooked by the chefs. With more than a thousand of us in the 3 Para Battle Group, now supported by signallers, gunners and engineers, living cheek by jowl, there was a real risk of bugs and infections spreading, so our hands were inspected before every meal to make sure that we'd washed them.

Each day brought new challenges. On 14 March, 3 Para were warned off for a potential air assault operation to seize crossing points on the River Tigris. The next couple of days saw intense activity as plans for the operation were drawn up. In the event it came to nothing, and the operation was cancelled. On a more mundane level, we also had to deal with a soldier who was sat on a wooden box latrine performing his bodily functions when another soldier chucked a lighted fag end into the latrine pit, igniting the chemicals and causing a flash of fire which singed the unfortunate soldier's private parts. He quickly assumed the nickname John Wayne, given the wide walk he had to adopt for a few days, but he was soon fine.

Sandstorms would sometimes blow in and interrupt the otherwise blazing sun. We initially did training runs in the early morning, before it got too hot, then progressed to marches carrying our equipment in the heat of the day. There was a great deal of uncertainty about what would happen. We still didn't know for certain that we would actually deploy into Iraq. Clearly, any such operation came with very significant risk. Sat there, in the desert, it was inconceivable to think we'd all make it home if we ended up fighting our way into Iraq. Some of us, possibly many of us, would be killed.

The Chemical, Biological, Radiological and Nuclear (CBRN) warfare training we conducted now assumed a much more serious edge. Only lip service had ever been paid to it before: it was pretty much regarded as a joke. But it wasn't now. Saddam Hussein had previously used chemical weapons against Iran and his own people and none of us relished the prospect of him deploying them at us. Wearing a respirator (a gas mask) and a thick charcoal chemical suit in the desert heat was no laughing matter – this equipment was disliked partly because it made you so hot and sweaty. Even back in the UK you could easily succumb to heat stroke. But nobody complained.

The signal to put on your respirator was when someone shouted, 'Gas, gas, gas!' One simple but deadly word,
repeated three times. You had just a few seconds to react
and grab your respirator from your pouch and put it on.
Any longer and you would likely succumb to the effects of
the gas. Wc practised the drills – what to do in the event
of a chemical attack – again and again. Time after time we
boiled in those suits, and we kept the respirators on for
long periods – it was hot, sticky and unpleasant. Nobody
grumbled because we all knew that these drills could
make the difference between life and death if – or, as we
believed, when – Saddam Hussein started lobbing chemical
shells at us.

I think we all quietly feared what a chemical attack could
do to us: we'd been shown harrowing footage of the impact
such weapons have on soldiers and civilians alike. Despite
the constant banter in the Regiment, much of which was
often dark, I never heard anyone joke about that.

In spite of the uncertainty, the battalion went about its
preparations in a highly professional way. We got ready; we
planned and trained for a range of different scenarios; we
packed kit, unpacked it, repacked it. The vehicles too were
packed, then unpacked, and then packed again. The drivers
practised driving through the desert sand by day, and then
by night. We built up our physical fitness with exercise.

We wrote 'blueys' – airmail letters home. We received
letters with news from home, and parcels. These were so
important for morale. Caroline sent out photos of our son
and wonderful letters. In one she wrote:

*It's been very cold but with the boiler fixed we now at*
*least have heating!!! Everyone has been so helpful and*
*supportive since you left and I'm trying to get the little*

*man into a routine. So far so good! Think about you*
*soo much, and hope that you and the others are staying*
*safe. Take care babe. LYF. XXX.*

She would also include a copy of the local paper and the
parish newsletter. I pored over them, craving the escapism
of a peaceful life back home and the pleasant greenery of the
British countryside. Not so much wishing to be back there
because I knew I had a job to do, but hoping at some point
I would make it back. Some people kindly sent sweets and
chocolate, which with the passage through the postal system
and in the desert heat melted into amorphous shapes. We
ate them anyway. One or two of the lads got 'Dear John'
letters, where they were dumped by girlfriends. They were
always rallied around and looked after.

We were able to make the occasional phone call home
too, though these were rationed to twenty minutes a week.
As the Adjutant I had permanent access to a phone so
if I heard of any soldier who for compassionate reasons
needed to call home I lent them the phone and didn't worry
too much about the twenty-minute rule (although I was
a bit more concerned when many months later I saw the
phone bill).

My own calls home were good in that it was wonderful
to speak to Caroline and hear our son gurgle, but bad in
that I missed them so much and felt so guilty that I wasn't
around to help.

Every night I listened to the BBC World Service to try
and keep up to date with the news (to this day the lilting
theme tune 'Lillibulero' makes the hairs on the back of my
neck stand up – and in an instant it takes me back to Iraq
in 2003). The Padre (the battalion vicar) conducted church

services that many people went along to, non-believers included. There was a lot of banter and some bravado, but there was also apprehension and fear. A quiet fear about what was coming and about how we would perform in the burning cauldron of war, when we expected to come under the most intense pressure. Fear, too, that some of us might not be coming home.

A few people sat down with the padre to discuss their fears privately, a few people came to me. I tried to provide calm, reassuring words, but given that I didn't know what was going to happen they sometimes felt a bit trite. Most bottled it up. Kept busy, got on with it and convinced themselves that either they wouldn't be killed or if they were it would be instant and they wouldn't know anything about it. The battalion felt very tight-knit; we looked out for others, knowing they would look out for us. This is what we did, this is who we were.

Once it became clear that the operation was a 'go', the uncertainty lifted to an extent. It was on. We were going for it. 'Let's get on with it and do our job' became the prevailing attitude. Any thoughts of protests back in the UK or concerns about whether it was the right thing to do were now banished from our heads – we had to focus on the here and now and what was coming.

The CO, Lieutenant Colonel John Lorimer (who had been my OC back in 1 Para), and his team gathered the whole battalion around a huge model made out of various salvaged and scavenged objects. Buckets represented the oil storage tanks buried in the sand. A set of orders were given to the entire battalion, so that everyone was clear about what the plan was and what their role would be. We would be advancing north through the desert following on behind the US Marines. The CO told us to prepare ourselves for whatever was to come. That we needed to be 'Ready for Anything'. Once the orders had been delivered I walked slowly back to my tent, lost in thought about what the hours, days and months ahead might bring.

Like everyone else I was quietly anxious about what was coming, and despite trying to focus all my thoughts and efforts on the task ahead I couldn't shake the deep-rooted thought in my mind that maybe, just maybe, one day, we, the UK, might lose a war. Recent operational experience had been characterised by 'victory' – we had successfully retaken the Falkland Islands, had participated in broadly successful deployments in the Balkans; the Sierra Leone operation had been a stunning success. Walking back to my tent, out there in the desert, it did not seem to me a foregone conclusion that we were definitely going to win this one. Might we suffer a large-scale chemical attack? Might we find ourselves in a Vietnam-style protracted conflict that attrited both our material capability and our political will? The risks were huge. I tried to banish these thoughts and focus on what I needed to be doing.

# 9

# Game of Ghosts

## *March 2003*

—

At H-hour (the time at which an operation starts), we drove in a long vehicle convoy out of Camp Longdon and headed north behind the US Marines out of Kuwait and across the border into Iraq. We manoeuvred our way through the acrid smoke of still-burning Iraqi military vehicles that had been recently targeted by devastatingly effective coalition air forces. The stench was overpowering. As far as the eye could see were burning oil wells. It felt surreal, like a scene from an apocalyptic film.

The US Marines in front of us were charged with securing the key oil infrastructure in the strategically important Rumaila oilfields. We took it over from them, and they then launched forward to Baghdad. The move went reasonably smoothly though it was frequently interrupted by Iraqi Scud missile attacks, which meant we had to spend long periods with our respirators and chemical suits on. Nobody ever flapped, we just got on with it.

The first time the Scud alarm went off I was sat in the back of a Land Rover, with my chemical suit already on, listening in to the battalion radio net. Somebody shouted very loudly, 'Gas, gas, gas!' This time it was for real. All around there was a frenzy of movement and like everyone else I hastily put on my respirator. I could feel my heart pumping its way out of my chest, but all I could do was sit and wait. We sat in silence. After a while I could feel the sweat dripping off my body on to the inside of the charcoal suit; it felt like I was melting. My core body temperature felt hotter than at any previous point in my life, and as the translucent plastic eye holes on my respirator fogged up, I thought about where the missile was going to land. It would have to land somewhere – would it be on us?

I felt utterly powerless to control it. I toyed with the idea of crossing my fingers so that it wouldn't land on us, but just like tip-toeing through a minefield, it seemed such a pathetically inadequate response that in the end I decided just to sit quietly and think of home, of Caroline and our son. Deep down I don't think I really believed the missile was coming for me, for us, on that first occasion, but there was still a nagging doubt that it might. After thinking about it some more, I changed my mind and crossed my fingers and like everyone else waited and hoped for the best. That's all any of us could do.

Although we never heard it land, that first Scud impacted several miles away so when the all-clear was sounded we just breathed a sigh of relief and carried on. There were to be many more missile alarms, more moments of anxiously waiting to see what would happen, but quite quickly we became attuned to it. We fell into the routine of soldiering in the desert. The logistic supply lines were long, but because of brilliant teamwork, we always just about managed to get the ammunition, water, food and supplies we needed. Sometimes we would sleep in the desert, underneath or close to our vehicle, other times we would occupy abandoned buildings. I ended up eating the same pork casserole ration pack for a total of fourteen days on the trot because that was the only one available. It was OK(ish) for the first week, but I quickly started to tire of it after that. Being handed another pork casserole ration pack for the fourteenth time was a genuinely low moment. By contrast, receiving a chicken pasta sauce ration pack the next day was a real moment of joy.

After the initial situation had stabilised, things calmed a little. There were occasional moments of frenzied activity, and all around was the distressing detritus of war, but mostly it was just difficult, hard, hot soldiering in the heat and dust. David Blakeley, who had been off with the Pathfinder platoon, had been involved in a serious accident when his Land Rover turned over in the desert at night. His injuries were significant, but I was very relieved to hear that he was receiving treatment and would be OK.

We had no idea of how long the war would last or of what might come next. During the next few weeks we patrolled the Rumaila oilfields and then moved on to Basra, before setting up a battalion HQ to the north of the city where we began to prepare for the follow-on units to take our place. Just like in Kosovo, it didn't seem long before we were heading home – we had been part of the first wave in, which meant we were among the first to head back. I had spent more time looking at photos of my son than I had actually seen him in the flesh so was desperate to get back and see him and Caroline.

The battalion had latterly been tasked to occupy and administer the Maysan province and city of Al Amarah and we established a routine of carrying out patrols, trying to bring some semblance of order and normality to the Iraqi people within our area. I had already turned my attention to addressing the mountain of administration that needed to be done and was stood talking to Matt, the Regimental Signals Officer, and Nick, an old friend on attachment from The Royal Scots, when I heard someone shout that a casualty had been taken. I dashed into the battalion HQ to be told that a young soldier from A Company had been shot and was being rushed into camp for treatment.

When he arrived he was taken into the field hospital, which consisted of a series of interconnected tents albeit well equipped and immaculately clean. Our Regimental Medical Officer (RMO) and our medics immediately went to work to treat him, but it looked like he was in a very bad way.

The duty watch keeper was told to radio Brigade HQ and request an urgent casualty evacuation by helicopter so we could get the wounded soldier into the main medical facility, where there would be a greater level of medical support. By now the battalion padre was stood by him, which I took as an ominous sign. I was told the helicopter would not be with us for thirty minutes. I sensed we didn't have thirty minutes. It would be too late by then, so I unceremoniously bundled the duty watch keeper out of the watch keeper's chair and got on the radio net myself.

'Need a lifter [helicopter] at my location ASAP.'

'Roger, lifter at your location in figures three zero.'

'Negative. Need a lifter now.'

There was a pause.

'That might be difficult.'

I could hear the concern in my voice as I spoke the words: 'Need. A. Lifter. NOW.'

'Roger, out.'

Very soon after the exchange on the radio net ended a helicopter screamed out of the sky and plonked down on the HLS directly next to the field hospital. The soldier was carried out to it on a stretcher by the Regimental Sergeant Major (RSM) and a medic. As they passed me, and although he was unconscious, I instinctively spoke to him: 'Do not die, Andy. That is an order.' It was the only time in fifteen years that I ever used the expression 'that is an order'.

The helicopter tore away with such force that the back draft blew the RSM clean off his feet.

Andy was just alive when he left on the heli, but tragically he died shortly afterwards. We were so near to getting away without a fatality, so near yet now so impossibly far. His funeral took place several weeks later, by which time I was back in the UK. I went to pay my respects. The church was in a stunning location overlooking the sea at Maker near Torpoint in Cornwall. A lot of people attended including many of his friends from school. Young people with the rest of their lives ahead of them to look forward to. I felt sick that Andy, who had had his whole life ahead of him, could not do the same.

He was eighteen.

Other than this one tragic death, we emerged from Iraq largely unscathed. Despite all the dire warnings that we would be gassed, despite all the fear and the risk, we returned feeling that we'd played our part in liberating the country. Saddam Hussein had been removed from power, the country's oil reserves meant it was in a position to prosper economically, and the situation was calming down. When I left Iraq in May 2003 I was hopeful for its future. My hope was misplaced, and what we would see over the coming months, and years, was a massive deterioration of the security situation.

As Adjutant of 3 Para, I took the decision to deploy to Iraq on trust. I was powerless to shape it, and I was totally committed to and consumed by getting our soldiers ready. There simply was not the time or the space to give it too much detailed thought. Since then, I've thought a lot about it. Two years later I picked up a newspaper which on its front page ran a story about the hundred British soldiers who had so far been killed in Iraq. This front page consisted of one hundred pictures of the fallen soldiers. I scanned across them. Included was Matt Bacon, who had been a good friend from Sandhurst. I counted nine more I had known reasonably well. Ten per cent – what a terrible game of ghosts this had become.

That was the moment I stopped counting.

I couldn't have been happier to be home, and after a demanding couple of years as Adjutant of 3 Para I was promoted to Major and posted to a desk job in the Army's recruit training directorate based at Upavon in Wiltshire. It was a relatively steady number which at least meant I got home every night. I sometimes got home earlier than that, because for the first time in my Army service I had a boss – Brigadier Jeff Cook, an enigmatic figure with a Military Cross – who used to walk round mid-afternoon and order people to go home and see their families. Jeff Cook was not someone to be messed with, and his basic ethos was very sensible – that you needed a decent work/home life balance. He knew that many of us, like me, had come from demanding posts or had recently returned from operational tours and while the work we were doing was important, many of us needed a bit of decompression from the shattering stresses of front-line soldiering. It was an enlightened approach, though it would have been unwise to describe it to him in those terms. He would stroll down the corridor with a golf club in his hand shouting, 'If you can't get your work done by now, I'll find someone else who can – go home and see your kids!' If people still had work to do they would hide in their offices, or go over to the camp café (the NAAFI) for a brew, and wait for him to go home before coming back to complete their work.

Shortly afterwards, in a characteristic Jeff Cook move he stunned us all by resigning his commission in order to take charge of security at Buckingham Palace. I had visions of him strolling down the palace corridors telling the Queen to go home and spend more time with her family. Not long after his appointment a Fathers for Justice campaigner dressed in a Batman costume climbed over the fence at Buckingham Palace, and we thought it would be funny to give him a call and sing the *Batman* theme tune down the phone. I'm not sure he shared the joke.

Just before he left, he did me a big favour. I was due to attend a two-year course at the Army Staff College. The first year was essentially a warm-up for the second year and I thought it was a waste of time. However, the posting system said that the first year was compulsory – no exceptions. I told Brigadier Cook this and he gave me an almighty bollocking. 'Who do you think you are?' he raged at me. 'There's a good reason why you do that first year, it prepares you for the second year.' I tried to explain that an opportunity had arisen for me to go and work at the Permanent Joint Headquarters (PJHQ), which would be a much better preparation. He was always telling us to 'think outside the box', and this is precisely what I had done. PJHQ was the tri-service HQ from which all UK operations were run. It was a brilliant opportunity and would be valuable experience – much more than the pedestrian first year at Staff College. He dismissed it out of hand and told me to 'bugger off'.

I did, but I didn't give up on it. I bided my time. A few weeks later I asked him again and got an even more curt response. Perhaps rashly, I thought I would give it one final attempt. Another few weeks on, I was walking past his office when I saw him practising his putting stroke.

'You're busy then, Brigadier,' I cracked. This was a highly risky strategy, and while he decided whether to laugh at my audacious joke or punch me, I quickly moved the conversation on to a piece of work I was doing that I knew he was interested in. We had a productive discussion about it, and I was just about to leave when I said, 'One more quick thing.'

'It's not about working at PJHQ, is it?'

'Yes.'

'You sure that's what you want to do?'

'Yes, sir.'

'OK, then I'll support you.'

'Many thanks,' I said, and walked off quickly before he could change his mind.

As I did, he shouted down the corridor: 'Perseverance, young Dan, perseverance.'

He was good to his word, and a few months later I was posted to PJHQ, where I was based in an underground bunker in Northwood, north London, working to Colonel James Everard who had been General Jackson's Military Assistant in Kosovo. It was a whirlwind of purposeful and operationally focused activity. The Armed Forces at their very best. The three services side by side working hard to get difficult things done. My role was newly created in the plans department and I set about the task of establishing this new role I had been posted into. I would start very early and in the dark I would go down into the bunker; by the time I had finished and I came back out of the bunker it was dark again.

I had been tracking progress in Iraq via the daily operational updates, and had watched with horror the descent into destruction. From PJHQ I went back out to Iraq in October 2004, some eighteen months after I'd last been there, to support planning work for the Iraqi elections. It was truly shocking to see just how dangerous the country had become. Al-Qaeda had flooded into Iraq (having not been there under Saddam – and they had thrived in the conditions of chaos that a power vacuum offers), and the level of violence against British soldiers was incredibly high. One hundred and seventy-nine would be killed and many thousands would be wounded.

I flew in a helicopter from the relatively secure British base at the airport to the Basra Palace base, which was mortared most days, with road convoys being attacked the whole time. The improvised explosive device (IED) threat was massive, and British soldiers were regularly being killed. The country felt very different from how it had felt when I left the previous year. Liberators had quickly become occupiers.

From 2009 the Chilcot Inquiry spent seven long years taking evidence and analysing the decisions that had been made. My own view was that winning the war – the direct application of military force – had, relatively speaking, been the easy bit; it was winning the subsequent peace that proved to be the tough fight. Judgements about the efficacy and morality of conflict are best taken over the longer term and come with the benefit of hindsight, but it looks like the decision to go to war in Iraq in 2003 and its aftermath will for the UK resemble, albeit on a smaller scale, the soul-searching the US went through after their Vietnam deployment.

Indeed, the decision to go to war in Iraq is likely to significantly influence the willingness of both British political leaders and the public to engage in future military operations, perhaps for another generation to come. In 2011, shortly after I was elected to Parliament, I spoke to Tony Blair about the decision he took as Prime Minister. He seemed convinced that it was the right one; that there was utility from staying close to the Americans (who were going anyway) and that we were best placed to shape what they did by being inside, rather than outside, the tent. Convinced that, based on the intelligence he was presented as Prime Minister, which we now know to be faulty, the attempt to remove a brutal dictator was the right thing to do.

The reality is that these decisions and the commitments that were made came with long-lasting consequences. There can now be no doubt that the intervention, although successful in removing a bloody dictator, also unleashed a range of forces which were unforeseen and have undoubtedly led to greater instability not just in Iraq but across the wider Middle East, and further afield. Looked at in that context, and remembering the hundreds of thousands of Iraqis who have lost their lives, it's impossible not to conclude that it was a grave error.

That our soldiers, including some of my friends, might have died in vain is something I still wrestle with. They lost their lives nobly serving our country, and their families can be proud of them and their service. But I cannot look them in the eyes and justify it when they ask me (as they have) whether their ultimate sacrifice was worth it, because for them I know that it won't have been.

If it is the case that it is now much more difficult than it would otherwise have been for Britain to take political decisions about the use of military force, then that also has far-reaching ramifications for future political decision-making. Some will conclude that this is definitely a good thing. If it's harder to go to war, then all the better. Inaction, though, has consequences too.

Decisions about the committal of military force are the most difficult and the most complex. They require not only the wisdom of Solomon, but a government with objectives, a strategy and a plan: political, diplomatic, economic, military. A government that can think long and hard about the potential consequences of their actions and prepare for and resource a range of different scenarios. That was one of the problems with Iraq: there was not sufficient planning for the reconstruction of Iraq after the initial intervention.

If any future British government contemplates a significant military commitment they must have not only a sustained focus in the lead-up to the committal of military force, but must understand that the commitment may run for many years the other side – we still have a military presence in Afghanistan having first deployed soldiers there in 2001. It is not just about the political will, and the financial commitment, over the period leading up to, and the first few months of, that committal of military force. It is a much longer, wider, deeper commitment, potentially over several decades, which involves addressing the root causes of the problems in that particular country.

It's never just a military solution.

We retain our Armed Forces because sometimes, in a complex, dangerous and difficult world, there will be occasions when we need to use force to defend ourselves and support the upholding of international law. I wish that was not the case, but we live in an imperfect world and that won't change any time soon; indeed there's good cause to assume that the world will only become more challenging over the next generation. Where force is used it must always be done in accordance with the rule of law and only ever as a last resort. In terms of Iraq, the long arm of history will be the final judge, but it is impossible at this moment in time to conclude that the world is a safer place because of that intervention, because it isn't, and no one should say it is.

I returned from Iraq despondent at its vicious spiral of decline but excited at the prospect of being a father again – Caroline was due to give birth to our second child, and on bonfire night with fireworks going off all around the hospital, our daughter was born. Caroline seemed only mildly irked that having disappeared to Iraq as soon as our son was born, I'd been dodging mortar rounds in Iraq until just a few days before she was due to give birth to our daughter. She had got everything organised but the deal was always that I would be back by early November, in time for the baby's arrival. I was a bit sandy but I made it back as agreed.

Married life in the Army and with two small kids was rarely quiet, but we settled into a relatively normal family routine and were happy and content, hopeful for what the future would bring.

# 10

# The C Word

## *April 2006*

—

'I think it is cancer' were words I never imagined I would hear. But in April 2006 the unimaginable happened: Caroline was diagnosed with bowel cancer. We were both of an age that neither of us thought such a thing would happen to us. For some time she had been suffering from what we initially thought was a bad case of indigestion. She'd feel uncomfortable after eating, and having endured it for several weeks went to see her GP, who said it might be irritable bowel syndrome (IBS). Accordingly, she made some adjustments to her diet, but the symptoms persisted and then, over time, got worse. She managed her symptoms, but clearly something was not right. There seemed a reluctance from the GP to acknowledge there might be a problem and both Caroline and I started to worry. Her health deteriorated, but typically she battled on up until the point where she was bedridden.

I called the GP out to see Caroline, determined that we

would get to the root cause of the problem, and eventually it was agreed that Caroline would go into hospital for some tests. Just a precautionary measure, or so we were told. We were relieved that at last action was being taken, but frustrated that we had had to wait until this point before it felt like our concerns were being taken seriously.

The tests were conducted and the registrar decided to admit Caroline into hospital. Again we were told it was just a precautionary measure – 'nothing to worry about at this stage'. Being told that you have 'nothing to worry about *at this stage*' guarantees only one thing: that you start to worry *at that stage*. Caroline was dozy from the drugs she had been given but I was now starting to get really worried. My concerns were eased when I was told that it looked like there was some sort of either blockage or entanglement in her bowel. Again, not to worry, we should be able to sort this out, I was told. I was relieved that finally the problem had been identified.

Then, something must have happened or someone saw something that hadn't previously been seen, because before we knew what was happening Caroline was having surgery, and an explorative operation was being conducted by a consultant called Andy Agombar. I waited for the operation to finish, somewhat bemused by developing events. I was concerned but calm. I was hopeful that the operation would identify whatever the problem was and that we could get it sorted, go home together, and get on with living our lives. I hoped that would then be the end of the matter. At that moment, this seemed entirely achievable.

After much pacing around a small waiting room, I was eventually told that the operation was over so I escaped the stuffiness for some fresh air. I was standing in front of Salisbury hospital, not really knowing what to do with myself, when Andy Agombar came looking for me. I was obviously hoping for and expecting good news, but there was something about his demeanour which betrayed the fact that he was about to impart bad news to me. I readied myself.

Very gently and sensitively he told me that he had been doing this kind of operation for many years. He paused. Although the 'blockage', as he described it, had been removed from Caroline's bowel and would have to be analysed in the laboratory, 'I think it is ... cancer', he said.

It took a moment for me to process the word 'cancer'. It was not a word I had expected to hear. I felt the colour drain from my face.

'Cancer?' I said, checking that I had heard him correctly.

Although we had come to understand that there was some sort of minor problem in the bowel, that it might be cancer just hadn't crossed our minds. Maybe it should have done. But it didn't – we hadn't even imagined the possibility. And now, from nowhere, completely unexpectedly, the 'C' word was being used for the first time.

I knew that I had to stay positive, though I didn't feel it. I was devastated. He let me pause for a moment to catch my breath and then we discussed how to break the news to Caroline. Andy said it would probably be for the best if he explained it to her. He walked back into the hospital.

In that moment it felt like a great cloud had descended and that our lives had just changed. I spent the night steeling myself for the moment that would see the bad news delivered to Caroline.

The next day, while Caroline was recovering from the anaesthetic, I was sat at her bedside when Andy appeared. He drew the curtain around her bed to give us some privacy.

'How are you feeling?' he asked gently.

'A bit groggy, doctor,' Caroline replied.

I took her hand. I knew what was coming and I was determined to be strong for her, though I felt utterly bleak.

Andy's bedside manner was superb. He exuded calm professionalism. He was compassionate but clear. In a gentle, matter-of-fact way he explained that although more tests were needed to confirm it, he was certain that the blockage had in fact been cancer. He paused to allow Caroline to begin to process this terrible news. He continued by saying that he thought he'd removed it all but he couldn't be absolutely certain. Though he was imparting devastating news, he did so in a manner that spoke of a calm, trustworthy authority. It was the very best of the NHS in action – a dedicated and exceptionally skilled professional getting on with a very difficult job.

I gave Caroline a big long hug. She was understandably very upset – this was a terrible shock for her – but she quickly regained her composure. I had already decided that I would be as ruthlessly positive as I could possibly be. I didn't want to unmask the terrible fear I felt because I knew I had to be strong for her. We agreed that she needed to rest and recuperate after the operation, and that we would both stay as upbeat as we possibly could be. Andy had said that he thought the cancer had been removed. That was a positive sign, and it gave us some hope.

Quite soon afterwards the doctors at the hospital in conjunction with the wider medical team decided that the operation had indeed most likely been curative, and that the cancer had been removed. A course of chemotherapy wasn't thought to be necessary. Though clearly we were not experts, we both wondered if chemotherapy might not be sensible, in spite of the side effects, just in case. But it was reassuring, in a way, to be told that it might do more harm than good, that regular blood tests were the best way of finding out if the disease had returned, or had spread elsewhere. We took it on trust.

Before Caroline was allowed to go home she was required to go for an appointment with an oncologist. This was standard practice apparently, and we thought it would just be a relatively straightforward chat. Having had a few days to digest the news and talk through the implications of it all, she was, all things considered, now in reasonably good shape. She was feeling better physically and mentally, and was absolutely determined to get back to full health and to get on with living our lives. I walked her through the maze of hospital corridors to the oncologist's waiting room. The reception staff were friendly and directed us to a waiting area. We sat and waited. And waited.

When we finally got in to see the oncologist he did not have the same calming bedside manner as Andy. There was something of the bureaucrat about him. He lacked empathy, appeared awkward and agitated, and very much gave the impression that Caroline was not a patient or a person but, as he went on to explain, a percentage. In the course of a difficult and upsetting meeting he clumsily and insensitively conveyed that although the operation had supposedly been curative, there was a real chance that the cancer would return and that 50 per cent of people (he repeated the '50 per cent' to ensure that the figure had registered with us) with the same condition would be dead within five years.

I thought for a terrible moment that he was going to repeat the word 'dead' as he had with the '50 per cent', such was the morose tone of his comments. His words were spoken in a very matter-of-fact way. I imagine he thought it was best to be clear about the longer-term prognosis, and not to offer any false hope. I can understand why someone in his position would feel the need to do that, but as Andy had demonstrated, there were ways of doing things more sensitively. I got increasingly angry at the tone he was adopting. Caroline became upset. It was very hard for us both to hear those words being spoken – made worse by the way in which they were spoken. They had a profoundly chilling effect.

To our relief, the appointment came to an end and I walked Caroline back out into the main corridor. It was a dark, miserable and austere place. A more gloomy spot would be hard to imagine. She looked at me and I could tell how upset and how worn down by it all she was. I took a moment to calm down and to steady myself. We had gone into the meeting genuinely hopeful for the future. We had come out petrified by it. 'We will fight this together, every step of the way,' I told her. We held hands and walked slowly back to the ward, now with what felt like the weight of the world on our shoulders.

We tried as hard as we could not to let that 50 per cent figure dominate every moment of our waking lives, but from then on, it was never far away.

I drove Caroline home through the quiet winding country lanes a couple of days later. The kids were there waiting for her as she walked in through the front door. It was an emotional moment for us both. We collapsed on the sofa and cosied up together as a family. The children were too young to understand what had happened, but sensed that all had not been well. From then on, everything felt different. Our hopes, dreams and ambitions for the future shrivelled. We hunkered down. Cancer now cast the darkest of shadows over our lives.

The 50 per cent figure was never mentioned again. Not

once. We agreed between ourselves that the way to beat it, to come through this, was to be ruthlessly positive – not necessarily upbeat, that would maybe be too much to ask, but just that we would try our very best to stay positive. Between us we had realised that in this difficult situation we had a simple binary choice: we could either be positive or we could be negative. There was a clear line that divided the two. In order to fight and beat the cancer we both agreed that we needed to try and avoid negativity, therefore we developed our own watchword which was 'Stay on the line'. To us that meant not allowing ourselves to cross over from positive into negative. I suppose from my perspective there was a familiar discipline to this technique – time at Sandhurst and then years in the Army had conditioned my mind to do things in a certain way. But it worked for Caroline too. Whenever one of us was feeling down or upset, the other would gently say, 'Stay. On. The. Line.' It would be easy enough to identify flaws in this strategy but for us it was helpful and comforting on countless occasions.

Caroline decided that she wanted to try and live the best possible life and did a lot of research into how to live healthily. She changed her diet drastically, becoming very careful and disciplined about what she ate. She stopped drinking alcohol (not that she had ever drunk much) and significantly cut down on her sugar intake (not that it was particularly high). Although there's no firm evidence to suggest that following a sugar-free diet will lower the chances of getting cancer, or raise the chances of surviving it if you are diagnosed, concerns had been expressed about sugar feeding cancer cells and helping them grow more aggressively. She tried to lead the most wholesome, healthy, stress-free life possible under these new circumstances we found ourselves in.

The diagnosis had a profound impact on us. All of a sudden, the future dimmed and we had to rein in our hopes and dreams. Fun, enjoyment, our ambitions for ourselves and our children – they all now seemed very far away. We stopped talking about what the kids would do when they were older. Those joyous conversations idly speculating about what jobs they might do when they grew up didn't happen any more, and we shelved our dream of designing and building our own home. We'd had an active social life before, but now we didn't go out anywhere near as much and we saw less of our friends. Our life no longer felt as if it was about enjoyment; now it was about survival. We fell back into the routine of work and tried never actually to speak the 'C' word. But it was always there at the back, and too often at the front, of our minds.

In such circumstances I found it tricky to stay on the line. I worried about the long term, about whether I could or should continue to serve in the Army. It was a massive commitment and for years it had been my life. I'd always craved the adventure and the challenge and had thrived on bouncing around the world, never really thinking about doing anything else. That had changed now. I questioned whether I shouldn't find a more sensible job that would mean I was around more, one that involved fewer risks. It felt like the world had closed in on us, as if it had now become a very different place. Which it had.

Neither of us had personal experience of cancer. I knew next to nothing about the debilitating effect it could have on people and their families. It had never occurred to me that anything like this might happen to us. We had a life insurance policy on me, not on Caroline. I was the one with the risky job, the one who knew countless people who'd been killed. The idea that she, not me, would be the one in danger wasn't one I had entertained until that moment, from nowhere, stood in front of Salisbury hospital, when the bombshell was dropped. Of course such diagnoses are terrible for the individual and it was absolutely devastating for Caroline, but there was a much wider impact on our whole family – we were all deeply affected by it. It was really tough for us to deal with it collectively as a family, and for me as an individual, because I naturally wanted to give all my attention to Caroline and not be self-pitying about the consequences for me.

I tried to cope by being useful and keeping busy. By trying to be the best husband and father I possibly could be. Up until that point I had been something of an absentee husband – in Iraq, in Afghanistan, back to Iraq, back to Afghanistan. On this exercise, in that country. Now, my view of the world had changed in that I'd always thought you made your own destiny, and that you made your own luck. Now, I was angry. Angry that Caroline, of all people, was having to go through this painful ordeal. An inner rage burned that she was having to endure this pain. I was desperately frustrated that there wasn't anything I could really do to make it go away for her. All I could do was soften the blow. It seemed so unfair. There was an all-consuming feeling of powerlessness and it proved very difficult to manage. For once I didn't feel as if I could just put it in my coping box.

Trying to cope with it wasn't something I ever felt comfortable discussing with others, though I wish now that I had done so more than I did. Despite the macho environment the Army undoubtedly is, there are some who have the gift of empathy, who just have a knack of being able to find a kind word at a tough moment, sometimes in a way that challenges the behavioural stereotype to which some men, particularly 'tough' men, think they ought to conform. A US exchange officer called Dan Enoch had a very American approach to it, much more up front than many British colleagues. 'It's shit, man,' he said to me, 'but we love you guys and we're rooting for you.' It helped. As did the comforting words of my old friend Zac Stenning: 'soldiers' hug' was his diagnosis as he administered a big man-hug.

Mostly, though, my coping self-medication consisted of longer and longer punishing runs over the hills to burn off the anguish. In the driving sleet, or whatever the weather, mile after mile, I would run myself nearly into the ground and return physically exhausted and caked in mud. This helped a bit – exercise always does – but there was no real escape from it. It was nearly always there. That worry. That concern. That deep and profound sadness. That fear that someone you love is having to endure the pain and uncertainty of worry. If I could have swapped places, I would have. But I couldn't.

There were also some self-pitying thoughts about what it meant for me. On occasions I couldn't stop myself from selfishly resenting the restrictions it placed on me. Above all, there was a deep, pervading horror that at some point Caroline might die. That I would lose her and be left on my own, trying to cope while mourning her loss and struggling to bring up our two kids. It was always the first thought in my head when I woke up in the morning, and always the last thing I thought about before falling asleep at night.

It was the starkest reminder of how precious life is and how fragile it can be. That however safe and secure you feel, you never know what's around the corner, so you have to make the most of the opportunities that come your way, or that you can create for yourself. But more than that, you also have to find time to focus on others, on relationships, and cherish and appreciate the people you love and the people you care about, and never, ever take them for granted. I thought about that a lot more than ever I had before – which wasn't hard, given that I had never really thought about it before. In the words of the well-known song written by John Lennon, 'life is what happens to you while you're busy making other plans'. We had been busy making other plans, but life had now firmly got in our way. Such experiences help shape your perspective on life. Those silly, silly little arguments about silly, silly little things – leaving the toilet seat up, putting the top back on the toothpaste – suddenly seemed so pathetically incidental and trivial.

Living under the dark shadow of cancer took its toll. Caroline's condition started to change her, but also me – in some respects in a good way. Along with everything I had seen in Iraq and elsewhere, recent events reinforced the notion and the importance of the sanctity of life, that you must value it, cherish it, never take it for granted. This manifested itself in different ways; positively in that both of us became much more straightforward in our outlook – there was no more beating around the bush. We had a much clearer understanding of the importance of relationships, of telling people what we thought (in a good way), of properly appreciating our family, friends and neighbours. It wasn't as though we now lived every day as if it was our last, because we didn't, but we understood much better than before the value of not leaving till tomorrow what you could do today. But there were also many negative impacts, in that the continued threat of cancer brings great uncertainty, pressure and stress which clog up your life and wear you down. It's a near impossible load to carry and you simply can't continue as you had before, and you have to be careful not to allow that seething resentment which you feel to consume your entire being, which it can do so very easily.

There's a well-worn expression, that 'you don't know what you have until it's gone'. We missed our old selves, carefree, relaxed and full of fun and laughter – those people who had previously lived a life untouched by cancer. Those folk were gone. Perhaps for ever. And we mourned them. We grieved their passing. We came to accept that we were now different people living different lives to the ones we'd had.

Rather than leave the Army, I decided that I should find a steadier role within it that would be less high-octane and would allow me to be closer to home, so that I could be around to help out more. I accepted a posting as the Second-in-Command of the Army Training Regiment at Winchester, training new recruits. It was hugely rewarding in its own way – not the job I'd have wanted under normal circumstances, but we had to accept that things were no longer normal in the way that they had been for us BC (before cancer). Caroline was adamant that I should continue to pursue my Army service in the way I'd always done. She was comforted by the stability of the life (once you'd accepted the uncertainty, the Army was a solid and respected long-term career). But she could see that, for now, it was more practical for me to work closer to home until life got back to normal, as we both desperately hoped that it would.

I quickly took to life at Winchester. It was a great team of people working diligently to train the next generation of soldiers. We believed in the value of what we were doing and I was determined to bring to bear the lessons I had learned not just from being on operations but from Sandhurst and Upavon, to ensure the training was as effective and as operationally focused as possible and delivered in a professional way. I worked hard, but for the first time (other than when working briefly for Brigadier Cook) ensured that I had something resembling a work/home life balance.

Despite everything that had happened to us, we were still determined to make the most of life and provide the very best start for our kids, and after a while – and it took time – we were able to re-establish some normality and a routine. Caroline went back to work, because she wanted to do that; it was important to her, and she got a lot of satisfaction from it and the company of the people she worked with. For a number of months life was steady. We got on and made the best of it. Caroline gradually began to feel reasonably well, and in time we reached an equilibrium. We were resilient people so we battened down the hatches and prepared for whatever might come next.

We didn't have long to wait.

As I opened my Winchester office door, the phone started to ring, and when I picked it up a voice at the other end said, 'How would you like to be Lawrence of Arabia?' It was my desk officer at the Army personnel centre in Glasgow. He had been sympathetic to my domestic circumstances and had helped arrange the Winchester posting to make it easier for me to be close to home. This offer came out of the blue and presented a big dilemma.

The posting I was being offered was the OC with a new unit, the Special Forces Support Group (SFSG), based at St Athan in South Wales; it was an amalgam of 1 Para supported with soldiers from the Royal Marines and the RAF Regiment. This new unit sat within the Directorate of United Kingdom Special Forces (UKSF). It would mean taking command of the B Company (my old company from when I had been a Platoon Commander) and deploying straight on a six-month tour to Afghanistan. If I accepted, I would be in command of a Task Force conducting a new, exciting and very challenging operation based in Helmand in southern Afghanistan. The purpose of the mission was to set up a base and recruit, train and operate a sufficiently capable Afghan force that could undertake complex and demanding military tasks alongside British and Afghan forces in Afghanistan.

The operation was being given to the SFSG to test their mettle – to see whether they had the wherewithal to effectively complete these kinds of complex tasks. The Parachute Regiment urgently needed someone they could trust to lead the operation and ensure its success, and even though they were aware of the pressures on me domestically, they decided to ask me to lead it.

Given my domestic circumstances I was surprised to be considered for such a demanding role. Professionally I was very keen to get back into the routine of leading soldiers on operations, and Afghanistan was the place to do that. Personally it was obviously going to be very difficult, if not impossible.

I spoke to Caroline about it that night. I didn't sugar-coat it and I was very straightforward about what it entailed. Without batting an eyelid, she said, 'You have got to do this. As much as possible I want us to lead a normal life, the kind of life we'd be leading if I hadn't had – well, you know what.' And she knew that I'd always hoped for an opportunity of this kind. She was more determined than I was, and after she had thought about it for a bit longer she was adamant that I shouldn't miss out on the opportunity. Our expectations of life had been lowered, but she wanted things to get back on an even keel and she craved the relative normality of our old life, a normality that involved me accepting the challenging roles the Army saw fit to offer me.

By the spring of 2007 Caroline was having regular check-ups but wasn't receiving treatment. She was feeling reasonably healthy and she was tough and resilient. Still, I was racked with doubt. Was it the right thing to be doing at this moment? How would Caroline cope while I was away? *Would* she cope? What happens if she becomes ill while I am away? What if I am injured? What if I am killed? What then? There were lots of questions. I thought long and hard about them all. Men and women in all professions regularly have to make difficult choices about whether to pursue career options at the expense of their family – and this felt like a very difficult judgement. I was torn. It was an extraordinary professional opportunity, exactly the kind of thing I'd joined the Army to do, and had been working towards for a long time. I asked Caroline to think about it some more. She did, and after further reflection she was still absolutely determined that I should go. So I called my desk officer back and accepted the command.

Arrangements were quickly made. The outgoing OC, the man I was taking over from, had persuaded his boss, the SFSG CO, to let him deploy the company out to Afghanistan to take over the base, which by this stage had already been established. It was called Camp Pluto. The plan was that I would join them there a couple of weeks later. To my mind this was far from ideal – much better, I thought, that I get to know the soldiers in B Company before deploying and do at least some of the vital pre-deployment training with them. But my predecessor had insisted and somehow persuaded the CO. Besides, someone still had to be found to take over my job training recruits at Winchester.

Crucially, this arrangement meant that I would not know

any of the company group soldiers – with the exception of the Company Sergeant Major (CSM), whom I had not seen for nearly ten years, and one of the Sergeants, whom I also had not seen for ten years. It would mean that I hadn't done the pre-deployment training alongside the soldiers I'd be commanding, so I would arrive in Afghanistan without the necessary situational awareness or the skills and knowledge required. It was obvious to me that this lack of preparation would make things unnecessarily difficult and put me at a huge disadvantage. I had a very strong sense at the time that it was not the best way to start and began to make attempts to persuade the CO to change the plan. My efforts were derailed when we received bad news about Caroline's health.

Tests showed that the cancer had returned, and very soon after that Caroline had another supposedly curative operation, to remove her ovaries. The operation itself was a major one which required a significant period of recovery. Despite this latest surgery, which we both convinced ourselves was a setback and nothing more, and despite the fortitude with which Caroline dealt with the bad news, it was a stark reminder – not that we needed one – of the fragility of her health.

I waited for the right moment to gently suggest to Caroline that given recent events I should no longer deploy to Afghanistan. I was reasonably certain that she would agree but she was even more adamant (if that were possible) that I should go. I made a misplaced joke about her wanting to get rid of me and immediately realised that it was the wrong thing to say.

'I just want a normal life,' she told me. 'I will miss you and I will worry about you, so much, but I don't want our lives ruined by . . . well, you know what.' The 'C word' was still very rarely spoken.

It was very hard to know what to do and my doubts intensified over whether I should be going or not. I was torn between family and professional duty. Family comes first, but this was the most difficult decision I had ever faced.

I take responsibility for my decision to deploy to Afghanistan in July 2007, albeit at no point (to my knowledge) did anyone in the military chain of command question whether I was 'in the right place' to take charge of what was clearly going to be an extremely complex and demanding operation. It was taken on trust that I would be fine.

# 11

# Long Way Away

## *July 2007*

—

Before I knew it, it was July and time to go. Getting ready to say goodbye, after everything that had happened, was heart-wrenching, much worse than it had ever been before. It's easy to say 'yes' to something months in advance, but the closer you get to the moment when you actually have to do it, the more you come to question the decision. I have since come to apply what I call the 'tomorrow test' – if it were happening tomorrow, would I want to do it?

I had continued to wrestle not just with whether I *wanted* to do it, but whether I *should* be doing it. Was it selfish? Should I be exposing myself to the extreme risks I would undoubtedly face in Afghanistan? Shouldn't I be at home to provide support for my family? Again I asked myself the question, what if I am killed? Where would that leave Caroline and the kids? Not in a good place, that was for sure. These questions continued to churn over in my mind and I hoped I was doing the right thing. I wasn't certain that

I was – I remained torn between a sense of responsibility to my family and duty to the Army.

While family should always come first, I did feel a strong obligation towards my Regiment and I had taken a very close interest in how the mission in Afghanistan had been progressing and wanted it to succeed. I had previously twice deployed to Afghanistan. When I'd been at PJHQ I had, in 2005, deployed on an operation to disrupt the flow of illegal drugs. I had also gone on the first recce to southern Afghanistan to scope the feasibility of shifting the UK's military effort from the more benign north to the likely more dangerous south as part of an expansion of the military campaign. As one of a small team led by an outstanding Major called Robbie McDermott we travelled to all of the provinces of southern Afghanistan: Kandahar, Oruzgan, Nimruz, Zabul and then Helmand.

We thought long and hard about where British forces could best make a contribution to the campaign. The Canadians had already 'baggsied' Kandahar, Oruzgan was mountainous and the lines of resupply were long and complicated, Nimruz bordered Iran and there was nothing much there, Zabul bordered Pakistan and the Americans were already there conducting counter-terrorism operations. Which only left Helmand. Helmand was the narcotics hub of southern Afghanistan, and the UK was the G8 lead for narcotics in Afghanistan. As we pored over a map in a small American military base up in the hills of Oruzgan it became clear that for the British, all roads would lead to Helmand.

This exposure to the country and the people served only to reinforce my view that there was a real risk we could get bogged down fighting an almost unwinnable insurgency campaign, unless we deployed a very significant and well-equipped and well-supported force with clear directions for what we wanted them to do, a clear mission statement that was achievable, and a plan to get them back home again. Whatever preparations we made, I sensed that we were about to poke a hornets' nest. In April 2006 the then Secretary of State for Defence John Reid said: 'We would be perfectly happy to leave again in three years and without firing one shot.' He would later come under criticism as some interpreted his comments as meaning that there was an expectation that shots would not be fired. The intention, though, had been to emphasise that the mission was about protecting the institutions of government and the process of development rather than to take on the Taleban. He was right that we would have been perfectly happy to leave without firing a shot.

I was therefore, having been there at the very beginning, invested in the southern Afghanistan mission. I agreed with the basic premise that we couldn't allow Afghanistan to be a safe haven for terrorists to plot their murderous attacks against the West and elsewhere. I thought the new SFSG unit had real potential – but that it needed to be nurtured if it was to succeed. I also believed that the operation had the potential to make a significant contribution to the ongoing mission in Afghanistan and I wanted to play my part in making sure that was the case. I felt an obligation, a duty to do my bit. Old-fashioned maybe, but it's what I felt. Set against my family commitments, all these points were factors in my decision on whether to proceed – alongside the more basic one of the appeal of the challenge of the job. It would undoubtedly be the most demanding task I had ever undertaken. I wanted to know what I could make of it. So, hard though it was, I started to focus on what I knew I had to do.

I had also asked myself the question, why me? The

Regiment were acutely aware of my domestic circumstances, they knew Caroline had now twice been treated for cancer, there were many other officers they could have asked – so why did they come to me? I don't know the answer to that. I didn't ask at the time and I've never asked about it subsequently. I suppose it was because the priority for the military always has to be operational success. I understand that. They will support people (and their families) to the best of their ability, but ultimately the system – the military machine – has to take decisions based around capability and getting the job done.

There was a general recognition from all involved that this was a difficult job; a judgement had to be made about who was professionally best suited to do it. Wider compassionate considerations were screened out of that judgement, even though it could be justifiably argued that they were materially relevant: how could someone be expected to take on such a complex role if they had compassionate issues that prevented them from giving it their full attention? Command of the operation needed someone who was more interested in doing the job than hogging the limelight – in that kind of environment there's really nowhere to hide and you simply can't bluff your way through it. That faith was being invested in me, which made it all the harder for me to turn it down.

The final few weeks before I went flashed by so it wasn't until the day before departure that I suddenly remembered I needed to update my will, which I hadn't touched since just before going to Iraq in 2003. It is always a sobering experience to read your will, particularly when you're about to undertake an activity in which there is a chance of you being killed. It inevitably focuses your mind on what would happen if you were to die. My will was now out of date but I just couldn't face getting into the detail of it there and then. I wasn't in the right frame of mind, and, well, I wasn't going to die, was I? So I didn't need to. I skimmed through it, and in addition to the serious stuff contained within it there were a series of light-hearted commitments. Prior to his deployment to Iraq in 2003, David Blakeley had left me various comedy items in his will, including half a bottle of aftershave. I had returned the favour by leaving him my second-best rifle cleaning kit.

Just as a precautionary measure, and to ease my guilty conscience that I wasn't giving it the attention it deserved, I scribbled a brief note to my father in red pen on my life insurance certificate, saying, 'Dad, if anything happens to me, make sure this lot accept their responsibilities and pay up so this all gets sorted for Caroline and the kids. Thank you.' I shoved the paperwork back into both a folder and my coping box and tried to forget about it.

The feelings of doubt persisted, though I shared them with nobody. On the Friday night before I was due to deploy on the Saturday afternoon, I was sat watching TV with Caroline (the kids were tucked up asleep in bed) when the phone rang. It was the Operations Officer from the SFSG HQ at St Athan. 'Dan, I know you're heading out tomorrow, and because you won't see any reporting of this on the news, I wanted to call and let you know that earlier today, Martin – Lieutenant Martin Hewitt, one of your Platoon Commanders – was shot and very seriously wounded in a firefight with the Taleban.'

I paused to absorb the news. All I could think to ask was, 'How is he?'

'It's bad,' I was told.

I thanked him for the call.

Caroline asked if everything was OK. 'Fine,' I

replied – no point telling her. It would only have made things even harder.

I continued with the pretence of watching the TV, but inwardly I reflected darkly that while I had not required any reminder of the risks of serving in Afghanistan, this had unhelpfully provided one. It sounded like Martin was in a bad way and I desperately hoped he would survive, knowing that his family would, at this moment, be beyond themselves with worry.

It was now Saturday morning. I was leaving that afternoon. Caroline was out doing some shopping with the kids, keeping things business-as-usual, no fuss, while I finished my final packing at home without the distraction of the children helpfully taking things out of my bags that I had just packed. Earlier that week I had been to the SFSG barracks in South Wales to be issued with numerous new shiny items of clothing and equipment, although I didn't know how half of them worked. I seemed to have so much stuff to take that there was barely any room left for personal items. I allowed myself a few family photos, including one of the four of us with Holly sat on the garden wall in front of our house, some paintings that the kids had done of the family, and a battered copy of *I Bought a Mountain* because I wanted to read about Esmé Kirby, the Welsh hill farmer who had been a friend of my grandmother's.

As I filled any remaining space in my bags with packets of rhubarb and custard sweets, I heard a sound from the kitchen. It was Holly whimpering. Something was clearly wrong. I went to investigate. She couldn't stand up. She was quite old, but terriers usually go on for ever and she had always been a healthy dog. This was the last thing any of us needed. I had a flight leaving in just a few hours. I was going to a war zone to take command of a rifle company of paratroopers who were already there and were waiting for me. The operation was underway. Casualties were being taken. I was already worried about leaving and now, to make matters worse, our beloved dog was unwell. Ringing up the SFSG HQ and saying 'Sorry, chaps, I can't make this flight because my dog isn't well' simply wasn't an option. I was just going to have to leave Caroline to sort out Holly.

Leaving was a familiar routine for me, because I had done it so many times before: dropping the house keys on the hook under the mirror in the hallway, walking out the door, closing it behind me. But this time, when the moment finally came, it felt very different. The kids were too young to understand where I was going but they were unsettled. Our son clung to my leg and wouldn't let go. The day before he had asked Caroline if 'Afghunastanley', as he called it, was a long way away. 'A long way away' I reflected when Caroline told me about it later – yes, at that moment it certainly felt like it was. Our daughter appeared completely unmoved by my imminent departure, which was just as bad as if she had been upset. Holly lay whimpering on the sofa. Caroline was slightly tearful but trying ever so hard to be strong. In the pit of my stomach it just felt awful, just awful, having to go. Even at this late stage, still turning over in my mind was the thought 'Sod it, let someone else do it. Be here for your family.' But I had given my word, and a lot of people were now depending on me.

I held the kids tight and we had a group hug. I kissed Caroline and said, 'I never want to do this again.'

'I never want you to do it again,' she replied. She was upset but in control. I suspected tears would flow when the door closed behind me.

It felt awful. Awful. I told them all that I loved them. Walking out of the door was the hardest thing I'd ever had to do. But walk out that door I did. Right or wrong, I felt I had to.

And as I did so, I considered the prospect that I might never walk back through it.

I walked to the car, my bags already in the boot. I got in. I sat there. I put my seat belt on. I turned the engine on. I turned the engine off. I took my seat belt off. I contemplated walking back into the house, closing the door, shutting out the world, putting the kettle on and just being there with the family that I loved so much. I suspected Caroline would now be crying. I thought about going back in to comfort her, but I had said goodbye. It was tough. It was very tough. But it was time to go.

Driving to RAF Brize Norton, I wondered if my flight would be delayed, as they often were, sometimes by twenty-four hours or more. If it was, I could spend another night at home. But I reminded myself that I had said my goodbyes, and going through all the heartache of those goodbyes again would be unsettling for everyone. Having driven there feeling utterly miserable, I arrived to find that, unusually, the flight was on time, and quite quickly I was airborne and on the long haul out to Afghanistan. I could see, looking around the plane, that I wasn't the only person weighing it all up, balancing competing emotions. Even with people you don't know you can see it in their faces.

The C-17 aircraft was basically a massive cargo plane, and while we were strapped into metal-framed canvas seats for take-off and landing the rest of the time we could take our sleeping bags out and try and get some sleep on the floor between the various bits of cargo that were being transported, which included a tractor (desert-coloured of course). I climbed inside my sleeping bag, or 'green maggot' as some in the Army call them. Others use the affectionate nickname 'horizontal time acceleration system' based on the notion that when you get in you are immediately transported three, four or even, if you are really lucky, five hours into the future (the idea being that you are usually so tired that you immediately fall asleep and know nothing more until you wake up). I pulled the bag right over my head, but there was no horizontal time acceleration for me. I couldn't sleep, my mind whirring at what I had left behind and what was coming next.

Hours later, as we eventually approached Afghan air space, still at very high altitude, everybody was told to pack away their kit and put their body armour and helmets on. There was a high threat of small-arms fire, and of rocket-propelled grenades (RPGs), but also of more sophisticated man-portable air defence (MANPAD) surface-to-air missiles being fired at the big, lumbering C-17. Long before you're in range of any of those weapons systems you're instructed to put your seat belts on. Then the lights go out and you sit in silence, in the darkness, waiting for the steep, dramatic *drop* rather than *descent* into Kabul. The pilot brought the aircraft sharply down in a corkscrew-like manoeuvre – not a way you'd ever land a commercial aircraft. Your head and heart go into overdrive as you sit there in the dark, your fate in the hands of the pilot, and hope that no one is waiting for you on the ground to take a shot at the plane as it comes into land.

Travel in Afghanistan is always time-consuming and prone to hold-ups. After a predictable delay in Kabul I flew on to Kandahar in an RAF C-130 Hercules aircraft. There were a number of others in transit to their units on the flight, all of whom scattered and went their own way when we arrived. There wasn't a connecting helicopter flight down to Camp Bastion – the vast British camp in Helmand (the largest province of Afghanistan, and one of the most dangerous places on earth at that time) and the logistics hub for British military operations, where some of our stores and supplies were kept – until the next day. I had to spend the night at the Kandahar military base, which had expanded massively since I was last there in 2005, in a huge canvas marquee tent that was on the edge of the runway.

I was the only person in there. No chairs or beds, and certainly none of the prized foldable camp cots (a valuable military commodity which helped ensure a comfortable night's sleep, but which were always in short supply and were highly sought-after items of kit). I found an old-fashioned narrow wooden bench with metal foldable legs, quite a precarious thing, not designed to be slept on. I lay in my sleeping bag on it. It was like trying to sleep next to the runway at RAF Brize Norton. I spent the whole night wide awake, blasted by the roar of landing planes and their associated clouds of dust, with my mind still racing, thinking about my family back at home and the challenges that lay ahead. It didn't feel like a great start.

In fact it felt like I was stepping into the unknown. I hadn't even seen a picture of Camp Pluto, where we would be based, partly because, for understandable reasons, there are strict rules within the military about not taking photos or doing anything that might cause sensitive information to leak out. Loose lips sink ships and all that. I'd been shown where the camp was on a map, but I had no real feel for what our surroundings were going to be like. I worried that I didn't have the required situational awareness. There's a German expression, *Fingerspitzengefühl*. The term means 'fingertip feeling' and indicates whether, in a given situation, an individual has the necessary knowledge to respond to the circumstances they find themselves in. I was acutely conscious that I simply did not have that fingertip feeling. This was not knowledge I could get from talking to people who'd been there or by looking at maps and reading reports. You needed to actually be there, on the ground, to have that 'ground truth' of what things were really like. Years later, this sense of needing to be there – to see for myself what things are like – informed my belief in the importance of politicians needing to burst out of the Westminster bubble in order to truly understand what's going on and what people really think.

When morning finally appeared – and after a series of delays because first the helicopter was diverted for an urgent operational task, then because of a minor technical fault, and then because it flew off to support a medical casualty evacuation (casevac) – I was eventually able to board a helicopter flight down to Camp Bastion.

There had been a mix-up over which flight I was on, so nobody was there to meet me. The SFSG camp within Bastion was supposed to be very discreet, so there was no sign to say where it was and it was a bit awkward for me to go round the base asking for directions. 'Excuse me, but could you tell me where the secret bit of camp is, which I'm in charge of?' was not a question I wanted to be seen asking. Eventually I tracked it down. I found the Company Quartermaster Sergeant (CQMS) very busy on the improvised weight-lifting machine. He was out of breath and seemed a bit flustered when I introduced myself.

'Ah, very sorry, boss,' he said. 'I thought you were getting here tomorrow.' The logistic convoy had already done its daily run, he told me apologetically.

'No worries,' I said, 'but to be frank, Colour, I do need to get there today.' I had been travelling for what seemed like a very long time and the prospect of yet another overnight stop did not appeal. I needed to get there and get sorted.

'Righty-oh, boss,' he said. 'I'll sort something out.'

He set about gathering together a small team of soldiers and a convoy of vehicles to escort me across to Camp Pluto. The CQMS issued me with a rifle from the armoury – I already had a pistol – and after a warm can of Miranda fizzy orange, off we drove, out of Camp Bastion.

For a few miles we stayed on the main highway road – the A50, which linked all the main towns in one big loop around Afghanistan. There wasn't much traffic, just the occasional very heavily laden lorry, overfilled both with goods and people, a few cars, and quite a few motorbikes. We slowed right down to pass through an Afghan National Police (ANP) check post. The policeman viewed us suspiciously before waving us through – the ANP were notoriously cor-rupt and bribery was second if not first nature to many of them. There had been numerous cases of the Taleban taking control of ANP check posts and using them to attack and extort money from people using the road.

A few miles further down the highway there now seemed to be virtually no traffic on the road and the CQMS told me over the radio headset that it was time for us to veer off into the desert. It was too dangerous to proceed further on the road because of the high risk of either ambush or IEDs detonated from culverts that ran underneath the road. We would complete the rest of the journey cross-country.

We were now entering bandit country. On the distant horizon was a rocky outcrop and I could just make out what looked like some sort of fort, which, as we got closer, turned out to be Camp Pluto. As the crow flies, it was only fifteen miles from Camp Bastion, but the driving was so slow off-road that it took us a couple of hours to get there. We pulled up to the gate, which was being guarded by Afghan soldiers, to find the camp pretty much deserted. Everyone was out, still deployed in the desert on the operation – the one Martin Hewitt had been shot on.

Camp Pluto was surrounded by a big wall made from huge sand-coloured wire-mesh containers with a heavy-duty fabric liner filled with rocks called HESCO bastion. The camp was divided into two sections, a British and an Afghan area. The British section was much smaller and was sectioned off by a wire fence with a lockable entrance gate manned by a sentry. It consisted of a series of Portakabins: accommodation, kitchen, stores, and the Operations or 'Ops' room and adjoining small office complex. Among the Portakabins was a series of reinforced shelters – essentially massive concrete toilet rolls, designed to provide some protection in the event of a mortar attack. The Afghan area consisted of larger accommodation blocks, a cook-house, a number of workshops with vehicles in different states of repair, and a HLS. A series of gun emplacements ran around the top of the walls, and the turrets on each corner were manned with heavy machine guns. The place felt like a cross between a French Foreign Legion base in the desert and the hideout of Colonel Kurtz in the film *Apocalypse Now*.

The British section, which covered about a fifth of the camp, was smaller than a football field. Out the back of the camp (as you approached it) was a high rocky hill feature with a rough gravelled track winding up it, with a large radio mast antenna and a sentry position keeping lookout on the top. In the other direction there was a mountain range in the far distance. Running through my mind was what I would do if I were the Taleban. I knew I'd seize the neighbouring hill feature and lob mortar shells and RPGs down on us. It all felt much too exposed for comfort.

The CQMS showed me to my Portakabin: as the OC

I was in the privileged position of not having to share. Somebody had helpfully printed my name on a piece of paper and taped it to the door; it was symptomatic of my current state of mind that my immediate reaction was that would be a very handy marker for the Taleban when they broke into the camp to murder us all in our beds. I dropped my bags and started to eye up the bed. It had been a very long journey and I was shattered. Then someone from the Ops room popped his head round the door to tell me that a helicopter was coming to pick me up in order to take me straight out into the desert to meet up with everyone.

This came as a bit of a surprise. I was knackered and had been hoping to unpack, get some sleep and settle in. No such luck. Instead, I only just had time to gather my desert kit together. Noticing that there seemed to be an internet connection, though doubtful that it would work, I quickly unpacked my laptop and to my surprise managed to get online to be able to pick up an email from Caroline sent on Saturday night. The words on the screen jumped out at me: 'So terribly sad to have to tell you that Holly has died. I will miss her so much.' I replied straight away: 'I'm so sorry to hear that. I've arrived safely. I'll be in touch. Love you.'

# 12

# Welcome to Helmand

## *July 2007*

—

I was deeply saddened to hear the news about Holly. She had been a wonderful companion and was part of our family, and I knew Caroline would be devastated. I also knew that I had to put it out of my thoughts for now. There wasn't time to think about it anyway, as the Chinook helicopter was already waiting for me on the HLS, rotors turning. With my bergan, chest webbing and rifle (which I hadn't yet been able to 'zero' or adjust on the range, meaning that it would be inaccurate if I had to fire it and was therefore all but useless), I walked up the back ramp of the helicopter and we took off and flew away into the desert. I didn't even know precisely where we were going.

After what seemed like just a few minutes we began to descend, and from the side window I could see, half hidden in the desert landscape, vehicles configured into what's called a 'harbour position', like homesteader wagons on the American plains positioned in a circle for overnight all-round protection. It was established practice that at the end of each day we'd configure ourselves in that way so that we could defend ourselves through the night before moving on before or at first light. The RAF loady (helicopter loadmaster) stuck up two fingers which meant two minutes till drop-off.

Green smoke from a smoke grenade on the ground showed the heli where to go. The pilot took us down. I was listening in to her talk to the loady via headphones and heard her say in a very measured tone that she didn't want to touch the heli down on the ground in case we detonated a mine. So I was instructed to jump off the ramp at the back while she skilfully hovered just above the ground – though not too close to the ground in case the down blast from the rotors set off a mine. It was only a few feet to jump, but first I had to drop my bergan. As I readied myself to jump, hoping *I* wasn't about to hit a mine, I wondered if this descent counted as an airborne insertion (the Paras hadn't conducted an actual airborne insertion since the Suez crisis of 1956 – it was a running joke that we were always looking for opportunities to do so). I thought better of making that joke to the group of bodies on the ground huddled together against the dust storm the heli had just whipped up.

Alistair, the OC, and Lee, the CSM, walked over to meet me. We shook hands stiffly given our less than formal sur-roundings (my arrival was the cue for Alistair's departure, and I sensed he was not chuffed to be leaving), and as the heli sped away, showering us all in dust, he led me off towards one of the vehicles, where we sheltered in a little shell scrape (a defensive position dug into the ground). 'The next time we shake hands will be to tell you that you're in charge,' he said in a very matter-of-fact way.

Someone handed me a brew – piping-hot tea with

powdered milk from a vacuum flask – and the CSM, whom I'd known from ten years before when we were both serving in B Company, said with a grin, 'Welcome back, boss.'

Everyone else there had been out in the desert for a week and had the grizzled look you get from not shaving or washing and from having been constantly sandblasted by the desert winds. I'd rocked up in my freshly washed uniform looking all clean and tidy. I was acutely conscious that all these soldiers, soon to be under my command, would be sizing up their new OC. The man who would likely determine whether they went home with a medal, or in a box. I self-consciously imagined that they would all be thinking: 'Oh, he's got his shiny new kit on.'

At that moment a sandstorm blew in and we hunkered further down in the shell scrape, which didn't afford much protection from the storm but was at least something if mortars started raining down. A hole in the ground has always been the soldier's best friend. As the storm receded, Alistair briefed me on the operation and pointed out various features on a large laminated map that the company Second-in-Command had pulled out of his smock. The purpose of the operation had been to conduct an initial ground orientation – basically to get a feel for the place and do a test run out, jointly with the Afghan forces, after a week's preparatory training in camp.

They calmly talked me through the recent 'contact' and described what had happened to Lieutenant Martin Hewitt. Martin was on his second tour of Afghanistan having been mentioned in dispatches during his first tour back in 2006. While leading his platoon towards a Taleban position he received gunshot wounds to the chest and to his foot from a machine gun. It sounded like he had been incredibly lucky not to have been killed. They also detailed a series of incidents in the first few days of the operation where several of the vehicles had struck mines. There had been a number of injuries to both British and Afghans, but thankfully no fatalities. I knew, though, that death and danger lurked around every corner in Helmand. Every track or road could have an IED placed by the side of it, every building could be booby-trapped, every Afghan was a potential suicide bomber.

I listened intently and tried to take it in. My brain was addled from lack of sleep and my very long journey. There was a lot to process.

As the briefing dried up, Juma, the Afghan force commander, came over with an interpreter, or 'terp' as everyone called them. He was friendly and positive. He'd known that a new OC was inbound, and he courteously referred to me as 'Major Dan'. (There was still caution about letting the Afghans know our surnames. Bonds of trust were still being formed.) After pleasantries were exchanged, the CSM took me round the vehicles, introducing me to the blokes. Although we were relatively securely ensconced in the desert, I was still getting my head around the actual level of threat, and at the back of my mind I worried that we could be attacked and overrun at any moment, or that I would stand on a mine or detonate an IED.

Meeting the soldiers who would soon be under my command felt a bit awkward and stilted, but was helped by the CSM who knew all of the blokes incredibly well – better than their own mothers did, as the saying went. As we approached each vehicle he muttered helpful details to me: that this soldier, for instance, had just had a narrow miss, walking away unscathed after driving over a mine that exploded under his vehicle; another one had just split with his girlfriend and was cut up about it; another had a heavily pregnant wife back

home. It was useful to know this sort of thing before enthu-
siastically asking someone how it was going. This was not
a moment to be airing the clichéd questions about whether
'boots fit and the mail is getting through' but to have a quick
word as part of a process of getting to know them. How
much easier would it have been if this had all been done
before deploying, I thought to myself.

Darkness soon fell, and after a few hours of much-needed
sleep in a sleeping bag by the side of a vehicle, before dawn
we began the long journey back to Camp Pluto. It was
chilly – the desert in Afghanistan is always cold at night,
even in the summer when it's been very hot during the day.
Moving vehicles over desert terrain is painfully slow and
requires great patience and skill. With lots of vehicles travelling in a convoy, you're at your most vulnerable if one of
them breaks down – 'you are only as strong as the weak-
est link in your chain' as the young Royal Electrical and
Mechanical Engineers (REME) mechanic became fond of
telling me. There were quite a few links in our chain.

Everyone was seriously twitched about the threat from
IEDs. We knew that in the desert there were both so-called
'legacy' land mines left over from the Soviet invasion of the
1980s, along with newer ones sown by the Taleban. Our
vehicles were conventional pick-ups. We all felt vulnerable
driving about in them.

On this return journey three vehicles broke down and I
was inducted into the difficulty of negotiating rough desert
terrain as part of a long convoy. One of the broken-down
vehicles could not be fixed and the desert ground was such
that it couldn't be towed, so we had to radio for a Chinook
helicopter to come and pick it up, and wait for it to do so
(this would be a low-priority task for the helis). We fixed the
other one – at one point I noted there were fifteen Afghans

helping the REME mechanic sort it. By the time the third vehicle broke down we were close enough to Pluto for it to be towed back into camp (albeit precariously, which further slowed the convoy down for the last few miles), the men and equipment from it crammed into the other vehicles. Throughout, the REME mechanic worked his desert-issue socks off. It was a nerve-racking few hours and we felt particularly exposed while we weren't moving.

When you're transiting through the Afghan desert the one thing you don't want to do is stop. The desert has eyes and ears, whether you're aware of them or not. The Taleban pay local men not just to fight for them but also to spot for them, and you see their spotters whizzing about on motorbikes trying to keep track of your movements before furtively speaking into hand-held radios. If they're organised they don't have to attack you directly, just start lobbing mortar rounds at you or laying mines or IEDs in your path. We had signals equipment called Integrated Communications or ICOM, which was a radio system that allowed us to listen in to the Taleban chatting on their insecure hand-held radios. While we were waiting for the second broken-down vehicle to be fixed I observed a grimace from the terp listening in. I asked him what was up. He told me that the Taleban were saying they were 'going to cut off our penises and shove them in our mouths'. 'Welcome to Helmand, Major Dan,' the terp added drily.

Over the course of the following months I listened many times to conversations that related specifically to our movements. It's eerie to hear the enemy discussing their often quite detailed plans to kill you. They sometimes spoke in florid terms but then could also be very matter-of-fact about what they planned to do to us. Some of them knew we might be able to hear them so did it just to try and intimidate us. I would later reach the point where I became sanguine about it – it was mostly just talk after all. But in those first few hours while I was still getting my bearings it was deeply alarming to hear such things.

We finally made it back to Camp Pluto late in the afternoon. After a quick shower and some hot food we sat down to conduct a detailed after-action review of the operation that had just finished. What went right, what went wrong. There was a lengthy discussion about the events leading up to the shooting of Martin. What lessons could be learned from that? I was exhausted but it was vital that I gained a good understanding of how things could be made to work better next time, particularly given that next time I would be leading it.

When it finished I was desperate to go and get some sleep. Alistair suggested we take a breather but he then wanted to brief me on the soldiers. We spent several more hours discussing the various people in the company – their strengths, their weaknesses. We talked through the mission to establish a highly capable Afghan force – more professional, adaptable and trusted than the Afghan National Army (ANA) – that could operate across southern Afghanistan, both with and without British forces. At midnight he and I shook hands, and finally I walked back to my Portakabin to get some sleep.

Technically, I was now in command of the operation. Back in my Portakabin I had a moment of real doubt where I felt overwhelmed by it all. The doubt seemed to flush over me in waves. I'm sure it was partly because I was tired, but in that moment my fears crystallised. I wasn't convinced that the operation was viable. It seemed like there were just too many risks. Our camp was in a vulnerable location, out in the middle of nowhere, and if a Taleban force wanted to attack us at night, it seemed to me that they'd have a significant chance of overrunning the camp and killing us all. At that point no soldier from the ANA had yet killed or injured a British soldier inside a camp. But there were subsequently to be many British deaths as a result of being shot inside camps by Taleban-supporting soldiers – so called green-on-blue attacks.

Standing in my Portakabin, I thought how risky this all was, how simple it would be for the Taleban to infiltrate our Afghan force – send in sleepers to lie low for weeks or months and then turn on us. I was also concerned about the amount of time it could take to get the Afghan force up to a standard where they could effectively operate jointly with British forces. There was a great pressure to make that happen sharpish, but I thought more time would likely be needed. Even though I was exhausted and not in a particularly good frame of mind, I hammered out a draft email to the CO detailing my concerns.

There was a travel kettle in the corner of the room so I made a hot mug of tea and sat down on my bed. Though shattered, I didn't think I would be able to sleep. Whirring round my head were the concerns I had about the viability of the operation, no doubt heightened by my lingering disquiet over whether I was in the right frame of mind to be leading it, and whether I should even be there at all. These were intensified by my unease over the lack of preparation and training I'd had to equip me to lead this most complex of operations. I was worried about Caroline and I was sad for Holly. I wondered what I had got myself into.

My mind was racked with doubt, but I eventually fell into a fitful sleep until I woke shivering at 4 a.m. The aircon had malfunctioned and my Portakabin now felt like a freezer. I couldn't suppress a weary giggle: here I was out in Afghanistan, assailed by concerns about the operation, about my family and about my lack of preparation, and now the bloody aircon wasn't working. I tried to turn it off, only to receive a bad electric shock. I couldn't catch a break. The giggle built to laughter as I opened the door to let the cold air escape and stood in the doorway admiring the first serene shards of an Afghan dawn.

After a while the tingling from the electric shock began to subside and I drew in a deep long breath, and then another, and another, and another. I started to feel a bit better. A bit stronger. I went back in and deleted the email to the CO – all the concerns contained within it were entirely genuine and reasonable, but rather than moan about it, why not get on and sort them all out? Rightly or wrongly, I was here now. There was *no* going back. Might as well make the best of it.

I kicked on my flip-flops, tucked my 9mm pistol into the back of my shorts and waddled over to the office.

Let's get this show on the road, I thought.

# 13

# Getting a Grip

## *July 2007*

—

Over the days that followed, I threw myself into the challenge and began to familiarise myself with every aspect of the operation. I started to get to know and understand the people, Brits and Afghans, and began to learn who was good at what, who I could trust to get things done, and who required closer supervision. I asked lots of questions and if I wasn't satisfied with the answers I asked a load more. I immersed myself in the detail. I established what the Army calls a 'battle rhythm' – a daily routine of briefings and planned activity.

Critically, I spent time re-evaluating my analysis of what I was there to do and my plan for how I was going to do it – what the Army calls 'The Estimate'. I'd spent time doing one before I left the UK, but when you're actually there, in the country, your understanding of the environment and the reasons behind your mission is far more developed. If you don't intimately understand the situation you're in, you can spend all the time on the detail you want, but it will be for nothing. You must be sure of the *ends* (strategic outcomes) you are working towards before you consider the best *ways* (tactics) to get there, and the *means* (resources) you will need. Never let the tail wag the dog. I made sure that not only was I clear about these key objectives, but that all my team were as well, and that they understood precisely what I required from them.

I decided that the training and development of the Afghan soldiers was a key component of the mission and I delegated to my Second-in-Command (2IC), a young, keen Captain, the task of drawing together a training plan, while in consultation with the brigade staff I planned a series of operations for us to conduct – though I wanted to ensure we were as prepared as possible before conducting them. Working with the CSM and Frank Gargan (who had been commissioned and was himself now a Major, and though based in the UK became a regular visitor to support us with our equipment requirements), we drew up a wish list of items that we needed but didn't have. There was a lot to do and a lot to take in. The independent nature of the command meant that occasionally I would seek guidance and advice from the chain of command above me, but mostly they left me to it, and I just got on with it.

The Afghan soldiers who had been recruited for the Task Force were culturally very different from my British soldiers. Like many young men, they could be determined, but also temperamental and stubborn. You needed to find different ways to motivate them. They didn't respond to traditional military discipline in the way my soldiers did. Like all soldiers throughout time, they performed better when they had good morale. I sensed it could be improved so I made some relatively minor changes to their contract of service, as well as improvements to their living accommodation. Quite small changes in the bigger scheme of things – quick wins – but ones which had a disproportionately positive effect; they appreciated the sentiment and it immediately helped forge better relations. Although they could be cantankerous, as I would come to learn, they were generally very brave and would dash towards the enemy without giving it a second thought. But that's hardly ever what you actually want. In a complex environment like Afghanistan, what you need is a highly trained and disciplined soldier who can respond effectively to orders. Success or failure depends upon it.

It's much easier to organise an attack, or a counter to being attacked, with your own soldiers, who you know (although I was still getting to know mine) and with whom you've worked and trained (again, this was work in progress for me). Introducing other forces with different languages and cultures into the mix makes everything much more complicated, and it's generally pretty complicated anyway – particularly in the dark and certainly under fire, when people are scared and confused and casualties are being taken.

Those first few days were long and hard going but at least we were all getting to know each other, developing a relationship of trust and comradeship. At this stage the Afghan force I had inherited consisted of 175 soldiers. The somewhat opaque process of recruitment had begun several months before I arrived on the scene. In the haze of the handover, nobody had properly briefed me on how the Afghan soldiers had actually been recruited or where they had materialised from, though there had been several passing references. At the back of my mind, among everything else I was trying to process, was a nagging doubt about it, that I didn't know enough about how that process had worked. I understood that some sort of arrangement had been reached with an Afghan 'warlord' who had agreed to send some 'volunteers' to sign up for the force but I knew that I needed to understand it better.

This was partly because I thought there was a possibility that at some point this arrangement might come back to haunt us. But also because in addition to training and mentoring our existing soldiers, in my mind I was already formulating plans to recruit more to grow the force when we felt ready and able to do so. It was clear that to satisfy the required operational tempo and to ensure a capability to have a constant presence out on the ground, we would, over time, need to recruit more Afghans to expand the force. But for now, the priority was to build the ones I had into a coherent force.

A week in, I felt as if I was slowly but surely getting a grip on things. I still had much to learn about 'ground truth' – about how things were out on the ground across Helmand – but I knew that would come with time. I was still getting to know the British soldiers in B Coy too, but so far so good. I was just starting to feel like we were making progress and that my head was above water, to the extent that I sent through an upbeat sitrep (a situation report, or update) to HQ in St Athan, which detailed the positive progress I thought we were making. Then, as is sometimes the case, just at the point where you start to feel in control, something happens which turns everything upside down.

I walked from my Portakabin over to the Ops room for the early morning briefing to be told by the CSM that ten Afghan soldiers had deserted overnight and more were planning to leave today. This was concerning news. The whole purpose of the operation was to build an Afghan force – we needed Afghans to do that. About an hour later the CSM returned to say twelve more had just walked out of camp with all their belongings. This was now turning into a crisis and was the last thing we needed.

The CO back in the UK had been very clear that time was of the essence and that the force needed to be fully operational as soon as possible. I was expected to deliver sharpish and was under intense pressure (admittedly some of which was self-induced) to train up the force and get it ready to conduct ever more complex operations, over greater distances, at night as well as during the day, and across a range of different military activities, from liaising with the local population to fighting the Taleban.

I needed to know what was happening and quickly; why the Afghans had left and whether more would follow them. Their contract of service was much better than those of the ANA (army) and the ANP (police), even before I had improved them. Through a series of often convoluted conversations via the terps with some of the more senior Afghans I was, after a while, able to find out that those departing soldiers were not doing so because they wanted to, in fact they were being 'ordered' to leave by the warlord who had originally supplied them. His nose was out of joint because he didn't think, as he had apparently described it, that 'his force' were being sufficiently loyal to *him*. This was local Afghan power politics playing out. Given that I didn't think it was 'his' force this was a peculiar notion, but clearly he carried great influence locally and was able to tell a number of the Afghan soldiers what to do and orchestrate their departure – it was self-evident their loyalty lay with him, not with us.

One of our brightest and best NCOs, a tough Scot called Corporal Kevin Mulligan, came in to say that a load more soldiers were now packing their personal effects and preparing to leave. We were haemorrhaging numbers. The CSM went to speak to the senior Afghan NCOs and I spoke to Juma, the Afghan officer, all of whom seemed reluctant to intervene, and in front of us fifteen more Afghans walked out the front gate of camp with all their belongings. This was now turning into a farce. If we lost many more the force would barely be sustainable. I had to try and stop them from going.

I sat with a hot brew in my office thinking about what I could possibly do. Being in Afghanistan came at huge personal cost to me; the last thing I needed was for the whole operation to go down the pan. I wondered if I should tell the CO back in the UK or the Brigade Commander in Helmand. They were both very experienced commanders, maybe they could give me advice. Realistically, though, there was nothing they could do. I was the person on the ground, in the hot seat, I was best placed to know what to do, so I decided I had to sort it out myself.

Nine more Afghans left.

The concepts both of the unit – the SFSG – and this particular operation were new ones. Both were under the spotlight. Some people in the military establishment back in the UK wanted us to succeed. But, at times, because of the rivalries that exist within the Armed Forces, it felt very much like there were some people who would have been supremely relaxed, even happy, to see us fail. The nature of the task was so complex and the moving parts involved so numerous that there were some within the British military hierarchy who just didn't think we were capable of pulling it off. They thought that only Special Forces soldiers could undertake such a challenging operation.

If the force deserted and the operation collapsed, I knew

there would be some back in the MoD who would celebrate
our failure and not be shy in pointing out that we should
never have been given such a difficult job in the first place.
Office politics don't just exist in the office. In terms of
developing a strong reputation for the SFSG the successful
completion of this operation was vital. And at this moment,
at this early stage, it felt like we were on the cusp of failure.
I couldn't allow that to happen.

Eleven more Afghans left.

A significant chunk of the entire force had gone. I had to
come up with some way of stopping this. Somebody brought
me another hot brew. What could I do? I had tried talking to
them; it wasn't working. I racked my brain for inspiration.

There was one thing that I could maybe try. It seemed
like a long shot but I was aware of an individual, who for
reasons that had never been explained to me (and I never
asked why) was always amusingly referred to as 'Simon the
fish', who might just be able to help us. I had briefly met
Simon, who worked for the Foreign Office up in Kabul. I
understood that he had been involved in brokering the deal
to recruit the Afghans in the first place. He was supposedly
on good terms with the warlord, and although I did not
particularly want to pander to the warlord, he needed to
understand that these were no longer *his* men. I needed my
soldiers back and sharpish, and maybe, just maybe, Simon
could help us.

As I prepared to call him to ask for his help, Corporal
Mulligan popped his head round the door to say that a load
more of the Afghans were packing their kit and planning
to walk out.

I called Kabul to be told that Simon was on leave back in
the UK. I could have his mobile number but only if it was
urgent. 'Yes, it's urgent,' I said. At that moment the satellite

phone line dropped out and it took our engineer forty-five minutes of fiddling with the aerial to get it working again. I used the time to go and speak to the Afghans who were preparing to leave. None of them would look me in the eye and it seemed that they too would soon be departing. Once the phone was working again, I called Simon's mobile number which rang and rang and rang. I sat there listening to it ring. It must have rung for five minutes. I just sat there hoping he would pick up. Eventually, Simon answered the phone. I didn't beat around the bush: 'Simon, I need your help.'

'I'm on a beach in Cornwall!'

'Sorry about that, but I've got a proper situation down here. I'm losing our Afghans, they're all deserting. I've tried to persuade them to stay but they are being told to leave. Please can you have a word and see if you can stop it from happening, or the whole operation will collapse.'

I think he lost signal at that point because the line went dead. I called back but it went straight to voicemail. I tried again but there was no response.

Twelve more Afghans left.

I'm not entirely sure what happened next, whether indeed Simon did do something, but early the next morning all of the soldiers who had deserted – or departed, depending on your perspective – were stood in a long line outside Camp Pluto requesting permission to rejoin the force. I never got to the bottom of exactly what had led to them returning and only fleetingly saw Simon again, many months later. It was a huge relief that they had returned – a full-blown crisis had been averted.

Despite us urgently needing them back, the CSM and I briefly toyed with the notion of not letting them return. We had to be clear that their loyalty was to the Task Force and to Afghanistan, not to anyone else. The CSM and I were both concerned that if we showed them leniency by letting them straight back in, with no questions asked and no consequences faced, that would send a worrying signal to them and to the rest of the force that they could just come and go as they pleased. We needed to build a force that was disciplined, and that risked sending entirely the wrong message.

In the end, though, there wasn't much of a decision to make. I desperately needed them back, but we still played through the theatrics of the CSM going out to speak to them. They formally requested that they be allowed to return, and he told them in a very clear CSM-like way that they had deserted, and that they had let us down very badly. That we had come to Afghanistan to risk our lives to help them fight against the Taleban for the good of their country. That we were supposed to be a cohesive force, fighting together against the enemy to build a better life for them and their families, and a brighter future for Afghanistan. He concluded by saying that given how seriously concerned we were at what they had done, he would have to speak to me about it.

We left them waiting outside for forty-five minutes before letting them back in. That night, in their cookhouse, I spoke to them all and told them that if they ever did it again there would be no more chances. They would be out and we would fight the Taleban without them. I finished my address with the rallying cry 'For Afghanistan!', at which point they all got so carried away with enthusiastic support that I thought we were going to have a riot on our hands. Clearly there was still some work to do to establish good military discipline.

We had resolved the immediate challenge, which was a huge relief, but it had been draining, it had wasted valuable time, and it had inflicted unnecessary pressure and stress, though it had at least resulted in me getting to know and understand the Afghan soldier psyche better. We now needed to put it behind us and get on with it. With the matter sorted, I decided that we should consolidate our training and bond the force with a gentle run out so that we could practise the skills and see what it was like operating jointly as a force out on the ground. We started to get ready.

# 14

# Killed in Action

## *September 2007*

—

I tried to be upbeat in my emails to Caroline. I wasn't allowed to say anything specific about what we were doing, so I mostly wrote about how hot and sandy it was in Helmand, but also asked lots of questions about how things were at home. Looking after two small children and worrying about your departed husband who was risking life and limb in a war zone was wearing, of course made worse by concerns about her own health. But in all the emails and letters Caroline sent she never once complained. She managed it all with grace and resilience. I knew how hard it was for her, though. At home Caroline had established her own daily routine of putting the kids to bed before then having a bath. She was normally so tired that she would then go to bed herself and read, but most days she would email or write to me. Her letters were a joy to read, but always reminded me of how much I missed them all. In one she wrote:

*The winks [kids] are now tucked up in bed, I think we read 7 or 8 stories!!! I'm now sat out in the garden with a cup of tea on what is a lovely late summers evening, there's a gentle breeze and I can hear the birds twittering away to themselves. We walked out to see Abbi [a friend's pony] today and saw a hot air balloon up in the sky which the kids loved. It reminded me that Holly used to bark at them when she saw them. I miss her very much. Miss you too babe. Stay safe and call when you can. LYF. XXX.*

It was wonderful to read her words; they warmed my heart and reinforced my resolve to make it back to them. Caroline sent updates about the children and I clung to every little detail. I would read them and re-read them. I missed them all so much, but there was barely a moment that I wasn't fully occupied. I would sometimes call them on the phone. It was of course wonderful to talk, but doing so reminded me of how far away they all were. The calls were made on a satellite phone, which didn't always work and would occasionally cut out mid-call. I usually wasn't able to warn Caroline that I would be calling so sometimes they would be out. I always wondered whether I should leave a message or not; it was good to be able to say something but it was always very disappointing to miss out on the opportunity to talk. If the kids were up, I would get to speak to them, which was always a joy. Caroline would dread me saying that 'I wouldn't be able to call for a while', which was code for me saying that I was deploying out from Pluto on an operation.

It was always a difficult judgement whether or not to let her know that I would be out of contact for a while. I knew she would worry, but then she would also worry if she didn't hear from me without any explanation. On balance it was better to know. If a British soldier was killed in Afghanistan – and twenty-four were killed between 1 July and 31 December 2007 – phone calls back to the UK would be suspended as the MoD wanted to make sure the next of kin heard the news from an official source rather than through the grapevine or on Facebook. I always thought that it was so much harder for those left waiting at home. At least those of us who were in Afghanistan knew what was going on. To be left wondering what was happening for long periods of time must have been agony.

We had gathered intelligence that a particular track through the desert was being used as a transit route by the Taleban to shift drugs, weapons and fighters through Helmand province. Throughout this period the Taleban continued to conduct brutal murders and attacks. They would target schools and behead teachers, just for teaching; they were ruthless in the methods of torture and killing that they employed. So we planned an operation which I thought would be a good run out for the force, and for me leading the force out on the ground. I didn't want anything too testing at this early stage, but I thought we needed to get out there and show a presence, which would also allow me to understand the complexities of operating a joint force out on the ground.

We planned to drive through the desert to a nominated holding area. It was just a spot in the desert some way short of the identified transit route. When there, we could covertly set up a position of over-watch from which we could launch a vehicle-borne operation to stop and detain any Taleban that we saw using the route. Out the back of Pluto we spent hours and hours carefully and methodically practising the move in to the holding area. We knew precisely where the route was, we'd rehearsed the operation to go forward and detain any Taleban we found, and through careful planning and an earlier recce we had worked out where we'd watch and wait.

When you're moving into an operation such as this it's absolutely vital to do it as quietly and discreetly as possible. Having driven through the day we identified an overnight stop, a couple of miles away from where we wanted to conduct the operation. The plan was that we would move in stealthily just before dawn broke, in order to be in position for dawn, which was when we anticipated that the Taleban would be most likely to pass along the route.

It was all going to plan as we painstakingly and very cautiously manoeuvred ourselves into position. 'So far so good,' I dared to say to my driver. The words had no sooner left my mouth than one of the Afghan soldiers managed to flick the wrong switch in his vehicle, which had previously been owned by the ANP. Though the flashing blue police lights had been taken off, it still had a very loud siren. Now the siren blared into life.

Sound carries a very long way in the desert, especially in the pre-dawn quiet. 'Turn that fucking thing off,' the CSM hissed, but the Afghan soldier couldn't figure out how to. Eventually, after what seemed a lifetime but was in reality about thirty seconds, he managed to silence the siren. It was one of those moments where you don't know whether to laugh or cry. Neither was an option at that moment and I had to decide whether to abort the mission or to carry on. We were all fuming that the work we had put in to get silently into position had been for nothing as the siren had advertised our presence to all from miles around.

The CSM raced his vehicle up to mine and we had a quick

conflab about what to do. We were both concerned at the possibility that it might have been done deliberately, either to scupper the operation or even to warn the Taleban that we were coming. We were still getting to know the Afghans and it was possible that there were Taleban sympathisers among the force, or some who had been paid to disrupt and report back. I decided that on balance it had most likely been an accident – cock-up rather than conspiracy – and that we were committed now and would just have to hope that no one reacted to the siren. But it was not an ideal start. To say the least.

We edged further forward, dismounted from our vehicles, which were hidden in dead ground beneath the ridge line, and crawled carefully forward into a position of over-watch along the top of a desert ridge line, with the transit route several hundred metres in front of us. It was now dawn. For hours and hours, nothing happened. We lay there scanning the horizon through our weapon sights. We waited, and waited. The CSM crawled over to me from his position, shot me a look and whispered, 'Duff intel?' Intelligence was not always right. Were we wasting our time?

You have to be very patient with these kinds of operations and sometimes you could expect to wait days just for a single convoy to pass by. But it was never our intention to be there for days and I considered pulling back out. We had all been lying in the sun for hours.

Just as I was about to terminate the operation, there was a crackle over the radio: 'Stand to, stand to.'

'Stand to' was the command to alert everyone of impending action and to get ready. Instantly everybody readied themselves. Several miles away was a convoy of vehicles speeding through the desert along the transit route. They were only visible because of the dust storm they were kicking up. The formation of eight to ten vehicles indicated that it was not an ordinary civilian convoy, but more likely to be Taleban.

'Prepare to move,' I whispered over the radio.

Everyone knew exactly what was required of them, and I launched forward a patrol of vehicles in a pincer movement to cut them off. I looked through my binoculars with some trepidation as our vehicle patrols with Brits and Afghans together screamed down the steep incline in front of us and raced forward to interdict the fast-moving convoy.

I wasn't sure exactly what was going to happen next but was confident that we had overwhelmingly superior fire-power if it all kicked off.

Our vehicles skilfully fanned out in front of the oncoming convoy and our soldiers dismounted and pointed their weapons. The CSM and I exchanged a glance.

'I hope they stop!' I said.

'We'll soon see,' he replied.

The convoy tried to veer away but the transit route constrained their movement and they finally came to a halt some fifty metres short of where our soldiers were stood. Our soldiers sprinted forward and surrounded their vehicles. There was then a bit of a stand-off until they all got out of their vehicles with their hands up. They were lined up, and I drove forward with the Sergeant Major. What we had to do now was confirm whether they were Taleban or not. Obviously, when asked they would say that they were not. We searched their vehicles and discovered a stash of opiates and some automatic weapons, but given the prevalence of both it was not sufficient evidence to confirm them as Taleban.

We then found ourselves in a confusing and farcical situation where none of us could make an informed judgement about whether they were actually Taleban or not. We asked a whole series of questions through our two terps. One of the terps, who insisted on being called 'California', walked over to me, looked me in the eyes and categorically assured me that they were all Taleban fighters – he was absolutely certain. 'No doubt about it, Major Dan. Taleban, every single one of them.' Conversely, the other terp told me, 'They're definitely not Taleban.' I then had the two terps arguing with each other about who was right. I didn't want us to hang around for much longer and had to decide if we were going to detain any of them. We could stop people who were behaving suspiciously, but there was a burden of evidence required if we wanted to arrest them. We relied on the Afghan soldiers to ask a series of questions about which village the men came from, which family and so on, in an effort to try and figure out if they were telling the truth.

Over the years I thought I had developed something of a knack, partly by gauging body language, for knowing whether people were telling the truth or not, but it was difficult and I don't know if the judgements we made were right or wrong. On this occasion we detained a number of the individuals for further questioning back at Camp Bastion. There they would be processed by the military system, and qualified and more experienced trained investigators would question them to ascertain whether they were Taleban or not. More often than not they would quickly be released, unless there was overwhelming evidence to support their guilt. We quickly became acutely conscious that the decisions we were making to detain could have real life-and-death consequences. Get it right, we were taking a Taleban fighter into custody, and that could mean lives would be saved. Get it wrong, and allow them to slip through your fingers, and they would likely be in a position to kill again and more lives would be lost. The stakes were high.

*

The run out had been useful but showed that we had much more work to do to get the force to the level of capability that would be required, and over the next few weeks we conducted a series of short missions, getting to know the ground and getting used to operating jointly. While deployed on these operations I had to concentrate intensely for protracted periods, keeping a close eye on what was happening. The simplest of mistakes could have lethal consequences; choosing a route that exposed the convoy to a greater threat of mine strike, an inability to react quickly enough when vital decisions needed to be taken, all risked severe consequences. But there were also moments of quiet calm, when I could stop to think. We kept camping-style folding chairs, desert-coloured like everything else, in the back of our vehicles, and when we stopped at the end of the day in a harbour position, in the middle of the desert, with sentries out, I'd bring my command group to the middle and we'd pore over a map, deciding where we'd go the next day and what our objectives would be. Once I'd given my orders I'd sit there in my chair, with a hot brew and a ration pack of food, looking up at the stars and wondering what the next day, next week, next month, next year would bring. I now felt relatively safe right out in the desert – it was an oasis of calm compared to the centres of population, where the level of risk was much greater.

I thought a lot about Caroline and the kids, wondering how they were getting on, and I vowed to myself that somehow I would get home safely to be with them again. I also took the time to think about what we were doing in Afghanistan. About our mission, and how I could make a success of it. Having now been there for a while I was much better placed to understand the challenges and work out how we could mould the force into something that could make a significant contribution to the campaign in southern Afghanistan.

I felt for the people of Afghanistan. It was a rugged and beautiful country but beyond that it didn't have much going for it. Riddled with corruption, it was close to being ungovernable. The Taleban ruthlessly exploited these circumstances for their own ends and it was increasingly clear that for Afghanistan to be able to enjoy anything resembling a peaceful future there needed to be rapid progress with both security and reconstruction. One couldn't happen without the other. But in the end we were never going to achieve what could qualify as mission success unless we left behind Afghan forces that could do the job of providing security without us. That's why this operation was so important, because it provided a means to do that. Even if I was sceptical about where their loyalties would ultimately lie, because for many that would no doubt be determined by who would pay them the most.

I took the burden of responsibility for my soldiers very seriously. I felt that I couldn't afford to falter or to let them down, not even for a second. I was supremely conscious that even a momentary lapse of concentration or a flawed decision could have fatal consequences. This was not a place to make bad decisions or silly mistakes. My overriding objective was first and foremost to bring all my soldiers safely back home.

But the longer you are in that kind of environment, the more you get worn down and the more you become tired. The constant need to be alert takes its toll, and for me the deployment continued to be made much harder by the lingering doubts about whether I should have been there in the first place. I tried to banish those thoughts to the back of my mind, but inevitably the fear and the relentless pressure

and exhaustion catch up with you. After the adrenalin high
of being out in the desert, playing a lethal game of cat and
mouse with the Taleban, came the exhausted low of being
alone afterwards, gloomily reflecting on it all, and wondering whether it really was all worth it.

Command is a lonely job. You are the boss, and the buck
stops with you, and in that environment you can't afford to
show any weakness or to share your doubts and worries. I
bottled mine up. After a tough mission the soldiers would
go and sit together in our makeshift bar attached to the
cookhouse and have a quiet fag and a couple of beers. But I
was in charge and couldn't easily go and sit with them – it
just wasn't how the Army did things. I could pop in, show
my face, but they didn't want the boss in there with them,
cramping their style.

I'd retreat to the solitary confinement of my office, or
my Portakabin in Pluto, where the anxiety would flush
through me in waves. I'd think about how lucky we had
been so far not to have sustained fatalities. I'd think back
to Sandhurst and Colour Sergeant Gargan talking about the
bank account of courage. Was I already running an over-
draft? Did I have the stamina to keep going for the duration
of the deployment? Would the combination of the pressure
of command and the added worry about Caroline and the
guilt of not being around for her overtake me and drag me
down? Would it impair my judgement, my ability to make
quick and effective decisions when under pressure? I was
acutely conscious of trying to protect myself as much as
possible, but out there, in that environment, the priority has
to be the mission and the soldiers, before yourself. There is
nowhere to hide.

I established the routine of spending a week out deployed
on the ground, followed by a week back in Pluto. The week

back in camp allowed everyone the time to get sorted after being out, before working up a planning cycle to prepare for the next week out deployed again, either in support of other British force activities or on a range of different tasks. In my week back in camp I was keen to ensure that we had a continued presence out on the ground so would give the Platoon Commanders and the 2IC the opportunity to take patrols out. It was good for their development, in that they got operational command experience, and good for the mission, in that we could show a constant presence, gather information and continue the training of the Afghans.

Early on the morning of 16 September I walked into the Ops room just to check there were no messages from the night shift and that the patrol out on the ground hadn't requested anything during the night. All was fine so I went to the cookhouse to get some breakfast. One of the oldest Army jokes is that the chef's course must be the hardest in the British Army – because no one has ever passed it. Yet in truth this is nonsense. Army chefs routinely turn out the most amazing standard of food often in the most difficult of circumstances. They needed to because, although it's a cliché, the army does march on its stomach. In our case, it was 'Junior', our ever-exuberant and hilarious Fijian chef, who was our hero for constantly providing it, despite the basic nature of the kitchen equipment and the infrequency of food supplies. As I walked in he was there, larger than life, nursing his fingers having just suffered a bad electric shock. He seemed completely unfazed by what had just happened and was in the middle of explaining his elaborate plans for rewiring the kitchen when I was told I was needed back over in the Ops room.

I hurried over just in time to hear the words 'Contact

wait out' over the radio net. Just like 'Gas, gas, gas', these three simple but stark words tell a story all of their own. 'Contact wait out' is the message that is sent over the radio net when soldiers find themselves 'in contact' with the enemy – when shots are first fired at them or if an IED or mine strike occurs. This initial short message alerts everyone else using the radio net to stay off the line and keep it free for urgent updates. It also warns the HQ that they are under fire. This initial message should then be followed up with a more detailed explanation of what is happening and whether the call sign on the ground has taken any casualties and is likely to require support. This more detailed message should come at the earliest opportunity, but given that the call sign on the ground is in contact with the enemy it can often be at least five to ten minutes before there is a follow-up update. Despite the obvious stress of the moment it is very important that an update is sent so that the higher HQ knows what's going on and can organise support where it is required. These procedures had been engrained into all of us over years of training.

The initial contact report came from the Joint Tactical Air Controller (JTAC) – someone I had come to know well. He was a calm, competent and highly capable individual. I could tell from the tone of his voice that something very serious was afoot. The CSM appeared, as did one or two others. We waited for the follow-up. And waited. After fifteen minutes I instructed the signaller to request an update, or sitrep.

'Hello Tango Two Zero Alpha, this is Zero, send sitrep over.'

At the other end, someone had pressed the setting on the radio that allowed a reply but no one spoke. Instead all we could hear was the haunting and unmistakable noise of rapid machine-gun fire, and the crump of explosions. A serious firefight with the Taleban was obviously underway. Still, I needed to know exactly what the situation was and whether they would require back-up. Were they going to be calling for air support? Had any casualties been taken? I instructed the signaller again to request an update.

A voice came back – 'Wait out' – indicating they weren't able to provide an update at that moment. The voice sounded panicked. Never a good sign. It was obvious that a major engagement was taking place. I looked at the CSM. We both felt powerless to help – they were going to have to sort it out themselves. The kettle went on and we sat down and had a hot brew and waited. And waited. I kept thinking back to the panic I'd heard in the voice earlier – it was a very bad omen. What on earth was happening that meant they couldn't let us know about the state of play?

I trusted their training and their judgement, and eventually we got an update over the radio: 'We are still in contact at this location.' They gave the grid reference. 'We have sustained casualties.'

Shit, I thought, and hoped they weren't serious.

I then heard the words 'We have at least one KIA [killed in action].'

'Shit.' At least one dead.

There was now a crowd of people stood in the Ops room listening in to the radio. They shouldn't really have been in there – you are supposed to keep the numbers down to those people who actually need to be there – but it seemed churlish to chuck them out. They were concerned for their mates. I looked over at the CSM.

'We need to know what's happening, boss,' he said to me.

I told the signaller to send a message to the Patrol Commander asking him to get on the net and speak to 0A (me). This was acknowledged, and shortly after that my 2IC, who was leading the patrol, came on to the net. He gave a pithy description: 'We are extracting from a major contact with the enemy. At least one of the Afghans has been killed. Multiple injured, Brits and Afghans. We are coordinating fire support from the air, will also need casevac helicopter – will send grid.' He sounded measured but deadly serious. I was relieved that he seemed to have a grip on the situation but was frustrated that I was not there with them to help. I looked at where their position was on the large map in the Ops room. They weren't that far away from Camp Bastion. Best that they recover back to there and get themselves sorted. I relayed this message back to the 2IC.

A couple of hours later the patrol limped into Camp Bastion. The 2IC called me on the secure landline phone. He talked me through what had happened. They had been advancing towards a small hamlet when all of a sudden they were pinned down by heavy and accurate automatic fire. Coordinated with the fire from the hamlet were mortar bombs that started to drop accurately all around them – they had come under a sustained attack from the Taleban who had, it seems, been sat there waiting for someone to ambush.

The 2IC seemed shaken but was coherent. I asked about our Brit blokes who had been injured; having sustained shrapnel wounds from mortar bombs, they were in a serious condition but would survive. I asked about the Afghans. He confirmed that a number were badly injured and along with our Brit casualties were already receiving medical attention in the field hospital at Bastion. And what about the P1 (fatality)? I expected the 2IC to say that he was in the morgue at Bastion. But he didn't. He paused, and then explained that they hadn't been able to recover his body and had been forced to leave him behind.

'Shit. You had to leave him? Are you absolutely certain he was dead?'

'I think he was.'

'You *think* he was? For fuck's sake, was he dead or not?'

'Dan, it was very confusing. There was accurate fire pinning us down, then the mortars came in. I think he was killed. The Afghans said he'd been hit.'

'Get back to Pluto now.'

I was devastated at the thought that one of the force had been killed, but that we couldn't say for certain was even worse. If we couldn't say for certain he was dead, then he might be alive. He could have been captured. He might be being tortured at this moment. The Taleban could already be in the process of forcing him to make a statement (under duress) that they could use as propaganda. Also, despite my concerns about the strategic implications of having lost a soldier and my obvious concern for his welfare, in my mind was the importance the Afghans placed on burying their dead. If we weren't able to do that for them there would likely be all sorts of repercussions.

The 2IC and the patrol arrived back. They were caked in a mixture of blood, sweat and sand. I could see from the eyes of some of them, from the so-called 'thousand-yard stare' (the distant look in a soldier's eye that tells you he has witnessed great trauma), that it had been a very tough firefight and that they were all processing what had happened, what they had just been involved in.

I wanted to make sure they were all OK but first I had to find out more about the missing Afghan soldier. The CSM took the soldiers away to get sorted out and I took the 2IC and the JTAC into my office for a hot brew. We sat down. They talked me through exactly what had happened.

They explained that one of our young British soldiers had time after time exposed himself to sustained and accurate enemy fire in order to rescue multiple casualties. Despite being ordered to take cover he had repeatedly ignored those orders and put himself in harm's way in order to rescue the wounded, both Brits and Afghans. This young soldier had got himself into various scrapes over the past few years including several drink-fuelled incidents in pubs and clubs. But on that day, in that moment, faced with the deadliest of circumstances and despite being ordered to take cover, his courage and conduct had been truly outstanding.

From what they knew, the missing Afghan soldier, Hama, had been shot, and was seen to fall to the ground. It was believed that he had been killed, but where he fell was just out of reach and given the furious firefight it hadn't been possible to get to him and recover him.

There was a knock on the door. Corporal Mulligan came in. 'Boss, sorry to disturb. Thought you needed to know: word from the Afghans is that one of them has heard that the Taleban do have Hama.'

'Is he dead?' I said.

'Yes, he's dead. And you're not gonna believe this, boss, but ... they say we can have the body back but we're gonna have to pay for it.'

I couldn't quite believe I was hearing this. 'Say that again – they're going to give us him back but only if we pay for him?'

What the hell was I going to do now? I needed to get Hama's body back but I couldn't entertain the prospect of paying money to the Taleban for it.

The information relating to the Taleban had come from Hamidullah, one of our senior Afghan soldiers. Hamidullah was a tricky character. He was useful in that he had an ency-clopaedic knowledge of Helmand, he understood the tribal networks and knew all the main families, and consequently was an invaluable source of information. He had all sorts of contacts and networks across the province and was known to be particularly close to the warlord we had previously had the run-in with. It was probably from him that he had gathered this information. But he was arrogant and lazy, and as I would find out later he was not trustworthy.

The CSM quipped that presumably I'd had training at Sandhurst as to what to do in scenarios such as these. 'I must have missed that lesson,' I replied.

We all agreed that we needed to act quickly to resolve the matter. The CSM and I went over to the Afghan section of Pluto to speak with Hamidullah. I knew it would be an all-round disaster if we couldn't retrieve the body, so with California translating, and the CSM standing next to me looking very menacing, I was very firm with Hamidullah.

'I'm not entirely sure what you have heard, or where you have heard it from, but I am telling you now, I want Hama's body back. I'm not paying for it, but I want it. Do you understand me?'

'But Major Dan, this will be impossible, I can't make it happen.'

I looked at him. There was something about the way he spoke to me that made me not trust him. I paused, looked him in the eyes, and slowly but surely said, 'You can and you will make it happen.'

This was something of a bluff on my part as I didn't know whether he could make it happen or not. I got a sense that it might be possible and I knew that I needed the body back, and in that fraught, pressurised moment he represented our best, perhaps our only, hope of retrieving Hama's body. However, it still felt insane that I was even having this conversation in the first place.

We glared at each other for a bit and then the CSM, California and I walked off. As we did so, a number of Afghan soldiers gathered round, desperate to know what was happening. They seemed curiously unaffected both by the casualties and the death of Hama, in part because most of them had been surrounded by death all of their lives, and people being killed was second nature to them and came as no surprise. But they were all seriously spooked that we didn't have the body to bury. One of them told me that if the body wasn't recovered they would be leaving, as they couldn't serve as part of a force that left its dead behind. I tried to reassure him that we were doing all we could to get the body back.

But to get the body back I was having to rely on a member of my own force to pass messages back to the Taleban. What a tangled web we were weaving.

I walked back towards the Ops room, and sat outside was the young soldier who had performed such heroics earlier on. He was talking to 'Rock', an NCO from our mortar detachment, sucking on a cigarette and sipping on a can of Miranda fizzy orange. 'Well done today,' I said, and beamed with pride. There was absolutely no doubt in my mind that his actions had saved countless lives.

'Just doing my bit, boss. Any one of the blokes would've done the same. Guarantee it.'

'Maybe they would, but you did well today. Thank you.'

I left him to finish his fag and his drink and to continue processing what he had seen and done and walked into the Ops room. The SFSG HQ back in St Athan knew all about the earlier contact and the casualties, but not that we were missing the body. I was going to have to tell them about it soon – goodness knows what they would make of it all – but I thought I would hold off for a bit just to see if there was any more clarity about what was happening. Bad news tends not to get any better with time, so as a general rule it's best to deliver it as quickly as possible, but it's also worth making sure you have as complete a picture as possible before you brief your boss. I decided to wait until I had some more information before calling him.

An hour later I got a message saying it would be possible to get the body back. About two hours after that I got another message saying it would not be possible. But the next day Hamidullah arrived with the body of Hama in his vehicle. I asked him how he had retrieved the body and where from, but he flatly refused to tell me. To be fair to him, he said that if he were to tell me, he would be killed. That he had these connections was on one level clearly deeply concerning, though it also meant that he was in possession of incredibly useful intelligence. I would have to attend to that later on.

Hama was wrapped in a white sheet and laid out on a table in a side room in the medical centre. His contorted face graphically illustrated the brutal pain of his death. There were many horrific wounds to his body. I hoped that they had been inflicted upon him by the Taleban after his death and were not the cause of it.

He had been killed on an operation that ultimately I was responsible for. He was under my command when he died, and although I wasn't with him when he fell, he was my responsibility. I felt a mixture of emotions: guilt that he had died on one of our operations, sorrow for his family and their loss, and anger at what the Taleban had done to him. Into the coping box it all went.

As part of the contract of service, we had in place an agreement whereby the families would be financially compensated in the event that an Afghan soldier was killed. I thought it was important to honour that commitment, and arrangements were made for Hama's father to come and collect his body. I asked to meet with him. He was, understandably, devastated at the loss of his son. We sat down together and through California I spent a long time talking to him. I thought about how I would feel if I was in his place. I told him his son was a hero who had died protecting his country and that he should be very proud of him. He sat with his head in his hands. Tears in his eyes. He listened to what I said with a terrible sadness written across his face. I repeated my heartfelt condolences. He thanked me for the words I had spoken about his son.

The Chief Clerk paid him the compensation, but a short while later I received a complaint from a bean counter in the MoD whinging about me having paid it. It was symptomatic of my darkening mood that they got short shrift from me in one of the very few rude emails I have ever sent. I never heard anything more about it.

Although we were still making good progress getting the force trained, recent events had underlined our vulnerabilities, demonstrated how much there still was to do, and reminded us all that the risks we carried were very real. I needed to get us back out on the ground. I thought the best way to do that was to keep people busy and get ready for the next operation.

# 15

# Certain Death Hill

## *September 2007*

—

The evening light was fading so rapidly that from the front passenger seat I could barely see the vehicle directly in front of us.

My vehicle was one of a long company convoy travelling north through Helmand province. The mission was two-fold: to prove new routes up into the northernmost parts of Helmand and gather intelligence while doing so, but also to test what progress the force was making and what level of capability we were now at. For the last hour we had been urgently seeking a place for an overnight stop in the desert but had found nothing suitable. I turned to Lance Corporal Lancaster, or 'Burt' as everyone called him, my trusted signaller and on this occasion driver, to say that I didn't think we could keep going for much longer.

'Too right, boss, it's darker than a very dark thing out there.'

I reached forward for the radio handset and flicked it

on to send. 'Hello all stations, this is Tango Zero Alpha. Prepare. To. Stop. Tango Three Zero Alpha [the rear call sign] acknowledge, over.'

There was a crackle over the radio net but straight away back came the reply: 'Hello Tango Zero Alpha, this is Tango Three Zero Alpha, roger, over.'

I paused for a moment to allow us to move forward a couple of hundred metres into what appeared to be a marginally better position before returning to the radio.

'Stop. Stop. Stop.'

The convoy halted, and I gingerly opened the door and stepped cautiously out of the vehicle on to the desert floor. I took out my night vision goggles (NVGs) from a webbing pouch and attached them to the metal fixing on the front of my helmet. I raised my rifle and scanned the hill straight in front of me through the night sight.

We hadn't moved as quickly as usual that afternoon. The broken ground – a series of irrigation ditches with few defined tracks that our vehicles could drive on – and the very high threat of IEDs meant we'd made slow progress and hadn't been able to make it to the stretch of open desert I'd planned to use as a night stop. A series of hamlets, scattered settlements and tiny villages in the north of Helmand, not shown on our maps, had given us a valuable opportunity to engage with the local population and to gather useful information and intelligence. But it meant we hadn't moved forward as quickly as I'd planned.

I now had to make a difficult decision. We could keep on driving into the pitch black of night – a hazardous exercise at the best of times, but even more so when our Afghan soldier colleagues weren't equipped with NVGs and didn't have experience of driving over rough ground in the dark. Or, we could set up an overnight defensive position where we were. The risk in that was we were much more likely to be spotted by the Taleban and attacked than if we were further out in the relative safety of the open desert.

In spite of the looming hill feature which dominated the ground we'd stopped on, and the reasonable chance that we would be attacked, the risk of trying to drive on in the darkness over difficult ground meant that on balance, I decided we should stay put. I communicated my decision over the radio net.

It was hard to think we wouldn't be attacked that night. We were sitting ducks. All of my soldiers knew that it was a tough call and accepted my decision. None of them whinged – at least not to my face – and everyone diligently got to work preparing for the night ahead in the highly professional way I had come to expect.

It looked like we had come to a halt in a large, open, dried-up river bed. My vehicle, along with the CSM who had pushed up from the rear of the convoy, was at the centre of our position. The rest of the vehicles adjusted to form a makeshift circle around us, no more than fifty metres away from our position in the centre.

I took a moment to try and analyse our situation. It was dark, there was an eerie silence, we were deep in hostile territory and parked up in front of a huge great hill which provided a perfect position from which to attack us. We were all exhausted and fearful as to what the next few hours would bring. I knew that if, or more likely when, we were attacked, we would almost certainly take casualties and that there was a very high probability that some of us would be killed. Our Afghan comrades, though determined, did not have the same soldiering skills or experience as us, and without the night vision equipment we had, their ability to fight in the dark – should we have to – was greatly reduced.

Apart from that, we were fine.

I quickly worked through a few worst-case scenarios in my head. We get attacked from the hill, and overrun by the Taleban; we are all killed. It starts to rain and we get hit by a flash-flood and have to abandon the vehicles and move off in the dark. Compared to the first scenario this was particularly unlikely given it hadn't rained for months, but the mind can slide into overdrive in these dark moments. The scenario that we all bedded down and had a peaceful night's sleep was not one that ever entered my mind.

The CSM appeared from nowhere in front of me. 'What do you reckon about us digging in, boss?'

If we dug shallow trenches or shell scrapes in the ground with our shovels they would provide some protection should mortar bombs start dropping down on us, but it would take time, and the noise of shovels impacting on rocks and stones would carry for miles in the silence of the Afghan night. It was another tough call. I was responsible for the safety of all these men, and my natural instinct was always to put as much protection around them as possible. But on balance, I weighed that the risk the noise would create was greater than the value of the protection it would offer. The CSM agreed, but like me, he wasn't exactly wild about being in this situation in the first place.

As he disappeared into the darkness, one of the Platoon Commanders emerged from it. I could tell he was anxious.

'Dan, could I have a word? I'm sorry we took longer than we should have done today. Given my platoon was at the front of the company convoy it is my fault and I wanted to apologise to you and take responsibility.'

'Don't worry about it, shit happens,' I replied. 'I should have pushed us along quicker. Anyway, it's done now, let's get prepped for the night.'

I could see there was something else on his mind.

'Dan, there is one other thing. The Afghans ... they're doing well and making decent progress, but you know they're not ready for this. If it kicks off tonight they'll be a complete liability. They'll be loosing off rounds left, right and centre – more likely to shoot us than the Taleban.'

He was right. Our Afghan counterparts with whom we had only been working for a couple of months were still at an early stage of their training and development. They weren't ready for a situation such as this and would be an absolute nightmare to try and control amid the chaos of battle at night. Given that my primary responsibility was the safety of my British soldiers I briefly considered the options and whether, in the absolute worst-case scenario, we should do our own thing without them. We had found ourselves in a situation for which we were not prepared. These things happen in war.

'I'm not leaving anyone behind,' I concluded. 'Let's get ourselves sorted and we'll talk more later.'

I reached into my desert smock pocket and felt for my emergency bag of rhubarb and custard sweets. If I was going to face a hardened enemy in the dark, at the very least I wanted some boiled sweets to help keep me going.

We needed to get organised for the night ahead, so I called the CSM, the Platoon Commanders and Platoon Sergeants – collectively known as the company 'head shed' – in for a briefing, and we hunched over the bonnet of my vehicle. In whispered tones, I began, 'Right, fellas, this is clearly not an ideal place to spend the night—'

'No shit, boss,' cracked one of the Platoon Sergeants.

I smiled and continued, 'But we're going to have to make the best of it. Let's make sure we have all our arcs of fire covered. I want maximum firepower directed up on the hill in case we need it.'

'Certain Death Hill, as the blokes are calling it,' interjected the CSM.

'We'll look to move off just before first light.'

I was trying to sound as nonchalant as possible, but everyone knew that this was nowhere close to business as usual.

'If the shit hits the fan and we do get attacked from, er, Certain Death Hill,' I went on, 'we will return fire and we'll call in air support.' I looked directly at the JTAC, an RAF Regiment soldier who would be responsible for giving the coordinates to either the fighter jet or helicopter gun-ship pilot who would hopefully be assisting us. He gave me a reassuring thumbs-up. 'If it looks like we're going to be overrun, we may have to abandon the vehicles and conduct a fighting withdrawal on foot. Await my orders over the radio.'

I paused.

'But I'm sure it will be fine,' I added, trying to convince myself as much as everyone else. I *hoped* it would be fine, but we were all acutely aware of the risks. 'Does anyone have any questions?'

'Can I have an alarm call, boss?' joked one of the other Platoon Sergeants.

There was a collective chuckle, broken by the CSM who grabbed the Platoon Sergeants and melted away with them into the darkness to brief them on the administration plan – to make sure everyone refuelled the vehicles from the jerry cans, cleaned weapons, ate some food and checked over the equipment. They then went off to site the sentry positions.

I was left alone. There was absolute silence. It was deafening. At any moment I expected that silence to be shattered by the clatter of heavy machine-gun fire, the thwack of mortar rounds, the whoosh of RPGs roaring down upon us. Surely it would come at some point soon.

Peering long and hard through my rifle night sight, I scanned the outline of the hill feature, which was now barely distinguishable from the dark sky behind it, searching for the silhouette of a Taleban fighter, readying himself for a deadly attack on us. I cursed the slow progress we'd made. I should've pushed us on faster, I shouldn't have allowed us to be in this situation. If we were all killed tonight it would be my fault.

I walked slowly and cautiously towards a spot where I knew one of our sentry positions had just been sited. You have to be extremely careful approaching sentries in the dark: many a friendly soldier has been mistakenly shot in this way. The paratrooper, who was laid on the ground with a GPMG pointing up towards the hill, whispered out the password: 'Tango Hotel.'

'Oscar Romeo,' I replied.

I padded forward warily and crouched down beside him. I had been in command for long enough to know that now was not the moment for a Churchillian pep talk, so I kept it simple.

'You all right? Have you had some scoff?' I whispered.

'Aye, nae dramas. Reckon Terry [Taleban] knows we're here, boss?'

'Probably. So keep 'em peeled.'

'Roger that. Boss ... if anything happens to me, there's a letter for my missus back in my locker in camp. You'll make sure she gets it?'

'Nothing is going to happen to you. You'll be telling your grandkids about this.'

'Right boss, yeah, but if it does, you'll make sure she gets it?'

'Yes, I will.'

I walked slowly back to my vehicle with a sense of utter

dread in the pit of my stomach, partly because of our dire situation but also because I hadn't written a letter.

My thoughts drifted back to home. I thought about Caroline. Our lives had been transformed by her cancer diagnosis and our worries about the disease returning. In that moment I knew that I was utterly powerless to help, and worse, would surely be the source of even more anguish. The time difference meant that Caroline would soon be giving the kids a bath before reading them a bedtime story and tucking them cosily into bed. I wished I was there with them. Wished I was reading the story. Wished I was there to support her. With every fibre of my being I hoped that she would be all right.

I visualised two people in smart military uniforms solemnly walking up the path and knocking on our front door to inform Caroline that I had been killed. It sent an ice-cold shudder right down my spine. I was determined I was not going to let that happen to her, or to anyone else. I tried to focus back on the job in hand. I looked back up at Certain Death Hill and reached for another rhubarb and custard sweet. I was now effectively chain-smoking them. We were in for a long night.

We had moved into the night routine. Occasionally above the breeze I heard the muffled shuffle of movement as our sentries changed over. The remainder huddled in their sleeping bags trying to keep warm and to grab some sleep. It was cold, the stars were out. The night sky looked truly magnificent but I was not in the right frame of mind to appreciate it. I'd had a boil-in-the-bag ration pack – pork casserole, which brought back a few memories – and having eaten, I was feeling a bit calmer and a bit more assured. In my mind I'd worked out exactly what we were going to do if we were attacked, how I would react and what steps we would take to return fire. There was nothing much more I could do. I knew that I should try and get a bit of rest myself – who knew what the next day would bring? – but I didn't want to get into my sleeping bag because I thought that if I did I might fall into a deep sleep and be slow to react if it all kicked off. So I sat in the front seat of the vehicle, peering up through the windscreen at the hill, straining to see any movement.

I sat and waited. And waited. An hour passed slowly. Then another one. I started to wonder whether maybe we would get away with it. Perhaps they hadn't clocked we were here after all. I closed my eyes for a moment; they felt heavy, and I yawned. I was tired and needed some sleep. I looked at my watch: it was still only midnight, so I decided to try and get a few hours.

I'd had my eyes closed for just a couple of minutes when the radio crackled into life. 'Stand to, stand to,' whispered one of the sentries over the radio.

All around I sensed activity as people were quietly woken up, sleeping bags silently discarded and weapons pointed outwards, everyone readying themselves for what was about to come.

Here we go, I thought.

I gently opened the vehicle door and flicked down my night vision goggles. I stood next to the vehicle and looked up towards the hill. I couldn't make out any movement but I could feel my heart pumping. I stood in silence, listening, waiting.

The CSM padded over. 'What's happening?'

'Not sure.'

Then over the radio came the message 'Stand down, stand down.' That was the signal to get back to the normal routine. I breathed a sigh of relief.

A moment later, out of the darkness crept one of the NCOs, who came over to the CSM and me. 'Just to let you know, boss, we sighted some movement at the bottom edge of the hill but we can now see that it's, er ... well, it's a fox, boss.'

'A fucking fox,' interjected the CSM. 'Right, thank God for that – everyone get back to normal routine.'

The CSM shrugged his shoulders and made a crack about how he didn't think the Taleban had yet been able to recruit foxes to the cause. I got back into the vehicle and drew breath. I was relieved that it was only a fox, but there were still a number of hours of darkness left: we weren't safe yet.

I decided again to try and get a bit of rest and dozed fitfully till 3 a.m. I got up and walked slowly around the vehicle. It was freezing. There wasn't much more than an hour of darkness left: so surely if they were going to attack us they would have done it by now. But then my mind wandered back to exercises at Sandhurst with Frank Gargan. The optimum time to carry out an attack was just before dawn: catch your enemy at the point at which they are most likely not to be ready and then consolidate on their position. Perhaps also the Taleban didn't have NVGs; maybe they were waiting till first light. This would be our point of greatest vulnerability.

At my bonnet briefing the night before I had said that everyone had to be ready to move for 4 a.m. so that as soon as it was light enough to move off we would be ready to do so. I stood and shivered for twenty minutes just waiting, hoping that we would get away with it. I just wanted to make it through this day – that was as far ahead as I could see at that moment. I wasn't bothered about tomorrow, or the day after, or next week or next month, and certainly not next year. Caroline was fleetingly in my thoughts but I didn't feel I had the luxury of thinking about home. I needed to stay sharp and sort out today before I could think about anything else.

It was still dark but from 3.30 I could hear the gentle rustle of sleeping bags being quietly packed away. By 3.45 everyone was ready to go. The CSM walked over to ask that I give him the nod when I wanted the sentries pulling back in, ahead of our departure. As he walked away, again over the radio came 'Stand to, stand to' – one of the sentries had seen something through his night sight.

'Another fox?' cracked the CSM.

'There's someone walking towards us from the village,' whispered the sentry.

One of the Platoon Commanders piped up over the radio, 'How many people? Any sign of weapons?'

There was a long pause, everyone now listening in and waiting to find out what was happening. I could feel my heart pumping again. My first instinct was to move into a better position so that I could see for myself what was happening, but I decided I should entrust it to those who were better positioned.

'Looks like a lone male, walking slowly towards us from the direction of the village. He's now about three hundred metres away.'

'Any sign of a weapon?' the Platoon Commander repeated.

There was another long pause.

'He's carrying something, but looks more like a stick than a rifle.'

'It'll be a shepherd, or someone coming out from the village to see what's happening – let's get out of here,' said the CSM.

'Agreed,' I replied. 'Get the sentries back in.'

Over the radio I gave the order: 'Prepare to move. Prepare to move.'

Vehicle engines hummed into life. We had already planned our route out of the river bed, and the formation, and despite an eerie early morning mist it was now just light enough to drive so we moved off as quickly as the broken ground allowed. The first ten minutes were tricky as we picked our way across the river bed, still wondering whether at any moment we would come under attack. I was worrying about how vulnerable we were to a mine strike, but at that moment all I could really do was hope that we could weave our way out to relative freedom on the other side.

Half an hour later the sun was up and we were well away from the dominating high-ground features and all neighbouring settlements and were able to park up in the relative safety of the open desert. Given the anxious night we'd endured I thought everyone – and on this occasion I included myself – would benefit from a decent breakfast stop, so to celebrate nothing more than the fact we were all still alive we took an hour to have a hot breakfast ration pack and a hot brew.

The CSM wandered over and sat with me in our folding deckchairs. We ate our boil-in-the-bag sausage and beans with our 'racing spoons' attached to our smocks with a bit of cord (so we couldn't lose them, just like little kids have their gloves attached to the sleeves of their coats). After a brief discussion about the events of last night, the conversation turned to our families and how much we were looking forward to seeing them again.

The working relationship between the OC and CSM is absolutely vital. If the company is going to be effective, these two people have to get on, and must be able to work closely together. We did. I had huge respect for him and greatly valued his experience, advice and support. I also liked him. I thought he was a top man, professional and dedicated.

Unrelenting in wanting both the best from the company and for the company, and never accepting anything less.

Throughout my time in the Army I'd never been comfortable with the protocol of soldiers and NCOs calling officers 'sir'. There's a reason for it, it's how the military discipline system operates – I get the logic – but sat there in the desert with nobody around, and after all we'd been through over the past few months, it seemed ludicrous to be observing such a protocol, so I dropped it and we spoke without the unnecessary formalities of rank. As our conversation drew to a close, I asked him how he was – was he tired?

'I'm all right,' he replied, 'but it's hard graft. Think all the blokes are knackered, but they'll crack on. They always do.'

# 16

# Cauldron of Chaos

## *October 2007*

—

I took out my battered old notebook and a pencil to jot down a few points to make at the morning briefing and noticed that scribbled on the inside back cover was a quote from Sun Tzu, a Chinese General born in 545 BC. Credited as the author of *The Art of War*, he is still studied today by historians and military strategists. The quote, which I must have picked up at the Army Staff College, read, 'Regard your soldiers as your children and they will follow you into the deepest valleys. Look on them as your own beloved sons and they will stand by you even unto death.' It struck a chord, not just because of the experiences of the last few hours but because throughout the deployment I'd been constantly wrestling with a conflicting sense of the love and duty I felt for both of my families – the one at home and the one out here. Very few people in the company had much knowledge of Caroline's condition. I'd kept it to myself, partly because it was personal but also because I didn't want anyone doubting my resolve to see us through the mission. The CSM knew, and sat there in the desert he asked me about it.

'How are things at home, it must be tough being out here?'

I paused. While it was tempting to shut down the conversation at that point, I was just brutally frank with him: 'Yes, it's tough.' I left it there and didn't say any more because even though I had a strong relationship with the CSM, the Regiment, the Army, was the ultimate macho culture. Within it, soldiers, men, were expected to be tough, always to be OK. They weren't expected to show weakness, ask for help or demonstrate even a faint hint that they might not be all right. We were all coping with adversity just by getting on with it. I daresay lots of very well-qualified people would say that this isn't the best way to deal with the traumatic experiences we were encountering and they are probably right. In the end, each of us charted our own course and coped as best we could.

In recent years I've been pleased to see that the Army has become a bit more enlightened in the way it supports its people who suffer from mental health issues including post-traumatic stress disorder (PTSD). Back in the summer of 2007 it was very much a crack-on culture, without too much thought given to what problems that might be storing up for the longer term.

We decided to give everyone another bonus hour to sort out their administration – as the Army saying goes, 'Admin is not just a place in China!' When you're deployed away from camp it is essential that you maintain all your equipment, the weapons and the vehicles, but also yourself. If you are deployed for weeks at a time your body can quickly degenerate if you don't look after it. Your feet are particularly vulnerable: caged within socks and boots, they sweat and need to be cleaned and powdered every day, otherwise they start to rot. We all busied about cleaning our rifles, powdering our feet and cleaning our teeth; there was no need to shave – nothing wrong with a bit of a beard in the desert. A small hole was dug in the sand as a latrine pit and those that needed to use it did so.

The company 'head shed' came in for a bonnet briefing, along with Juma. The atmosphere was now much more relaxed than the night before. I reminded them that although the immediate danger had passed we were still deep in Taleban territory, the risks were high, and nobody should drop their guard. Not for a second. Everyone understood. Over the time we had been in Afghanistan together we had bonded as a team. I was surrounded by outstanding people who were prepared to, and had to, put their lives on the line for each other. We had built a bond of trust and it was down to me to get the most out of them so that collectively we could do the best job. We pored over the map and decided that we would go and recce a small village showing on the map some ten kilometres away. If it felt like there was an opportunity to meet with the village elders then we would try and have a meeting.

On the edge of this remote village I decided to send forward some of our Afghans to make contact with the locals and see if they would be prepared to meet us. Word quickly came back that they would, so I made my way forward into the village. I was invited into a building for a meeting, or 'shura', and offered some black tea. We sat cross-legged on the floor opposite the village elders who had hastily assembled. They were friendly, curious to know who we were and what we were doing. We asked them about the Taleban, and they told us that from time to time they would show up and threaten them, that they would confiscate crops and tell them that they would all be killed if they ever supported the Americans or the British, or the ANA and the ANP.

While our medic tended a bad cut on a little girl's arm we continued our conversation. It was clear that they had only the most modest expectations of life: they just wanted to be left alone to get on with tending their crops and living their lives in the way they had for generations. Their lifestyle had altered very little over the years. There was no electricity, and water came from a primitive-looking well in the centre of the village. There was no school and no medical facility. These were people who had very little, but when we arrived on their doorstep they went out of their way to make us feel welcome as their guests. I came away hoping that at some point, all of our efforts, alongside the work of so many others, would help improve their lot in life. Time would tell.

We'd been on the ground for a week so I decided it was time to head back to Pluto. After the painfully slow progress of the previous day and the high drama of last night, we made surprisingly good time and were back in camp by nightfall. After some hot food and our standard debrief, the blokes took themselves off to unwind, and to make phone calls home. I retreated to my room, where I reflected on the night before, on the tension of just sitting there waiting to see if we would be attacked. Hoping to make it through the night. The amount of nervous energy burned off was huge.

We were now roughly at the halfway point of the deployment. Rest and Recuperation (R&R) had already kicked in, which meant that at different times all of the soldiers in the company would be returning home for two weeks to be with their loved ones. I hadn't yet decided what to do about my R&R. I wanted to go home and see Caroline and the kids, but I worried that if I did it would make returning to Afghanistan so hard, for them and for me.

I knew, though, that I could feel myself starting to tire. The shattering stresses and strains of it all were starting to tell. Each day, particularly those deployed out on the ground, was a marathon, physically and mentally. The heat, the cold, the danger, the fear, the uncertainty, the doubt, the burden of decision-making under extreme pressure – all this, over time, wears you down. The constant requirement to focus and concentrate was mentally exhausting. There's also something all-consuming about fear. You get used to it to an extent – you can manage it, deploy mechanisms to distract from it – but eventually it gets under your skin and into your system. I could mostly manage the fear when out on the ground. In the heat of the moment, I knew I needed to be calm and stay sharp. But back in camp, afterwards – that's when it really came for me. However tough, however determined you think you are, these constant pressures take their toll. And they were taking their toll on me. I decided that I should head back for some R&R but only when the CSM returned from his.

Despite the fatigue, the pressures, the complexity and sometimes the chaos of working with the Afghans, I genuinely felt we were making real progress. Notwithstanding all my initial concerns, the force was shaping up well. We had greatly enhanced their capability in terms of both performance and equipment, and Camp Pluto was already virtually unrecognisable from when I had first seen it. Some of the Afghans were now really starting to excel; they were keen and working hard. It was starting to feel as if all the graft was paying off and that we had come together to form a united, cohesive force, determined to achieve our mission. This was heartening.

But, as is often the case, there are always those – in this case, one – who are troublesome. The fly in the ointment.

I had always believed that to get the best out of people you needed to treat them with respect, be clear about what you expected from them, and give them the freedom to get things done, while reviewing their progress and providing constructive feedback. That all sounds hunky-dory in a management handbook and maybe it's fine in an office environment, but out in Afghanistan, in the desert, in the cauldron of chaos that a combat environment is, things don't always quite work out that way.

I had known from previous deployments and from my studies that corruption was endemic throughout Afghan society; it permeated every single level of government and the judiciary, extending into the Army and the police and into every walk of life. No exceptions. Every aspect of Afghan life was touched to a lesser or a greater extent by it. Corruption was, and is, the biggest enemy of the people of Afghanistan. At the root of so many of their problems was poor, inept, corrupt governance. Wherever you went, wherever you looked, there was corruption. Around every corner and under every stone was corruption. It had long been part and parcel of Afghan life. Perhaps unrealistically, I was determined to ensure that our Afghan force remained immune from it, at least as much as possible, but it would have been naive to expect at this relatively early stage that we would be free of it. The recruitment process had done some rudimentary screening of candidates to try and weed out both those who might be unsuitable and those whose allegiances might lie elsewhere. Particular attention was paid to those Afghans who were occupying more senior roles within the force. But the truth was we didn't really know much about the backgrounds of our Afghan soldiers.

Hamidullah, our trickiest Afghan NCO, was a constant

source of concern. I had always had my suspicions about
him. I thought at best he was a bit fly – he didn't seem to
have the same level of dedication as most of the others and,
as the Hama incident had shown, he had all sorts of very
dubious connections. More recently, the CSM and I had got
wind of stories that he had been mistreating some of our
younger Afghan soldiers. We hadn't got to the bottom of
exactly what had been happening over on their side of the
camp, but there were whispers that he had physically bullied
some of them. Concerningly, there were even rumours that
there was some sexual element to the misconduct.

There's an Afghan term, 'bacha bazi', which is slang for
a variety of sexual activities that sometimes occur between
older and younger men in Afghanistan; it had very loosely
been translated into the expression 'Man Love Thursday'.
In essence it meant some older Afghan men using their
power and status to have sex with younger Afghan men. I
was concerned that this might have been going on and that
Hamidullah was a key part of it.

It was something I could have done without. It would
have been easy to turn a blind eye, accept that you couldn't
effect significant cultural change overnight, and justify
it by saying you were there to win a war and that there
were higher priorities – this was after all Helmand, not
Harrogate. This would have been the easier path to tread.
If I had done that, probably nobody outside Camp Pluto
would ever have known about it. But I'd always been clear
that I expected the highest form of conduct. It wasn't the
right path to tread.

Not for the first time, though, this did present something
of a moral dilemma. I reflected back on the night in front
of Certain Death Hill and the conversation with one of the
Platoon Commanders about whether, if it all kicked off,

we should leave the Afghans to fend for themselves. There was an undeniable logic to doing so, if we'd come under sustained attack, if we were taking casualties and having soldiers killed, if deserting *them* might have saved *us*, but would it have been the right thing to do? You can justify from a moral standpoint a decision to leave them and a decision to stand with them. My view was that they were our comrades and that we were in it together. On that occasion and under those circumstances I couldn't morally justify, at least to myself, abandoning them.

These are, however, difficult, fine judgements – easy enough to cogitate on them from the luxury of an armchair, a bit harder when you're out there in the desert living it for real. So, did I tolerate certain behaviours from an individual who added important capabilities in other areas? Although there were whispers about Hamidullah's conduct, not yet proved but with reasonable grounds for concern, there was virtually nothing that he didn't know about Helmand. He appeared to know all the personalities, he understood the tribal make-ups of each town and village, and his knowledge of Taleban activity was such that there was no doubt he was a valuable asset to the force. A mine of useful intelligence. But doubts about his personal conduct persisted and increasingly I was of the mind that despite his value in some areas, the concerns over his conduct meant he was a liability, which, in all good conscience, I couldn't continue to tolerate.

I had discussed it with the CSM before he departed on R&R. We were in complete agreement that we had a duty of care to the Afghan soldiers and had both spoken to Hamidullah to let him know that while we valued his contribution we would not tolerate anyone breaking the rules and that under no circumstances would we accept mistreatment of any of the Afghan soldiers. In the CSM's absence, I decided that I would find a moment to confront Hamidullah about it. I chose the wrong moment to do it.

Earlier that day I had been told that the Taleban had apparently placed a $50,000 bounty on me, either for my capture or for my head. My initial reaction was: good – that showed what we were doing must be having an effect. It wasn't a huge amount of money, but looked at in the context of Afghanistan it was a king's ransom. It would have been enough for any Afghan to immediately retire and not only never have to worry about money again but to live in relative luxury. Under those circumstances, who could say for certain that one of our Afghans wouldn't betray us? Although I wasn't initially too concerned about this personal threat, the more I thought about it, the more it undermined my morale.

I was working in my office when I was told that Hamidullah wanted a word with me. I was now, as I said, feeling increasingly worn down. I could feel the tiredness in my eyes and I sensed that it was starting to show. My attention span seemed shorter than normal and I was becoming very impatient and irritable. I should have said no, should have waited till the following morning at least, should have definitely waited till I was in a calmer frame of mind. But I didn't.

He waltzed into my office and demanded to be promoted. He told me that he was a prize asset, better than all the other Afghans, and that he was deserving of not only higher rank and greater status within the force but that his efforts deserved more money. Maybe he was right, and I tried patiently to explain to him via California that he had a future with the force, but before there could be any discussion of promotion or a pay increase he needed to accept our rules – nobody was above them. I expected everyone, *everyone*, to treat others with respect. No exceptions.

He protested and continued to argue that we were disrespecting him with such paltry wages. I tried to remain calm but I could feel myself getting wound up. I explained that the terms and conditions were more than generous, better than the ANA, better than the ANP. I went on to say that my motivation for being in his country was to make it a better, safer place to live and I hoped he would continue to work with me. I could and should have left it there. But I didn't.

'Furthermore,' I continued, 'given that we are having this conversation, I want to ask you directly: have you at any point mistreated any of the other soldiers?' In my mind was the shame of what had happened at Deepcut Barracks, and while we were a world away from Surrey, I wasn't having any of that kind of behaviour on my watch. I'd grown increasingly angry at the prospect that it might be happening and that he might be responsible for it.

He tried to make light of it and fob me off by telling me that I didn't understand what he described as the 'Afghan way', at which point I did something which I have very rarely done. I lost my temper. I was tired, I was worn down, I was not in a mood to be messed with. I looked him in the eye and said, 'Quite frankly, I don't give a fuck whether it's the Afghan way. You're part of this force and it's our way or the highway. Those are the rules, and if you don't like it, pack your bags and fuck off.' California struggled a bit with some of the translation, but I think he captured the gist of it.

Fortunately Hamidullah stormed off and I was left alone to calm down. The encounter was unnerving. I started to worry about what I would have done next had he escalated it. I couldn't say for certain that it wouldn't have properly kicked off. Although I was not in the best frame of mind I should have gone about it in a different way. The success of the operation depended on my ability to raise the Afghans to a high degree of competency: I needed their good will and their support to make that happen.

I decided I would walk over to the Afghan section of camp to gauge the mood. California and Corporal Mulligan came with me for moral support. Hamidullah was there in front of the cookhouse bemoaning his treatment by me to anyone who would listen. I suggested we sit down and talk about it, but he didn't want to. He stormed off, packed his bags and left. We never saw him again.

That night the Afghans had a massive party to celebrate his departure.

I needed a break from it all so arranged to fly back home shortly after the CSM arrived back.

I had contemplated not taking any R&R. The force still needed so much work to get it up to anything resembling a full operating capability and I had arrived a couple of weeks after everyone else, but I needed to get back home to spend some time with Caroline, to check how she and the kids were doing. However much you might think you're indispensable, you're nearly always not – better to recharge the batteries and come back refreshed. Plus it was a good opportunity for my 2IC to get the experience of taking charge for a week or so.

The flight back to the UK on the same C-17 aircraft that had brought me out was sobering. On it was a very seriously wounded British soldier being flown back to Selly Oak hospital in Birmingham for emergency medical treatment after being very badly wounded in an IED blast. He lay on a sophisticated-looking medical trolley, what looked like a massive incubator, surrounded by a dedicated team of medics who kept a constant watch on him. I asked one of them how he was doing. He shrugged wearily and replied, 'Not looking good.' I climbed into my sleeping bag to escape from it all. I was so tired that I fell into a deep sleep and woke up a few hours later. I could see everyone else in the plane immersed in their own thoughts and emotions, processing what they had seen and done in Afghanistan over the past few months. Some just sat there staring off into the far distance.

From RAF Brize Norton I drove to the M4 and, as I had done numerous times before, had to turn right to HQ at St Athan rather than left to head home. I desperately wanted to go left but I had agreed to debrief the CO on the progress we were making. Once that was done, I went home. I pulled up outside our house and paused for a moment to take it all in. The greenness and freshness of the English countryside seemed so alien and an assault on my senses given how accustomed I had become to the sandy, dry desert. I walked in through the front door to a wall of love and hugs and more than a few tears.

The kids were ecstatic, and it was unreal to be back. The kettle went on, and then with a cup of tea Caroline and I walked out into the back garden. It was wonderful to be home but I was steeling myself for the upset that would come – it was the first time we had been together since Holly had died. Caroline's father had buried her in the back garden. We stood together in front of her little grave and I hugged Caroline. I hated the fact that I'd not been around to comfort her. I could see from the strain on her face how difficult it had all been.

While it was wonderful to be back, it was hard to readjust. Just a matter of hours earlier I had been out in

Afghanistan, amid the death and the destruction of it, and now I was at home with my family in a peaceful little village. Caroline had established her routine while I'd been away. The kids went off to nursery, and for a couple of days I didn't really know what to do with myself. Mostly I slept and ate, recovering from the effects of months on the go with so much nervous energy expended.

Caroline and I went into Salisbury and sat outside a café in the sunshine having a coffee. I watched the world go by, good people just going about their daily business. But I found myself starting to resent them and their normal lives, untouched by the brutality and carnage of war, just carrying on like we weren't out there risking our lives every single day. For them. Didn't they care about us? Weren't they bothered? We were out there putting our lives on the line, our friends were being killed and maimed, yet here they were just pottering about continuing their safe everyday lives as if nothing mattered. Caroline, as she always did, calmed me down and was the voice of reason. She reminded me that I was the odd one out, not them. I was the one who had chosen the path to serve. The problem was very definitely mine, not theirs.

Caroline was absolutely right, and I snapped out of my misery. We walked around Salisbury Cathedral, lost in the splendour of it, then sat peacefully inside. But my mind was constantly wondering what was happening back at Pluto. The camp dominated my thoughts, and although it was wonderful to be home, I couldn't stop thinking about the fact that I would soon have to go back and that there was still much to do. It was hard to relax, knowing that in just a few days I'd be back there, amid the chaos of it. Although we didn't discuss it at the time, a few months later, at the end of my tour, Caroline referred to this period of R&R by saying that I was 'there, but not there'. She was right. I was there, but not there. Although I tried my best to get back into our normal routine (such that we had ever had one), I just wasn't able to.

Before I knew it, it was time to head back. I was almost relieved to be getting on with it. Although we had, as a force, largely been lucky, as a result of a lethal cocktail of IED strikes and Taleban bullets, British and Afghan soldiers had been falling all around us in Helmand. I was dreading Caroline asking me to guarantee that I'd be OK, to tell her that I would come back safely. Even if I had been able to speak the words that I would be fine, I suspect my face would have told a different story. Fortunately, Caroline never asked me the question. Perhaps she didn't want to hear the answer. Perhaps she didn't want me to lie.

It was easier than before to walk out the door, because I knew I had to go, I had to get back there, so without great ceremony or delay I headed off. Caroline and the kids waved me off, and within a matter of hours I was back in Afghanistan.

# 17

# Long Way Home

## *November 2007*

—

R&R had given me some short-term respite, time to sleep
and to eat, but it had done little to address the long-
term fatigue we were all battling against.

Nonetheless I slipped quickly back into the routine and
was pleased to see that good progress had continued to be
made in my absence. It's amazing what people can achieve if
you trust them to get on with things. The Army often talks
about what it calls 'mission command', the basic idea being
that you make sure people know your intent – what it is you
want to achieve – and they then get on and deliver it, and do
so whether you are there or not. Sometimes this is preached
more than practised. But on this occasion, my brief absence
had given the company a degree of autonomy, and I was
pleased with the results. A series of low-level vehicle patrols
had harvested lots of valuable intelligence and planning was
underway to provide direct support to a big forthcoming
brigade operation that was going to take place in Helmand.

As the capability of the force increased we were inevitably (and rightly) tasked with ever more difficult and dangerous missions as we continued the work of supporting British brigade operations across Helmand. I developed a ritual each morning as I woke up, whether I was in Pluto or deployed out in the desert, of repeating under my breath the simple mantra 'none of us will die today, none of us will die today'. At the end of each day, I would repeat, 'none of us died today, none of us died today'. Each and every day that none of our people died was a bonus, to be savoured and cherished, but I was mindful of the fact that we would risk it all again tomorrow.

I received an email to say that someone called Tom Tugendhat was being sent down from the British HQ in Kabul to 'help'. My initial reaction was one of suspicion, that he was being sent to see what we were up to and to keep an eye on us. He turned up regardless and despite our initial scepticism within a short space of time had made himself invaluable. He had developed a comprehensive understanding of the tribal networks and was able to replace some of the expertise we had lost with Hamidullah's departure. He also proved to be both good company and a source of good sense, and having someone else there, outwith the chain of command, with whom I could talk things through proved to be extremely useful and helped reduce the loneliness of command. I decided to take him out with us on our next operation so he could get a feel for the ground and provide me with real-time advice while we were deployed.

The night before we were due to head out at dawn, I phoned home. I got to speak to Caroline and went through the now established code of saying that I wouldn't be able to call for a few days. I spoke to both of the kids, and during the conversation with my son, in part perhaps because of the crackle and feedback from the satellite phone line, he said that 'it sounds like you are a long way away', an expression he had used before when asking about Afghanistan. It reinforced in my mind that at that moment, I was. I was a long way away and it was a long way home. As before, I knew I had to try and banish it from my mind, but it now felt like there wasn't space in the coping box to put any more stuff in there.

Early the next morning, things didn't get off to a great start. My pre-dawn brief to the Afghans had gone well, though. For reasons of operational security – in other words to ensure that none of them leaked any of the information about the operation – they were only briefed on where we were going just before we actually drove out of the camp. It was, however, impressive how much they had grown in stature over the months. They had a new-found confidence and professionalism and now for the first time it felt like they were a true partner, an asset rather than a liability.

Soldiers can sometimes get quite superstitious on and around the battlefield, with many choosing to follow meticulous rituals as part of the process of trying to keep themselves safe and alive. I'd always worked on the assumption that I was lucky and would continue to be lucky, though now, a number of months into the deployment, I was feeling less so than before. I had developed the habit of carrying a green handkerchief in my desert camouflage trouser pocket. It had been a present from Caroline years before and I carried it partly because in a practical sense it was useful for blowing my nose and for wiping the sweat and dust off my face, but also because it reminded me of her.

Over the period July to November, I had indeed been fortunate. There had been death and destruction all around, but as yet it hadn't quite directly touched me. I've never been superstitious but the longer I spent deployed in Afghanistan, the greater the attachment to and the greater the affection for this green handkerchief became. Maybe it became my talisman, perhaps a mini comfort blanket, in part I think because my addled mind clung to any little crumb of comfort, any little thing that might help me navigate through the challenge of command. Under those unique circumstances, many of us were prepared to suspend a sense of disbelief about the efficacy of a lucky mascot. It all helped. Consequently, the green handkerchief went everywhere with me to the point that I would not have contemplated deploying out on an operation without it.

With our long vehicle convoy lined up inside Pluto all ready to go, I felt into my trouser pocket for the reassuring feel of my green handkerchief. To my dismay, it wasn't there. I must have left it behind in my room. The CSM bobbed up to my vehicle having confirmed that everyone else was ready to go, and said, 'Boss, we're all ready – you good to go?' In that moment I didn't feel that I could say 'Oh sorry, CSM, I've left my lucky green hanky behind, can you hang on while I nip off and get it', so I gave the order to move and we set off. I took it as a bad omen. I'd left my hanky behind, and with it went some of my hope that I would continue to survive unscathed.

This operation we were embarking upon was the most complex yet in terms of planning and logistics and going into the unknown. There was a series of identified supply routes from northern Pakistan up through Afghanistan along which Taleban leaders and fighters, weapons and supplies, would be transited. Our mission was to drive down through the desert and conduct reconnaissance of a target believed to be a key transit hub for the Taleban, drug smugglers and traffickers. (In my mind I conjured images of the Cantina bar in *Star Wars* where all the bad guys from the different galaxies congregated.) It was deep in ungoverned Taleban country in the southernmost part of Helmand province, in an area known as the 'Fish hook' because of the shape of the river winding its way through the desert. This was as wild country as it got. There was no rule of law down there. It was the rule of the bandit.

The operation was intended to gather more detailed intelligence about the fort and potentially, subject to progress, to disrupt movement in and around it. It was a journey into the unknown. In part this was because of its remote location – not only was it difficult to get to, but because of the distance we were outside the coverage of helicopter medical support. This meant that if we took a casualty, either through contact with the Taleban or indeed through an accident, we couldn't guarantee to get the heli all the way down to pick up the casualty. Even if we could get a heli there, the distance meant that we were outside the 'Golden Hour' travel time: any serious injury needs to be treated in the critical first hour to minimise the likelihood of death. I'd chewed through all of this as part of the planning process. Some advised it wasn't worth the risk, others made the point that we needed to get down there and take a look, and that the risk of not doing so was greater and more dangerous over the longer term. It had been a difficult judgement and I took time to weigh up all the factors in my mind, before deciding we should do it.

Because it was such a long way to get down to the fort we had planned an overnight stop in the most southerly located Forward Operating Base (FOB). These small defensive camps used by UK forces were rudimentary, the size of half a football pitch, basically just the shell of a protected wall of

The helicopter flight from Camp Pluto into the desert to meet up with B Company.

Two minutes till drop-off.

Deployed in the desert with our Afghan comrades.

Two paratroopers from B Company sorting out their equipment prior to the next phase of an operation.

The British section of Camp Pluto.

In front of my Portakabin in Camp Pluto.

Pictures on my Portakabin wall to remind me of home.

Dawn in the desert.

Dusk in the desert.

Sitting in my reasonably comfortable foldable chair in a Forward Operating Base, planning the next phase of an operation.

With my two
outstanding
signallers, who
not only ensured
we had good radio
communications
but also provided
constant banter
and an everlasting
supply of Miranda
fizzy orange.

Talking tactics with
Tom Tugendhat.

Giving a briefing
to our Afghan
comrades ahead
of deploying out
of Camp Pluto on
an operation.

Having a much-needed breakfast stop after a long and difficult night under Certain Death Hill.

After conducting a 'shura' with elders from a remote village in northern Helmand.

Precious family time on a beach in Cornwall.

Running for office.

Along with Ed Miliband meeting Mrs Violet Booth for the first time. She would become a good friend.

With Andy Burnham and John Healey, shortly after the by-election result had been announced.

Now the Member of Parliament for Barnsley Central.

With Rachel in the Rhinog mountains.

HESCO bastion. No running water or electricity. We were due to arrive at the FOB before dusk.

Everything was going swimmingly until about ten kilometres north of the FOB when the ground suddenly became much softer and we had to slow right down as we transited around and over the more dune-like ground. This required the most skilful driving. Our young driver was struggling with the conditions and we started to detect the pungent and concerning smell of burning choke.

We slowed down further as all the vehicles in the long convoy struggled to negotiate their way through the terrain. We stopped a number of times to dig out vehicles that had sunk into the soft sand. It was slow going, and the clock clicked remorselessly on. I was supremely keen not to get us into another Certain Death Hill scenario. I needed us to make it to the relative safety of the FOB, ideally during daylight, so I kept pushing us on as fast as we could possibly go. Gradually, though, I could feel the clutch failing on my vehicle, until eventually we accepted that we had a problem and stopped.

Our REME mechanic came up to take a look. 'Your clutch is buggered, boss,' was his technical assessment.

We were now about five kilometres north of the FOB, so I decided we needed to get there and sort ourselves out; this was not the place to do it. While I was deciding precisely what we were going to do, California came over to speak to me. He had been listening to ICOM chatter over a hand-held radio (though this had previously proved an eerie experience, we were now pretty much sanitised to it). The chat he'd been listening to had been quite specific: the Taleban were apparently tracking our movements and had been talking about us travelling down through 'their' territory. Concerningly, they seemed to know that one of our vehicles had broken down. Although we couldn't be a hundred per cent certain they were talking about us, there were no other UK forces for many miles around, so this was alarming. We now knew that in all likelihood we were being watched and followed.

It was dusk, and the CSM and the REME mechanic decided which vehicle would tow my vehicle on to the FOB. Because of the difficulty of towing another vehicle through soft sand we had to remove as much of the weight from our vehicle as we could and transfer it into the other vehicles. By the time this was done it was dark. I busied myself ensuring that the three other occupants of my vehicle, our driver and two signallers, along with their equipment, were sorted. The driver stayed with our vehicle to steer and I physically placed the two signallers into two separate vehicles. Having put everyone else in their lifeboat, I then turned around for mine.

It had disappeared.

Amid the melee of allocating who would go into which vehicle to move the final few kilometres to the FOB, somehow I found myself without a vehicle to jump into. I had been peripherally aware that behind me was a vehicle I'd intended to get into, but in the confusion and darkness, when I looked for it, it wasn't there.

It was at this moment that all the radios stopped working. They just went dead. So, no vehicle, no radio.

When I first realised that I had been left behind my instinctive reaction was to laugh. Straight away, though, the magnitude of the situation dawned on me. This was seriously dicey. The convoy had already moved off, but given that they were moving relatively slowly I thought I would be able to run after them and catch them up. But the darkness that had descended was disorientating, and amid the

rolling sandy ground I could hear only the occasional hum
of a vehicle's engine, increasingly far away in the distance.
It was just my bad luck that the convoy had quickly reached
the end of the softer sand and were making better progress
on harder desert floor. I wasn't going to catch them. I was
now on my own.

I dropped down on one knee and fumbled into my chest
webbing for my NVGs. I put them on, then took out my
hand-held GPS so that I could chart a course to the FOB.

As I was fumbling with the settings I swore repeatedly and
told myself that this would never have happened if I hadn't
left my bloody green hanky behind. For a moment or two,
and despite knowing it wasn't that far to the FOB and that
our vehicle convoy had been heading directly towards it, I
was overtaken by events. Lost in dark introspection. It felt
much worse than back in Pluto when, having just arrived,
I'd wondered what on earth I had got myself into. This time,
I was much more exposed.

I took a moment to gather my thoughts. I had been left
behind. I was five kilometres away from the FOB. On foot.
In the dark. Radio not working. I then thought about what
California had said about the ICOM chatter and the risk
that we were being followed. Shit. My tired, stressed mind
started to make calculations about what I might do if the
Taleban cornered me. Would I let them take me hostage? I
knew what they would do to me. Was I going to let it get
to that stage? Was I? Really? In a moment of profound personal anguish I debated whether, if it came to it, I should
shoot myself rather than be taken captive. I then started to
think that even if the Taleban didn't get me, there was a real
risk of being shot by friendly fire from my own side, either
by my soldiers or by those guarding the FOB.

Again, I allowed myself a moment to calm down. There

was nothing else for it, I just had to get moving. I knew that I needed to try and stay cool and started to move in the direction of the camp. So, with my NVGs on, a route plotted on my GPS and my rifle pointing forward, I was on my way.

My mind wandered back to Nepal and the night David Blakeley and I had a hair-raising walk out of the jungle after our jeep had broken down. Here I was again, walking this time through a pitch-black desert, all alone. Just like before, waiting for something to launch out at me. Scared but composed, I plodded on.

After about an hour, having cautiously worked my way through the dunes, I was just able to make out the silhouette of what looked like the shape of the FOB and walked warily up towards it. I knew there would be ANA guards on the gate and I didn't want them mistaking me for the Taleban and shooting me so I walked towards them slowly and then called out, 'British, British, British.' The sound jarred against the quietness of the night and the surprised Afghan guards cautiously gestured for me to come forward. Then, when they could properly see me, they welcomed me in, albeit with a bemused look on their faces. I didn't hang around to explain what had happened and walked in mightily relieved to have made it.

With the radios down, and amid the confusion of the move into the FOB, nobody had yet clocked that I was missing and that I had only made it there on foot. This came as a massive relief and I decided that I would spare myself the humiliation of anyone knowing that I had allowed myself to be left behind and keep it to myself. The move into the FOB had been chaotic. I was mortified, not least because we had Tom Tugendhat with us, that we had arrived looking like a rabble. We worked late into the night to sort ourselves out. The CSM stowed my vehicle with its burnt-out clutch in the corner of the FOB and we repacked our equipment and fixed the problem with the radios. We repaired one of the other vehicles that had been damaged and reorganised, knowing that my vehicle was not serviceable and in time would have to be recovered back to Pluto. We ate some food, and then I did my normal bonnet briefing before getting a bit of sleep.

Having put the chaos of the previous night behind us, we then demonstrated what we could do. The next day we drove south into uncharted territory, and after a night laid up in the desert we finally reached a spot from where we could observe the suspected transit hub. We'd left the vehicles behind (with a small team to guard them) and advanced cautiously on foot. Having identified a route along a drainage ditch to the fort we crawled slowly for a long distance so we could get closer to it and then carried out a detailed reconnaissance, monitoring movements in and out, so that we could get a feel for the comings and goings.

All of a sudden there was a loud bang: it sounded exactly like someone firing a mortar bomb at us from the fort. We dived for cover, waiting for impact and expecting to be showered with deadly shrapnel, but no mortar landed. To this day I don't know what the bang was but we then had to endure several very tense hours, at any moment expecting to be seen, expecting to come under fire, expecting it all to kick off, though it never did. We gathered the information we needed and I decided it was better to quit while we were still ahead than push our luck further, so we made our way back to the vehicles.

Despite everything – the increasing fatigue, the increased risk – all of a sudden our morale seemed to be sky high. We had got to know each other so well and were now so used to our Standard Operating Procedures (SOPs) that everything ran like clockwork. Despite the unwieldy nature of a large

British-Afghan vehicle-borne force, we manoeuvred about the desert as if we had been doing it for years; the constant exposure to the sand and the wind meant that we had all long since assumed the look of desert nomads blasted by the elements. The Afghans had developed to the extent that they could be trusted to go off and do smaller, less complex operations on their own, and when we came back together we were a joint force to be reckoned with.

Over the days that followed we bounced on to multiple tasks in different parts of Helmand and got on with collecting valuable intelligence, arresting suspected Taleban and supporting other operational activities. We conducted a planned meet-up with a squadron of The Light Dragoons in the middle of the southern Helmand desert in order to discuss how we would work together on a joint operation. Their heavy guns on their hulking armoured vehicles were to be used in support of our search of an Afghan village. We marvelled at the protection their heavily armoured vehicles afforded them and they pitied the pathetic protection we had from our seat covers. Though the culture and ethos of the Light Dragoons was different from the SFSG, they were very professional and good company. We stood among them in the desert drinking tea and sharing stories, then headed off on to the task.

Throughout this period, as had been the case previously, I had to take the most difficult decisions. In that kind of complex environment you have to make hard choices. I was always guided by a simple principle: do what you think is the right thing, in accordance with the law. It's relatively easy to go round blowing things up and loosing off rounds without too much thought. But it's the wrong way to behave. A US General, Stanley McChrystal, had summed it up when he spoke about exercising what he

termed 'courageous restraint'. He was right. It's easy to pull
the trigger if you are in doubt, much harder not to. I made
it clear to all my soldiers and to our Afghans that often the
bravest thing to do was not to fire, not to drop the bomb.
Only if you were absolutely certain that you needed to did
you do so. There are very strict rules – Rules of Engagement
(RoE) – that govern a soldier's conduct in an operational
theatre; you carry an actual card in your pocket with them
written down so nobody can be in any doubt. They give you
the legal and the moral legitimacy to act and to use lethal
force should you need to. The card was our bible, we followed it to the letter.

Sometimes the use of force, including lethal force, is necessary, which is why it's important to have rules governing it.
Soldiers need to exercise their 'moral compass' to make sure
that they do the right thing and follow the rules. Proximity
to death and violence, and to those who do not acknowledge the rule of law (which certainly included our Taleban
adversaries), both challenges your belief in the importance
of these laws and reinforces the need for them. Adhering
to such laws can at times be difficult: courageous restraint
requires extraordinary moral resilience and fortitude.

But how we utilise force is what differentiates us from
our opponents. I knew, and I made sure my soldiers knew,
that we lose our legitimacy if we sink to the level of the terrorists we face, and that such legitimacy is only maintained
through the rule of law. Soldiers are taught that for force to
have legitimacy it must (a) distinguish between those who
pose a threat and those who do not, (b) be proportional in
terms of what you are trying to achieve, and (c) be born out
of the need to protect life and prevent further suffering, not
a desire for retribution.

The UK and our Armed Forces have sometimes got it

wrong and broken these laws. Under such circumstances it is right that the International Criminal Court investigates claims against British soldiers. The UK is not, nor should it ever be, above the law. Our answer to the threat that terrorism brings must be unequivocal, but it must also be legal. Because the rule of law is key both to the society we are defending and how we defend it, if our response to terrorism is to destroy human rights and the rule of law, our opponents have already won. I was absolutely determined that on my watch, they weren't going to win.

After what seemed like forever deployed in the desert, but was in reality ten days, we made it back to Pluto. We had supported a number of different operations and gathered a significant amount of intelligence. Crucially, what we had also done was prove the concept of the force. To all those who said it couldn't be done, we had shown that it could. We had built a force of Afghan soldiers that had developed the competence and the confidence to conduct a wide range of military tasks. Yes, there was still more to do – the training never stops – but it was clear that we had made good progress and the force was now in demand to provide support to both British and Afghan military and security activities in southern Afghanistan.

Back in camp, we again decompressed after the stresses and strains of being out on the ground for a lengthy period. We phoned home. We sorted out our admin and had some food and sleep. Indications of our frailty and fatigue were now obvious to see. Physically and mentally, we were running on empty. I suffered from endless mouth ulcers and cold sores. Goodness knows what my blood pressure would have been – I would never have allowed anyone to take it.

By now my eyelids were so heavy and dragged down by

the gravity of constant activity and mental exhaustion that for the first and only time in my life, at any moment of the day I could have taken myself off into a quiet corner and fallen immediately into a deep sleep. But I never once was able to. On occasion, when I needed it, I had been able to draw down boundless amounts of energy – but there was always a counter punch. If your adrenalin kept you sharp for twenty hours or forty hours, or however long you needed it to, it would always catch up with you at some point, when tiredness would engulf you.

As we neared the end of the deployment I found myself edging towards complete meltdown, having run myself into the ground for nearly six months. With three weeks left of the tour, I wondered whether I would be able to keep going. Each day was now an ultra marathon, mentally and physically; the days used to take so long to get through. But I knew I had to get through them. One day at a time. The more tired you get, the more questionable your judgement is; when you're worn down, mistakes become more likely. Fortunately for me, the impact of 'leaders' legs' kicked in: you are tired, but knowing you're in charge, that you are responsible and it's down to you, helps motivate you to keep going.

For those final few weeks we consolidated on the progress that had been made. We continued to train the Afghans and we developed a plan to recruit more. We continued to patrol across Helmand, conducting operations. We skirmished with the Taleban – we did everything we could to play our part in defeating them, as they did to us. Although I loathed their ideology and despised their conduct, it was hard not to have at least a grudging respect for their soldierly stamina. I don't bear any great bitterness towards them as individuals. To an extent we are all products of our environments;

they were caught up in their fight, as were we. I hope that at some point in the future there might be an opportunity to sit down with them and better understand why they did what they did. We'll see whether that happens.

I was determined to ensure that my handover to the incoming OC was as near perfect as possible. I wanted the next company to have the best start, so we got ready to hand everything on in good order. We were expecting C Company from the SFSG to be in position to take over from us by the middle of December so that we could get back home for Christmas. The C Company group arrived and we handed the operation over to them. I shook the OC's hand as Alistair had shaken mine. It was now down to him. Before we left we held a farewell parade with the Afghans and afterwards shook their hands and in many cases hugged each other. We had become a band of brothers and we had bonded through the extraordinarily difficult times of the last six months. They had become our allies, but also our friends. That said, we could also see that understandably they were keen to forge new links with our replacements from C Company – they were now their future allies. We had done our bit. It was time for us to go.

We wished them all well and we left them to it. It was theirs now. I was one of the last from B Company to depart Pluto. We drove to Bastion. I looked out of the window across the desert and wondered whether this would be it for me, whether I would ever return. Would I ever be back in an environment such as this, back in Pluto, back in Afghanistan, back on operations?

The vehicle dropped me off at the SFSG hub where I had arrived all those months before. The CQMS and the storeman were there, all packed, all ready to go home. We picked up our bags and walked in silence towards the HLS where we were due to get on a heli. The setting sun provided a stunning backdrop to our final view of southern Afghanistan.

I sat on the floor of the C-17 aircraft lost in thought. Utterly drained. I'm not sure I could have kept going for much longer. Not sure I would have lasted another week. It had consumed me. All the things we had done flooded back. The effort we had put in, the risks we had taken. The British and Afghan lives that had been lost. I really did hope it had all been worth it. Time would tell.

In my sleeping bag, I thought back to my earlier deployment to Afghanistan in 2005, where as part of a small reconnaissance team we had planned which southern province should become part of an expanded British mission. We had talked through the options with our team leader at a tiny US base amid the stark beauty of the Oruzgan mountains. Standing there, surrounded by those Afghan peaks, I knew we might have to fight. I also knew that if fighting was all we did, we would fail. On that same reconnaissance we had strolled leisurely through the bazaar in Sangin in Helmand – the province where our troops would be deployed. When I returned there on this most recent tour, the only way to get in without getting shot or blown up was by helicopter. How the situation had deteriorated over those two years. Where would we be in two more years' time? I wondered.

My thoughts on whether it was worth it have been further informed over the years by having had to make difficult decisions in Parliament about the use of military force. I often reflect on the heroes of our Armed Forces who served in Afghanistan and remember the 453 British soldiers who never came home. It was, is, a campaign in which the UK has been engaged for longer than both world wars combined.

Britain's withdrawal from Afghanistan is still not yet complete – we have people deployed there today, so we don't yet have the neatness or finality of knowing who has won or who has lost. Whether it's all been worth it or not. Dredging for the positives, there are some flickers of hope. A political compromise has secured a broad-based government, the Taleban have been engaged in meaningful negotiations with the US administration, and the Afghan security forces continue to grow in capability. Nor should we ignore just how much progress has been made since 2001, with significant improvements in, for example, health indicators and the education of girls.

Yet the situation remains incredibly fragile. The suicide bombings and attacks continue. Fighting intensified in 2019 and spread to new areas. Corruption and political abuse continue to be widespread, and it is unclear whether the current or any administration can tackle it. Successive elections have been marred by serious fraud, and the authorities in the provinces are still seen as lacking legitimacy. The basic truth is that the war that Britain gave so much to win is still being fought, and its outcome remains uncertain.

Looking back, there are aspects of the Afghan campaign that could and should have been done differently, right from the loss of focus after the intervention in Iraq (where for a period the Afghan campaign didn't get the attention it needed). These include the empowerment of abusive warlords, the handling of the counter-narcotics issue, and the failure of the international community to prevent their own spending fuelling corruption.

The conflict in Iraq has been subjected to the most microscopic attention from the Chilcot Inquiry and many others, yet our commitment to Afghanistan cost significantly more British lives, consumed more resources and has gone on for much longer. Despite that, we've dedicated relatively little time to discussing or analysing the campaign, trying to make some sense of it and identifying lessons even to consider learning. I think more should have been done to look at the conduct of the campaign to inform future foreign policy decision-making. I think that partly because it's just obvious, but also for my own selfish reasons. I lost good friends in Helmand. I think we owe it to them to consider what went wrong and what lessons we can learn to inform how we combat complex threats in the future.

The outcome of the wider war was only ever partly in the hands of our Armed Forces. Our fight was always about creating space to build a lasting political solution rather than purely defeating the Taleban. We were too slow to realise this. Not ruthless enough in seeing the bigger picture, too focused on a conventional military operation when what we needed was a more unconventional approach. But we didn't see it. We allowed a 'conspiracy of optimism' to pervade among our political and military decision-makers – that one more heave, another six months, would see us over the line. I lost track of the number of times we were told that this was to be the year we resolved the conflict, that this was a pivotal moment for Afghanistan.

Although other matters have consumed our national political debate, we should find time to ask the hard questions. Why more was not done to make use of the space for political progress that Afghan, British and International Security Assistance Force (ISAF) troops bought at such great cost – and how we can best adapt the support we are still giving to match that goal.

The public expect this level of analysis to happen, and it is only by demonstrating to them that we've done it that we will begin to regain their trust to make important foreign policy judgements in the future. Ultimately, the measure of success in Afghanistan is not meaningless statements about how many Taleban are killed but whether the country has a political settlement that reduces conflict rather than creates it; whether the rule of law is strong enough to keep corruption and abuses from fundamentally undermining the state and alienating the population; and whether the government is representative and responsive enough to hold legitimacy in the eyes of its own people.

But these questions apply beyond the borders of Afghanistan. In our struggle against Islamic State and radical Islamism across the world there will be debate about military action, but we should, of course, only contemplate it if it is an absolutely essential element in a wider, coherent political strategy. The nature and character of conflict shifts over time and has always done so. We have come a long way from the attritional static warfare of the trenches of World War One. The front line is now less likely to be a trench in a field and more likely to be in our own towns and cities, or online.

In Afghanistan, our soldiers played their part with honour. They deserve our tributes. But part of that process should be to soberly examine the conflict in which they put their lives on the line, and how it shapes Britain's future. It's the least we can do for those who aren't now around to do it.

The Afghanistan campaign raises some challenging questions for national government but some tough ones for me too. Having analysed what mistakes our governments might have made, it's only right that I subject myself to the same scrutiny, however uncomfortable that might be. I have to accept that perhaps I should have tried harder to overrule Caroline's desire for normality. That I let soldiering and service get too much under my skin, that I became too caught up in it, to the extent that I could not see the wood for the trees. I have also to accept that I just got a bit too comfortable with the risks and with the danger. The heady mix of adrenalin and fear, the rush of the operation, the high that comes with surviving when you thought you might not, was a drug on which I became dependent and had on occasions overdosed. Perhaps I got it wrong. Maybe I shouldn't have taken the risks I did by putting myself in the line of fire. These are questions I still wrestle with.

We returned from Afghanistan just in time for Christmas. Again I landed back at Brize Norton, again I drove to the M4 and instead of turning left to go home went right, to St Athan. When I arrived back in camp the Christmas party was in full flow, with happy, drunk friends having the time of their lives. Although we were greeted as returning heroes, I wasn't in the mood for a party. At the earliest possible moment I slunk away to my room and started to unpack my kit, all still coated in sand. I stood under a hot shower for an age, washing the sand away. I must have been there for an hour.

The next morning I gave a presentation to the unit about the operation. I stood in front of them all, hundreds of people. Normally an occasion such as this would have brought at least a few butterflies in the stomach and a flurry of nerves, particularly when faced with such a sceptical and hard-to-please bunch as a battalion of grizzled paratroopers. I didn't feel any nerves at all. I felt utterly Zen about it. I wondered whether there were now no nerves left, that all the butterflies had long since fluttered away. Goodness knows how much stuff I had tried to shove into the coping box. I certainly wasn't in the mood to open it any time soon.

In a matter-of-fact way I talked them through what we had done and outlined the progress that had been made. Despite my initial concerns about the viability of the operation we had proved it was workable. Through our blood, sweat, toil and tears, and despite the dust, the heat, the cold, the fear and the risks, we had turned an embryonic concept into an actual functioning operation that gave the Afghans what was perhaps their best hope of taking control of their own security, without which not much else could be done. We had also cemented our wider reputation within the UKSF community.

But I felt obliged to end with a sober warning: the war in Afghanistan was nowhere near to being won. I was sadly certain that many more British lives would be lost out there in the sand, and that unless our government ensured that the operation was properly resourced as part of an international coalition, there was a great risk that ultimately we would fail. It wasn't what some people in the audience wanted to hear, but I felt I had a responsibility to be straight about it.

Looking back on this period, it is worrying how little consideration and attention was actually given on our return to ensuring everyone was going to be able to cope with their experiences in Afghanistan. Before sending people off on leave I had been explicit that anyone struggling to cope should come forward and that we would provide every support – but nobody did. Off people went on Christmas leave, and the moment they were back in the New Year we were straight away getting ready for the next adventure. Conventional troops undergo a formal process of 'decompression' when returning from operations in Iraq or Afghanistan. They fly via Cyprus where they spend forty-eight hours discussing their experiences and being briefed on what the tell-tale signs of depression and PTSD are. We didn't do any of that; it was Pluto, Bastion and home. Just a matter of hours from war zone to family kitchen (in my case) or pubs and clubs (in the case of many of the soldiers).

I got in the car and drove home. I was greeted at the front door by Pip, a very enthusiastic little Patterdale cross terrier. Caroline had decided to get another dog. It was wonderful to be home, although I struggled to take it all in. The decorations were up and the kids were very excited about Christmas and very pleased to see me. So used to the privations of life in the desert was I that everywhere seemed stuffy and too warm; although it was December and cold outside, I had to keep going out to cool down and draw in fresh air. After a couple of days of trying to settle down I was able to get back into the routine of being around and enjoyed the festivities and atmosphere of a family Christmas.

However, it took time to readjust. In my mind I kept turning over the events of the past six months: the things we'd done and not done, the risks we'd exposed ourselves to; the decisions we had taken and the consequences of those actions. What had we achieved? I wondered how the Afghans were getting on. I kept turning it all over in my mind.

So it took time to get back into the swing of family life. You don't just waltz back in after six months away. There's a routine in place that doesn't involve you, and it's easy sometimes to feel that you're in the way. I was also exhausted, physically and emotionally. It takes a while to recover from that, and I slept and ate a lot. But my mind kept wandering off. I knew that I had come back a different person.

Although I would never have admitted it to Caroline, there were aspects of being deployed on the operation that I missed, and craved. I suspected that I might never find myself back out there under the same circumstances and I was sad about that. It had been the most intense experience, the best and the worst of times, and though draining, terrifying and exhilarating it had also been extraordinarily satisfying professionally. That comradeship, that sense of purpose – I'd never experienced anything quite like it, before or since.

Although I'd never been closer to death, I'd never felt more alive. It's what I had joined to do, it's what I had trained to do (albeit not as much as I needed to), and it did feel like it had been worthwhile – like, despite everything, we had been given the chance to make a positive difference, and that we had made the most of that opportunity. I was proud and satisfied with what we had achieved. Much as I was glad to have returned home, some of me was still out there.

# 18

# The Punishing Routine

## *April 2008*

—

The ruthless tempo of the planned military activity or the 'forecast of events' within the unit meant that in the New Year of 2008 I was straight back into it, and tasked with getting B Company ready for a major joint exercise. Already we had begun the process of psychologically moving on from what had gone before in Afghanistan to what might come next – whatever and wherever that might be. We prepared to assume the 'stand-by' commitment which meant that we would be on ultra-high readiness, on just a few hours' notice to deploy anywhere in the world to undertake a wide range of military tasks, from peace keeping to war fighting. As part of our readiness training we went on an exercise embarked on the Royal Navy ship HMS *Bulwark* where we sailed off the west coast of Scotland and launched a series of practice assaults on targets up on Cape Wrath. It was all-consuming and kept me very busy for several weeks. In the occasional moment of down time I would stand on the deck of the ship and admire the beauty, both of the rugged Scottish coastline and of the swirling seas. I thought of home, yearned to be back there, and was sad that yet again I wasn't.

I returned to find out from Caroline that her oncologist was arranging further tests. The blood tumour marker, which we had been assured was the best indicator of potential cancerous activity, had gone back up to a worrying level. It sounded and felt like bad news, and it was. It seemed likely that we were going to have to battle it all over again. I knew that I needed to free myself of the huge responsibility of a 'stand-by' commitment and be closer to home to provide love and support and to help out. I was not going to walk back out of that door again, certainly not under these circumstances, so I had no choice but to request that my command tour with the SFSG be brought to a premature end. I was sad to be cutting it short but I knew that I needed to support Caroline, and B Company deserved an OC who could give them his full attention. The unit CO and the wider system were supportive and understanding and a new posting was found for me in the training directorate of the Army's HQ at Salisbury (where I'd previously worked for General Jackson), just a few miles away from our home.

The test results showed that the cancer had returned. Devastating but unsurprising news which came as a terrible blow. Caroline was distraught. Worry surged through my veins. We had so hoped not to be back in this place. But we were. Again, reasonably quickly we absorbed the terrible news and re-committed our efforts to fight against it.

This time chemotherapy was prescribed and Caroline began the punishing routine. She would have the chemo which would make her feel very poorly, gradually the effects of it would wear off, but by the time she was starting to recover from it, it would be time for the next cycle. I would take her to the hospital for the treatment. I would drop her off and park the car, walk slowly from the car park to the ward. Stop outside. Take a deep breath. Go inside. I would sit next to her while it was administered. She was usually the youngest person in the room and we tended to be surrounded by much older people, accompanied by their similarly old partners. What on earth are *we* doing here? I would wonder. The nurses and the doctors were all friendly, caring and helpful but I hated the place. Hated that we had to go there. Hated the way it made Caroline feel. Despised the unfairness of her having to go through it all.

Over the period spring 2008 to early 2010, this was our life. We cobbled together as much of a routine as we could. I would go into work and selfishly enjoy the distraction of being able to focus my mind away from the unfolding horror of events at home. We worked to keep Caroline as healthy as possible, and she was incredibly careful about her diet and routine. We spent all our savings and incurred considerable debt from the cost of exploring alternative medical options, including going to Germany to trial a developing treatment. We tried everything; we left no stone unturned looking for anything that might offer even the faintest glimmer of hope of a solution. Throughout that time there were low moments, but more positive moments too. Every minor victory was savoured. To me, it felt like a deadly game of chess. The cancer would make a move, we would respond. Then it would respond. And on it went.

For New Year's Eve 2009/10 we went as a family to Cornwall. We stayed in a little wooden chalet and when the weather allowed we walked along the beach in our wellies, enjoying the sea air and being together as a family. When it was too wet or too cold to go out we huddled in front

of a fire and watched family DVDs. It felt like very precious times. Although neither Caroline nor I would have
ever described it in this way to each other, I think we were
both secretly wondering whether this would be our final
family holiday.

We returned home, and over the next few months
Caroline's health began to deteriorate. The GP and the
supporting medical system continued to be there for us,
but I sensed they thought that we were now fighting a
losing battle.

We tried to keep the show on the road, but it became
harder and harder with each day. A profound moment of
terrible realisation was the point when it was decided that
Caroline needed a permanent oxygen supply at home. From
that moment on it was literally impossible to pretend that
we had anything resembling a normal life. Impossible to
pretend that we weren't up against it. Impossible to pretend
that this wasn't a horrible situation to be in.

As much as we could, we tried to shield it from others.
From the kids, from family, from friends, from neighbours,
from work – from the outside world. We didn't want people
to know. Caroline didn't want the pity, she didn't want
people to worry, she wanted us to deal with it ourselves
as much as we could. We didn't want people to think of
us as being anything other than a happy, loving, normal
family. I think for both of us there was also an element of
self-preservation: it was hard enough dealing with our own
terrible concerns about what was happening, we didn't want
to have to deal with other people's as well.

Throughout this difficult time Caroline remained mostly
stoic. There were moments of desperate fear, anxiety and
depression, but as much as possible we tried to keep our
lives on an even keel. But it was hard. Each day brought

its challenges. We discussed a lot of things throughout the period, but we always stopped short of discussing the worst-case scenario. Neither of us wanted to accept that it was now likely, or inevitable, or even an option at all. We just didn't want to accept it. I didn't feel that I could raise the spectre of Caroline dying with her because I never wanted her to think that somehow we couldn't still beat it. If, as some couples do, we had sat down to plan a funeral, we would have abandoned, or at least very seriously undermined, our positive approach, and I always believed that was the thing above all else that we had to hang on to. We had to stay on that line. So we never broached it.

As Caroline's health continued to deteriorate, there was a distressing shift in our relationship: as well as being her husband, I became her carer. I tried to put all my efforts, all my focus, into looking after her. I didn't have any experience of caring and it wasn't something that came naturally to me, or something I had ever imagined having to do. I rolled up my sleeves and got on with it as best I could, but I hated it. Hated our situation. I just felt so desperately sad that we were having to go through it all.

I never ever gave up on Caroline, but there came a moment in my mind when I had to acknowledge where this was leading us to. I had to start accepting that the cancer was probably going to win. That it would take her from me. That I would lose her. That I would be left on my own with the kids. That I would have to suffer the pain of bereavement. I felt I had to start thinking about what on earth I was going to do, how I was possibly going to cope. I'd always been a planner. I had always looked around the corner to think about what was coming next and to try and get ready for it as best I could. But for the first time ever, I just

couldn't bear to look round that next corner, nor was I able
to shove it all away in my coping box. Maybe it was because
the box was full, or maybe because this didn't belong in the
box. I don't know which it was, I just knew that I couldn't
discard the worry in the way I always had before.

I continued to juggle being at work and caring for
Caroline. Once the kids had gone to school she was usually
keen for me to go into the office, so as much as possible I
did. While there I engrossed myself in what I was doing. It
was a more than useful shield, an opportunity to focus my
mind on something other than our ever-deteriorating situation at home.

My remit in the Army training policy directorate was to
ensure that the training being carried out across the Army
was what was required, and if not, to develop it. I was able to
draw on my previous experiences and, when I was there, add
some value. I remember seeing an extraordinary letter from the
Health and Safety Executive, the gist of which was that we, the
Army, were not taking enough risks with our training. Their
rationale, which I agreed with, was that ongoing operational
commitments in Iraq and Afghanistan were so dangerous that
more lives would be saved over the longer term by making
the pre-deployment training more realistic (and by extension,
more dangerous). They were right, and it countered much of
the nonsense that has been talked about so-called 'elf-n-safety'
over the years. It provided me with a useful context for developing some of the ideas about how to improve our training and
how, based on my experiences from Afghanistan, it could be
made more realistic and more effective.

I had something of a eureka moment. My boss Brigadier
David Homer and I were observing a jungle warfare tracking course in Brunei in June 2009. I watched them teach a
technique called Ground Sign Awareness (GSA) – basically

an ability to track and see where movement has been made by the enemy in a jungle environment. I told the Brigadier that it would have been extremely useful to have had those skills and that awareness while operating out in the deserts of Afghanistan: if you knew what to look for you could more easily spot where IEDs had been laid by the disruption to the ground around them.

We both agreed that we needed to integrate the training into the pre-deployment training package, and from then on that became my mission. Every spare moment I had away from home I dedicated to developing the case for having GSA integrated. This was not a simple task and it took a lot of hard work to draw up the case for it and convince others of the requirement. The pre-deployment training package was, a bit like a school curriculum, a set length and very difficult to change. If you wanted to put something in, you had to take something out.

At this difficult time for me, I channelled all my professional energies into it and was stubbornly determined that I would get it done. A few people told me to forget about it, it wasn't going to happen, but I persevered and eventually we achieved it. I could see the value that the GSA training would add. I was convinced that it would save lives, potentially a lot of lives. Perhaps deep down I was thinking that if I was losing a life at home, I needed to save some at work; I'm not sure. What I do know is that it provided a vital professional diversion from what was a very testing time domestically. I know it saved many lives. It might have also saved me because it provided that much-needed distraction. Perhaps not for the first time, a hole to hide in. I think it helped keep me sane.

Soon after that we had another difficult meeting with the same oncologist with whom we had previously had difficult meetings. He was clearly an expert in his field, knew his stuff and had seen it all before. But we felt like he had decided there was basically not much more that could be done. Maybe he was right, but we didn't want to hear that. We weren't giving up and we resented the fact that he seemed to be doing just that.

Through our own research we had found out that there might be a possibility of some additional treatment and we asked him about it. He seemed dismissive of it, brushed it off, saying he wasn't sure if it would be available. He seemed cagey about it, though, so I rang him afterwards and left a message for him to call me back, which he did. I was in the middle of handing over my job to my replacement at the Army's HQ when he rang me. I challenged him, asking why he wouldn't support us over this additional treatment; didn't he understand what we were going through? Why was he not being more positive, more helpful?

Perhaps because we were speaking on the phone, and Caroline wasn't there, he was even more blunt than usual. 'There's no point,' he told me in the most matter-of-fact way possible. 'By the time the treatment becomes available your wife will no longer be with us.' In a way I appreciated his candour, but it was probably for the best, at that moment, that we were talking on the phone and not face to face.

'Your wife will no longer be with us'. Those words reverberated around my head.

*No longer be with us ...*

As I put the phone down I felt the last vestiges of any hope draining from me.

I then felt obliged to go back and carry on with the meeting I'd left in order to take the call. Looking back now, I think, why on earth did I do that? Why didn't I just go home? I spent the next few hours handing over the job.

I had planned to be there all that day, but it was clear that my mind was elsewhere so it was agreed that I would head home early. I suppose the handing over of the job had been another useful distraction. I felt mind-numbingly exhausted and furious at the unfairness of it all. It was agreed that I would go on immediate compassionate leave so that I could be at home full time to support Caroline. I steeled myself for what was to come.

# 19

# The Last Smile

*June 2010*

—

The final few weeks were just awful. I was caring for Caroline at home with some medical support from a nurse who came in every day. It was utterly draining, horrendous. But I knew enough by that stage to expect that, and knew that I had to be strong, resilient and supportive for Caroline and the children. I had to keep myself together. Now wasn't the time for me to be losing it.

In her last weeks, Caroline needed oxygen around the clock. I came to hate that oxygen machine. It was incredibly heavy, and we only had one of them, so every night I had to carry it upstairs to the bedroom and every morning back down to the living room. Caroline and I had talked about moving her downstairs, but what she wanted was normality, and that meant sleeping in our bedroom. While I was taking the oxygen machine up or down, Caroline had a smaller portable device. It was always nerve-rackingly worrying that we were going to run out of oxygen. We depended on cylinders being delivered and the resupply timings seemed to work on a just-in-time basis. Maybe that was acceptable for a manufacturing company, but not when it was an essential supply.

On one occasion during a hospital visit Caroline's oxygen supply in the smaller portable device started to run low. We were sat in a waiting room. I reported my concerns at reception. Nothing happened. Again, I politely explained that my wife's oxygen supply was running very low, please could someone help us. I pleaded with them, and there was a promise of help, but again nothing appeared. The staff were fiendishly busy but Caroline understandably began to get very concerned. As the oxygen dwindled in the tank, I could feel the anger welling up inside me. Just at the point at which I was about to go ballistic, an oxygen supply finally arrived and we both breathed a huge sigh of relief. It had been an exceptionally stressful and draining thirty minutes.

As much as possible we strived to maintain the normal routine, with me getting the kids ready for school and then bringing Caroline downstairs, where I would make her as comfortable as possible before getting on with everything that had to be done. On a beautifully fresh summer's morning at the end of June we made it out into the garden and sat in deckchairs with a coffee. Caroline had her sunglasses on, and despite everything she had endured was still beautiful, graceful and delightful company. Despite everything – the oxygen, the terrible sadness – in our little garden we were able to enjoy a wonderfully precious and beautiful moment of peace and calm. We sat and enjoyed the sunshine and each other's company and I took the opportunity to tell her how much I loved her. We treasured the experience.

Caroline noticed that there was a stirring of activity in the little rose bed by the side of the house – something was digging its way up through the soil. It was a mole, and gradually it worked its way to the surface and, after a few moments, popped its sleepy head out. It paused for a moment, as if to enjoy the lovely warm sunshine, before deciding that it was perhaps better off underground and so back down it went. In that brief moment we were completely transfixed by it, everything else forgotten. We savoured that moment, the distraction, the fleeting escape from our grim reality. Caroline recounted the tale to the children when they returned from school later that day and was so excited to tell them about it, as they were to hear it.

It was the last time I saw her smile.

In the weeks that followed she declined with terrifying speed. The South African cancer nurse – who, like all the nurses we dealt with, was amazing – came back after a long weekend off and I could see in her face just how concerned she was about Caroline's deterioration over the few days she had been away. Although I still didn't want to accept it, it was becoming increasingly clear to me that this was a battle we were going to lose, and sooner rather than later. Deep down, I'd known it for several months, I just didn't want to face it. I wanted to escape it. I no longer felt that I could.

The rate of decline accelerated and I battled to hold it together and to be strong for Caroline and the kids. It had been decided that Caroline would go down to Southampton hospital to see a radiotherapist, and again, we both drew comfort and strength from the hope this trip provided. That something, anything, even at this late stage, could be done. We clung on to that hope. It wasn't to be. The day before the appointment it became clear that Caroline would not be well enough to make the journey. I phoned to cancel the appointment. A new appointment was offered in a few weeks' time. I said I would get back to them. I felt sick to my stomach.

On a Friday morning in July, Caroline became very short of breath, even with the oxygen supply. I rang the GP, who told me to call 999. An ambulance came and took Caroline away and I grabbed an overnight bag for her and followed on in the car. Before I could set off, the GP called me back to say, 'I think you need to be aware it's highly likely that Caroline will not be returning from hospital.' It seemed to me that they'd made their minds up. She was being taken into hospital to die.

From then on I was on autopilot. The past few months had been so intense, so draining. I was tired, run down, and so worried for Caroline. As I walked out the door to follow on behind the ambulance, I considered the prospect that Caroline might never walk back through it.

I sat by Caroline's bedside on the ward for several hours. She had been given all sorts of drugs and was in a deep sleep. She hadn't had a drink or eaten anything for some time. I went to one of the nurses and said, 'I know that you might think this is a strange thing to ask, but I'm asking you, for my peace of mind, to put a saline drip into my wife so that she's receiving some kind of hydration.' I could tell they didn't think there was any point and only did it because I'd asked them to.

All day I could see and feel Caroline sliding away. I was incredibly tired, partly from the stress of it all and partly because I'd barely slept for days. One of the nurses persuaded me to try and get an hour's sleep in the rest room. I lay down on the floor and tried to rest, but my mind was racing, turning it all over, and then before I knew it a nurse came in to say, 'I really think you should go and sit with your wife.' I understood her to mean that the end was close.

I sat with Caroline holding her hand all night, and for most of the following day. In the morning I called her parents to tell them to come and see her. It was an incredibly difficult time for all of us. A time of the most profoundly deep and unshakable sadness. That afternoon I could feel her going, and at 3.30 p.m. she died.

I had no idea what to do. I went outside for a moment and had a quiet cry. 'It's not fair, it's not fair,' I could hear myself saying. For a moment I was just lost in the sadness of it. Then I had the strangest of experiences, where it felt like I was looking down on myself – a spectator watching this horrible nightmare play out.

I told myself that I had to pull myself together. I went back into the ward. I sat with Caroline for a while. After I had collected my thoughts I phoned her parents, who had returned home and were sat by the phone awaiting news, to tell them – that was such a hard thing to do. To speak the words that she had gone. I felt the need to do something, anything, so I went back outside and made some other calls to family and friends, completely on autopilot. I heard myself say over the phone 'I've lost her – she's gone'. I could hear myself speaking those words but I just couldn't believe, despite everything we had been through, that it had actually come to that. That the worst had happened. Despite all the time I had spent thinking about it, trying to prepare myself for this moment, I wasn't ready for it.

Some of our close friends were particularly shocked to hear the news, in part because we had deliberately kept Caroline's recent deterioration to ourselves. We had not wanted to have to explain it all, but that meant that some people I was telling were devastated by the news I was delivering. I think it was at this point that the adrenalin kicked in, and I realised that there were a number of things I now had to do. What about the kids? They had been staying with Caroline's parents. When was I going to see them?

And what would I say to them? How would I break the terrible news?

I sat back down at Caroline's bedside for a further moment of quiet reflection. But also because I just wanted a bit more time with her. Just a few more moments together. I didn't want to let go. But quite soon afterwards the medical staff politely explained that they wanted to take Caroline down to the morgue. I think they needed the bed. They asked me if I wanted to go with her. I thought about it and decided that, yes, I definitely did want to go with her.

I tried to compose myself to escort her down into the depths of the hospital. I followed behind along the long, dark corridors. My mind was drawn back to the lovely walks we had enjoyed together, on the beaches of North Wales, over the chalk downs of Wiltshire; now we were walking this final walk through long, dark, oppressive corridors. We arrived at the door of the morgue, where I was told, again politely but firmly, that I couldn't go any further. Caroline was taken in on a trolley and the doors closed behind her. That was it. The woman I adored and loved with all my heart was gone.

She was gone.

I lingered for a brief moment, but I knew that I needed to get out of there. I didn't want to be in that place any more. So I walked back up to the ward, thanked the staff for their care, collected Caroline's few belongings and walked slowly out to where the car was parked. It was in exactly the same place I had parked when Caroline had given birth to our son, and the same place I had parked when Caroline had given birth to our daughter. That seemed a lifetime ago. I couldn't help but think about the happiness I had felt on those two occasions, having been with Caroline in that same hospital, being with her through two labours, and the relief and joy of walking back out both as a new dad for the first

time and then again for a second time. How happy I had
been, what pride we had felt. Now there was just a gut-
wrenching, visceral despair.

I was holding a small plastic bag containing Caroline's
belongings – her dressing gown and a washbag I'd made
up with a few toiletries. I'd arrived at the hospital with
my wife, I was leaving with a plastic bag. I had never felt
lower. I had never felt more consumed with sorrow, anger,
frustration – with grief. 'What am I going to do, what am I
going to do?' I kept thinking. Round and round the question
went in my addled mind. We kept chickens – Caroline had
always liked being surrounded by animals. What the hell
was I going to do with the chickens? My mind fixated on
the chickens – probably as a defensive mechanism to occupy
my troubled mind.

I drove the short distance back to our house, opened the
front door and walked in. That's when the magnitude of it
hit me – like a shock wave washing right over me, a force
field of anguish and hurt. Years later, a constituent stopped
me in the street to tell me about the impact the death of
her husband had had on her. She described it as like going
over the edge of a waterfall. That is just how it felt for me.
There was an acute feeling of being trapped in the water,
being swept uncontrollably in a fast-flowing river towards a
waterfall edge. Then that moment when you're pulled over
the edge and into a terrifying free fall. Stood in our family
home, at that moment, that is how it felt for me. In the
weeks and perhaps months leading up to Caroline's death
I had been in that river, being drawn ever further down-
stream, ever closer to the lip of the waterfall. On this day, at
3.30 p.m. when I lost her, I was sucked to the edge. Arriving
back home, I was swept over it.

I walked into the kids' bedroom and sobbed uncontrollably. I looked at their little beds. I thought of them. How cruel and unfair that they had lost their mum. I couldn't make it stop. I couldn't make it go away. However strong you think you might be, however much you think you might be prepared for such a moment, you're never really ready.

I knew I couldn't be in the house any longer. It had been our home, but being there alone, it was too much, just too painful. I tried to compose myself and went round to one of our neighbours' houses. I didn't want to tell them that Caroline had just died, but it must have been obvious to them that something very bad had happened. I must have looked dreadful. So I was straightforward about it, blurting out to them that the worst had happened, that I wanted to go and see the kids, and, please, please, could they feed our chickens. Yes, they said, of course they would.

I wasn't sure if I should drive, but I knew I had to be where the kids were and there was no other option. I got into the car and told myself that the last thing anyone needed was for me to crash the car, so sort yourself out. I drove over to Caroline's parents' house, but by the time I got there the children were already asleep at their uncle and aunt's nearby. The kids hadn't been at home to see their mum taken away in an ambulance, but even young children are quite canny, they soon get a sense when things are not right. But they can't have been expecting this.

I was exhausted but couldn't sleep for thinking about how I would break the news to them, how we might get through it. Caroline's mother gave me a whisky, and for the first and only time in my life I took a sleeping pill and went to bed. The pill knocked me out for four or five hours. And so ended the worst day of my life. Then I was up, thinking, 'Right, where are the kids? I've got to do this.'

A little later, Caroline's mother brought them out to me in the garden. The conversation we had then was the worst thing I've ever had to do. I'm still haunted by it. No kid should ever have to be told they've lost their mum or their dad.

Afterwards, as it was starting to sink in, we all went for a walk together through the surrounding fields. We made a fuss of the kids: they had quite a few chocolates and we tried to wrap them up in a blanket of love. But that first day was just awful, a terrible, terrible day, as the reality of it began to sink in. Eventually it came to an end – and we prepared for the second one. We got through that as well. It is a well-worn cliché but we took it one day at a time, and I tried to ease us into a routine of keeping busy, getting on with things as much as we could. I thought it would be helpful for all of us.

I knew Caroline's funeral was going to be hard to get through. Along with her family we had spent a lot of time planning and organising it – that had helped keep us busy. Given us a focus. I wanted to get on with it as soon as was practically possible but it didn't take place until two weeks later in the village church where we'd married nine years earlier. I hadn't been back since then, and as I walked in the memories came rushing back.

After Caroline had died and as part of the planning for the funeral I had written a eulogy, to be delivered during the service. I toyed with the notion of delivering it myself. While the words had been easy to write, I imagined they would be difficult, perhaps impossible, to deliver. I just wasn't sufficiently confident that I would be able to hold it together to do them justice. So I decided to ask our local vicar, Canon David Henley, to read them on my behalf. He did so perfectly. I was enormously grateful.

Caroline had always been very environmentally minded,

so the coffin we had chosen was a woven wicker basket, beautifully decorated with wild flowers. Her father, her two brothers and my brother carried her out of the church, while I walked behind with the kids and Caroline's mother, down a steep little winding path to the quiet, narrow village road.

After what had been an uplifting and positive service, very much a celebration of her life, came the burial. I found that much harder to cope with. I'd arranged for my parents to take the kids away at the end of the church service. I didn't want them to be there for the committal; I didn't want them to see their mum being lowered into the ground. I think it was right for them to be at the funeral, to experience the love for their mum, but on balance I didn't think they needed to be there for the final bit. I also wanted to be there on my own – a private moment to say my goodbyes.

As everyone drifted away, I remained by the graveside. One of my closest friends, Ed Sandry, an old mate from the Regiment, stayed with me. We stood there in silence, I don't know how long for. I said goodbye to Caroline. We moved back from the graveside, but I didn't yet feel ready to leave her. The grave was about to be filled in, and I wanted to make sure that the soil was put carefully into the grave – I didn't want it to be just dumped in. Ed talked to the man doing the job, who said, 'Yes, of course, I'll be very careful.' For which I was grateful.

In difficult moments, when you're upset, your mind can play tricks on you. A mad, mad thought came to me. My grief-stricken mind became convinced that the coffin hadn't been put down properly in the ground, that it wasn't straight within the grave. Without a flicker of hesitation, Ed dropped down into the grave in his immaculate pin-stripe suit and shifted the coffin so that it was just that bit straighter. I'm incredibly grateful that he did that. I thought it needed to be done so he did it, no questions asked. In that moment it made me feel much better. It was true unconditional friendship and I'll never ever forget it.

Ed and I wandered slowly back through the quiet country lanes to Caroline's brother's house, about a mile away, where people had gathered. I was in no rush to get there and we walked mostly in silence, listening to the birds singing and appreciating the rolling green countryside. It gave me time and a bit of space to draw myself together. It was peaceful, and I was calmed by it. The service had been what I'd wanted it to be – a fitting tribute, an opportunity not just to grieve but also to celebrate the life, albeit one cut so cruelly short, of a wonderful person.

We got back to find the kids tearing about in the garden, playing with their friends and cousin, which was a great relief to see. They were screaming about on bikes, doing what kids do. My daughter was riding too – something I had never seen her do before. I was temporarily confused by this. How, when, had she learned to ride a bike? It showed that for the past few months my mind had been entirely fixed on supporting Caroline. It was, however, precisely what I needed to see at that moment and it gave me a flicker of hope for our future.

# 20

# A Dark Place

## *August 2010*

—

Grief is the price we pay for love, and most people know what it's like to lose a loved one. It is harder to bear when the loss is unexpected or seems to go against the natural order, when people suffer the loss of a loved one at an earlier age than might have been expected – especially, of course, the terrible tragedy of losing a child.

When I got married, I never imagined that I would lose my wife a few years later. It was something that never occurred to me. Why would it? But by the time of Caroline's death I had been steeling myself, and was more prepared for it than if it had come out of the blue. She had been unwell for some time after all, and towards the end I knew what was going to happen; I hoped for a miracle and for the first time in my life suspended disbelief about miracles happening, but I'd been readying myself for some time, and to an extent had begun a process of grieving even before she died. Long before she left us, the wonderful, vivacious woman

I had married had disappeared. She had become someone else, as had I.

Even so, over and above the aching sadness, I was seething that someone so lovely, someone who had lived such a good, decent and wholesome life – someone I loved so much – should be so cruelly taken away. It seemed unjust to her and unfair to those of us left behind. For a while I was engulfed by the pain of that, lost in a choking fog of grief and despair. The world felt like a dark place. But I also knew, from early on, that I couldn't afford to be consumed by the pain. I wasn't able to go up on the Wiltshire downs and howl into the wind and rain, I had to be there for our kids. I had to help them through it. I had to hold what was left of our family together and get them into a new routine. It was tough but we had to try and keep going.

Caroline's battle against cancer had been an ever-present worry. Nearly always there, never far from my mind at any time. Part of this worry rested on the uncertainty – would she recover, would we have a normal life again, what would it mean for the longer term, how would it affect our kids? That had now given way to a different emotion. There was now at least certainty about our circumstances. Caroline was gone, she wasn't coming back. That would never change. Still, there remained uncertainty about what that meant for our future, and a worry about how we would be affected by the loss. There was also the deep sadness of it all. I tried to keep busy. Tried to be the best parent I could be. Tried to get on with making a normal life for the kids. But it was hard. There are no short cuts through the fog of grief, there is no easy route through. But you have to try and find a path, even when your heart is aching.

Caroline's clothes and her possessions were still scattered around the house. It took me a couple of months before

I could bring myself to look in her wardrobe. I knew at some point I would have to open those doors, sort through her clothes and the memories that would trigger. I felt as if there was no rush, and on a number of occasions I put it off. I stood in front of those wardrobe doors on countless occasions staring at them, wishing that I wasn't about to open them, and time after time I didn't feel I had the strength to pull them open and look inside. I think I felt that the moment I did that would be the final acceptance of the fact that she was gone. That she really wasn't coming back. I *knew* she wasn't, but part of me still wasn't ready to accept it.

Eventually I did. I was confronted by her clothes hanging neatly on coat hangers, her shoes neatly arranged in their boxes. A wedding dress. Maternity clothing. A dressing gown. I shut the doors again and walked away. Later, I returned and sorted and packed every item away for safe keeping. It felt like I was packing away more than clothes. I was packing away a part of my life that deserved to be kept open. I didn't want to close those boxes, but close them I did.

We had two cars, but we now needed only one. I couldn't bring myself to sell Caroline's, so I sold mine instead.

A while later I opened her bedside drawer. I was immediately struck by a waft of her favourite perfume. For a moment she was with me again, and then she wasn't.

I think 'society' has a certain view, an expectation about what is appropriate behaviour for people coping with bereavement. Generally people are more understanding of emotion displayed by people who have recently suffered a loss. I dropped the kids off at school one day and one of the mums came over to ask how we were. I couldn't find the words. I felt myself getting upset. I just didn't want to be having a conversation at that moment. The mum was very understanding, could see I didn't want to talk, and put a reassuring hand on my shoulder, telling me that they were all thinking of us before leaving me to it. A simple act of kindness to help me feel better.

I was thirty-seven years old when my wife passed away. There are, thankfully, relatively few young widows and widowers. As a society we are accustomed to much older people having lost their wives, husbands or partners. So, because there are fewer younger widowers, I wasn't clear in my own mind what I should do, or what people expected of me. Was it, for instance, OK to go and have a drink in the local pub? I was permanently concerned that people were discussing how I was reacting. I'm sure I was being over-sensitive, but I was acutely conscious that some people might be judging me.

It is at tough times like this that you find out who your real friends are. Some turn up with a home-cooked lasagne, but some don't turn up at all and go silent on you, for whatever reason. Most of those who had been *our* but were now *my* friends stepped up and were superb and brilliantly supportive. Card after lovely thoughtful card arrived. I read them all and they made me feel a bit better, because they reassured me that there were a lot of people thinking about us, and also offering practical help.

Over the years since 2010 I've had cause to send many letters of condolence to people who have been bereaved. Thoughts and kind words go a long way, but actual practical support and advice are invaluable, that was what I appreciated most. Food parcels on the doorstep were a frequent source of comfort. Several friends, though, were nowhere to be seen. I don't know why, but they weren't there for me; in my hour of need they went absent without leave. I guess they must have had their reasons – too busy or whatever; maybe they didn't want to confront the magnitude of the situation; perhaps it triggered bad memories for them or concerns about their own mortality – but I have never been able to think of them in the same way. What are friends for after all?

These were a tiny minority though. The majority were brilliantly supportive, which reminded me that while you can't choose your family, you can choose your friends – so choose them wisely and never take them for granted.

A few close friends recommended that I get some grief counselling to help me cope. I was instinctively cautious. It didn't neatly fit with the life I had led. I had lived and worked in a military culture which (although to a slightly lesser extent than in previous generations) still saw counselling, or talking about your concerns, as a sign of weakness. You were expected to keep going through the tough times. Setting all of that aside, though, my primary concern was a practical one: I just wasn't personally convinced that it would work, or help. I knew what the problem was, knew that there was nothing I could do to change what had happened, and thought that the way to make things better, and to dull the pain, was to look after the kids and get on with our life as best we could.

A volunteer with the support unit at the hospital had left a series of messages, asking me to phone him back. I never did. Then one evening the phone rang, and then flicked on to answerphone. It was him again. He started to leave a message, sounding so concerned that I hadn't phoned him back that I found myself feeling quite sorry for him. I hovered by the phone, unsure as to whether to let in a stranger, but then – and only because at that moment there was calm in the house – I picked the phone up to speak to him.

We talked for forty-five minutes. I think we both felt better for it, though it was a bit awkward at first.

'How do you feel?' he asked.

'Well, not great to be honest. My wife has died and I miss her terribly.'

'Oh . . .'

But he went on to tell me that his wife had died too. That gave him credibility in my eyes, in that he knew what he was talking about and maybe understood what I was going through. On that basis, I thought it worth having the conversation.

It helped, and although we never spoke again, I think there is great benefit in having conversations like that; in finding someone you feel comfortable with, and trust to talk to about your feelings. Talking to someone about the process of grieving helped me realise, if nothing else, that maybe, probably, hopefully, at some point in the future I could get myself into a better place. The deep sadness would always be there, but perhaps I could learn to adapt, to cope, to live a life resembling some form of normality.

The kids responded in different ways, as kids do. Mostly they wanted to play and see their friends and get on and do the kind of things any normal kid wants to do. They were now seven and five, and given their young age I think the true horror of what had happened to us had to an extent been lost on them. I have often thought that if they had been teenagers it would have been even harder, but at that age they quickly adapted. I was naturally very protective of them, though I also knew that I simply could not wrap them up in cotton wool. I read to them before bed and got them to read to me. I tried to get them to talk about their feelings, and would try regularly to draw the conversation towards their mum. I wanted to keep her memory alive for us all. But it was a particularly tough moment when the first drawing came home from school that had just the three of us in it.

There were numerous other tough moments. Four simple words, 'I want my mummy', now conveyed a cataclysmic sense of loss and grief. To hear them screamed out chills the soul. On another occasion I was struggling to do my daughter's hair. I didn't know how to do it – Caroline had always done it. The frustration was such that I wanted to scream and cry, but I didn't, because I didn't want my daughter to see that I was upset. I was dreading the first of the kids' birthdays. I was terrified that it might be a moment when Mum was missed even more. I am sure that I was worrying about it more than the kids were. When the time came, I carried in the birthday cake with lit candles and felt consumed with sadness that Caroline wasn't there. But it wasn't the moment to reflect on that – it was a kids' party and I had to ensure they had a great time.

I had to work out how best to guide them through. I would try different things, test and adjust to see what worked best. An early sign that we might be making progress came a couple of months after the funeral, when I took the kids down to the Dorset coast for an afternoon on the beach. It was a perfect late summer's day, the sparkling blue sea shimmering. We took a picnic and had a nice time. But while driving home I began to feel incredibly upset about the fact that there were only three of us in the car. I knew how much Caroline would have enjoyed the day. The kids were asleep in the back. I pulled over into a lay-by, got out and stood by the car, trying to draw in the evening air until the sorrow and rage drained away. I remember looking at the kids in the back of the car, fast asleep. So sorry that they were going to have to grow up without their mum. How unfair it all seemed. I got back in and drove us home in a very dark mood.

I felt that there was a lot of pressure on me now. How was I going to cope with the challenges of the future? But I knew that retreating inwards wasn't an option. The kids needed me to cope. There wasn't much time or space to grieve in. And Caroline would, I know, have rightly expected me to get on with it and to do the very best for our children. In the end, like she had been, I am a practical person. I concluded that I only had two options: sink or swim. I chose to swim – the kids meant there wasn't really a choice.

So I tried to get on with life. I think you have to. I employed the same tactics as I had in the Army; I didn't really know any other way. Try and hold things together in the heat of the moment, work through the tough times, keep going, try and stay cheerful, never give up, and when you can, work out what you're going to do and then get on and do it. Simple. Well, maybe not always.

By the autumn we had started to find a routine as a family of three, not four. Every morning I did the school run. In the afternoons it was mostly mums at the school gate. They used to look sympathetically over at me. They would be stood chatting waiting for the kids to come out, I would fiddle with my phone to avoid being drawn into the conversation. I had some help from relatives and friends, because while any parent will tell you that being a parent is the hardest job in the world, being a single parent is even harder.

On one occasion I returned home from work with the kids to a mountain of washing and all the cooking and cleaning to do. They went out into the garden to jump up and down on the trampoline. I cooked a meal and called for them to come in for their food. I called again – no response. They kept jumping. I started to get annoyed. I shouted for them to come in. They kept jumping. I walked out into the garden. They kept jumping. Again I said, 'Time for tea,' calmly, but it was clear I now meant business. They kept jumping. There was so much to do, I didn't need this, but at the same time getting cross probably wasn't going to help. I walked over to the trampoline and now, less calmly, said, 'Time. For. Tea.' They kept jumping. Next time was louder: 'TIME. FOR. TEA.' One came in at that point, but the other was still jumping as I walked back into the house.

At moments like that, the practical impact of there being three and not four of you, one adult and not two, comes home to you. I was now outnumbered. I hadn't just lost my soulmate, I had lost my workmate too. There's so much more to do, and when things go wrong there's no one to back you up or help you out. You've lost your back-up, your safety net. Being a parent doesn't come with a job description, you don't need a licence, and 'full-time' doesn't nearly cover it. From dawn till dusk, from their first steps till the moment they walk off into the big wide world (and forever afterwards), your kids are the most important part of your life. Always responsible for them, always worried for them, always hopeful for them. It's hard enough to bring up kids as a couple, it's doubly hard as a single parent. All of the pressures are magnified.

So while I found myself trying to get organised and establish a routine, I was constantly in fear of disruption to it. Even with a daily routine (and I didn't want to turn our home into the first five weeks of Sandhurst) you quickly learn that your world can be turned upside down by something as seemingly incidental as a cold or a tummy bug. Trying to keep the show on the road whenever one of the children was unwell and had to miss school was always a scramble. Rearranging work, calling in favours, asking for help. At the same time, the worry at the back of my head was always, 'What if *I* get ill? How on earth will we manage then?'

I always found the mornings really hard: getting the kids out of bed, washed, fed, dressed, out the door, in the car, and safely dropped off at school. It doesn't matter how organised you are or how helpful the kids are (which they *mostly* were), there's just always a lot to do. However practised or slick the routine is, there is just *always* so much to do.

All of that said, and despite the difficulties of keeping all the plates spinning, I took huge strength from the kids. They helped me to get through the loss, partly because they are great kids, but also because there are so many joys to being a parent. The really hard part comes when you don't have anyone to share it with. The good days, and the days you'd rather forget. Even the basic everyday things, like being stuck in a long traffic jam on a packed motorway with one of the kids on the back seat desperately needing to go to the toilet. These difficult moments really do test you, not just as a parent but as a person. They continue to demonstrate to you an obvious and incontrovertible truth: that as a parent, life is so much harder on your own.

I missed Caroline more than ever in these tough moments – we all did – and I also wondered just how she had managed to cope in similar situations when I had been away. It gave me an even greater respect for what she'd done for us, for me. The evenings were the hardest time, after a busy day and the kids were in bed. I would be sat alone, thinking, feeling lonely. Missing her. Over the years a lot of people have talked to me about their personal experience of bereavement and coping with grief. Men in particular are susceptible to retreating into their metaphorical cave. A widowed man who would never have previously thought of wandering about in the dark supping milk directly out of a milk bottle can quickly find himself doing it. I know.

In some relationships, one of the partners may have relied heavily on the other for certain things, whether that's cooking and paying the bills, or doing the banking and cleaning. Most co-habiting couples split the jobs and people take responsibility for 'their' roles. All of a sudden, it's just you. You are on your own. All the jobs are yours and you have to do everything now. The shopping, the cooking, the cleaning and tidying, the washing, the paying of bills, the garden, putting out the rubbish – all these things need to be kept on top of, before you can get to the more fun stuff. The running of any household, particularly one with kids in it, always brings a lot of work. That's life, you accept it, but if there's two of you the load is more than halved; on your own it's a constant battle to keep up with it all, and each and every day brings with it so many tasks, just to keep your head above water.

The Army was supportive, and fortunately my next posting wasn't a normal military position: I already had in place a long-standing offer to go to university to study for an in-service Master's degree. It was quickly agreed that it was no longer feasible for me to study at Jesus College Cambridge, where I had a place. But daily commuting to King's College London was just about doable. I arranged for Liz, a wonderfully kind and caring child-minder, to pick the kids up from school and I began the routine of travelling into London. It was always a mad dash to get the kids ready and off to school before driving to the station to try and find a parking space before jumping on the train. The timings were always tight and I never drew breath until I was sat on the train, but it was refreshing to be in a new routine. Good to be meeting new and different people. And great to be having my brain exercised in a way it hadn't been for some time.

After years in a highly disciplined and very structured Army environment it felt strange, but stimulating, being back in what now felt like a supremely casual and relaxed world. At King's I met Harry Parker, an impressive and personable young Army Captain who had recently lost both his legs in an explosion in Afghanistan. We were, I think, good foils for one another.

He had lost his legs, I had lost my wife.

We were both damaged goods, though in different ways. We cheered each other up as we adjusted to our new environment.

We sat in the student union nursing a pint, both feeling somewhat self-conscious and out of place surrounded by much younger and much cooler student colleagues. Harry told me about the opening lines to the best man's speech he had just given at his brother's wedding: 'I always knew that I would be legless at my brother's wedding.' It was a devilishly funny and brilliant opener which unsurprisingly had not left a dry eye in the house. It was deeply humbling that he could find it within himself to draw humour from the catastrophic misfortune he had suffered. When he told me about it I didn't know whether to laugh or cry. It could have gone either way, but I laughed. It was the first time I had laughed since Caroline had died. After laughing, I felt guilty – that I was laughing just three months after Caroline had died. But Harry had cheered me up. He had shown me that despite everything I had retained at least some capacity for joy, and that was something I could build on.

After Caroline died I had a number of big decisions to make. The most important one was how I was going to structure our lives so that I was best placed to look after the kids and make sure that after suffering the loss of their mum they had all the love and support they needed to have the happiest possible home life and the strongest possible start in life. A crucial part of my ability to do that rested on whether I should, or could, continue to serve in the Army.

I had to decide whether I was prepared to put myself in harm's way again. Was I really going to go back to Afghanistan, or to the next place, wherever that might be? The kids had lost their mum; could I ever really justify putting my head back into the lion's mouth, allowing myself to get into a position where it became more likely that they would also lose their dad? Would that be fair to my kids, or indeed to those people under my command? On an operational deployment, in war, you need a commander who is prepared to take risks. Sometimes it's the risks that make all the difference – that flash of raw nerve, courage and daring that results in achieving success and averting defeat. If I was back in the field, having to make those decisions again, would I be able to make them, or would I play it safer because I was trying to protect myself more than I might otherwise have done? Fundamentally the question was this: did I still have it within me to take big risks? I thought that I probably did – and that scared me, because I knew where it might lead, how things might end up.

I could have pursued a desk-based career in the Army, taking staff jobs close to home, and in many respects that wouldn't have been a bad option. It would have provided some continuity, financial security and stability. But deep down I knew that it was time for a fresh start and a new challenge. Of course I wanted the best for my kids, but I also knew I had to think about what I wanted to do next – I wanted to be professionally satisfied and needed to find a way of achieving that while at the same time putting my kids first. After much deliberation, I concluded that after all those years of service in the Army it was time for a change and I must now do something different. But what?

I had always been interested in politics. My parents had been politically active for a while, and as a child I had been taken along to various events and demos including a Campaign for Nuclear Disarmament (CND) rally in Hyde Park. From an early age I had a developed sense of right and wrong, and at secondary school I was elected as our class representative. Our teacher, Mr Rick, told everyone to close their eyes and raise their hands to vote for their preferred candidate. I wasn't entirely convinced by either the process nor the result, but John Rick had just given me my first taste of 'democracy', and my first job in politics.

I had studied politics modules at university as part of my International Relations degree, and although life in the Army had kept me focused on other things, I had always kept an eye on what was going on politically. For some time I had been considering getting into politics when I left the Army, although I'd always assumed this would be another ten or fifteen years upstream.

On the night of the 2005 General Election I had been in the British Army HQ in Kabul. I sat up all night listening to the BBC World Service on the radio, as the results dripped in. It came at the end of what had been a frustrating month away from PJHQ, spent supporting a counter-narcotics operation down in southern Afghanistan. Although it had been high-octane soldiering, it had also been deeply unsatisfying. Partly because I don't think we really achieved much – a bit of disruption for certain, a few arrests, some confiscated opium and some good stories. We made ourselves, and the system, feel like we were having an effect, but really it was more of a sticking-plaster solution than treating the gaping wound that lay underneath. I was becoming increasingly frustrated at this short-term approach and in my mind started to question the direction of travel policy-wise, both in Iraq and in Afghanistan. I remained fiercely proud to serve in the Army but had come to appreciate that it was only in politics that you really got the opportunity to shape and change things – to make things happen.

It also became abundantly clear that we in the Armed Forces were a very long way down the decision-making food chain. I had twice been out to Iraq and three times to Afghanistan with no control whatsoever over the decisions that been taken before I (and countless thousands of others) went there. I was starting to think that some of those decisions were underpinned not by evidence or experience but by expediency. However good the people in the military were, we were only as good as the political decision-makers sat above us.

To be fair, though, it wasn't just the politicians who were to blame. Among some, though not all, of our senior military there seemed to exist an innate belief that almost whatever the circumstances, our military effort would prevail. On occasions this manifested itself in advice being given to ministers which, looking back, had in some cases more to do with inter-service rivalry and a desire to convince ministers that our Armed Forces were invincible. If the government wanted concurrent commitments in Iraq and Afghanistan, we, the Armed Forces, could do it, and, crucially, do it with the existing resources. Maybe they thought that was the case, but I didn't think so, and it was becoming increasingly clear to me that the answers being given by senior military to questions being asked by politicians related less to hard-tested evidential truth and more to a desire to please. I wasn't prepared to play those sorts of games.

It felt like whatever the task, we would sort it; however scarce the resources, we would make it work. The military is an extraordinary 'can do' organisation, and that culture works incredibly well on the ground when you're trying to get difficult things done, but if politicians are asking you to do difficult things there is an absolute responsibility to ensure that the advice offered is grounded in a deliverable reality. And first among the questions that need to be asked when discussing new commitments should always be: do we have the resources to do this? If the honest answer is no, the politicians need to be told that, and have it explained that if they want it done, $x$ amount of extra resource will be needed, and $y$ amount of extra risk will be incurred.

As a Major I was, in the bigger scheme of things, very junior to the most senior commanders. The culture of the military, then and still today, does not lend itself to more junior people questioning the judgement calls of more senior people. I understand why that is the case, but increasingly I was questioning the wisdom and logic of some of the big decisions, despite the individual brilliance and character of many of the people. The culture just didn't allow the opportunity to scrutinise or even discuss or question the big judgements that were being made. Consequently, I was becoming increasingly frustrated by a system that I thought was too rigid, too unwilling to accept change or constructive criticism.

But I think this was only in part a systemic cultural issue. The Army was also, as the expression went, 'running hot' – so consumed by the operational tempo and the commitments that it had accepted that there just wasn't the time, the space, to step back, to have what some in the Army refer to as a 'Condor moment'. The term stems from a 1980s TV commercial where a pipe smoker doesn't allow the stresses and strains of life, or the inconvenient or unwarranted interruptions of others, to prevent him from having a moment of quiet, reflective calm. The basic point is sound: however busy you are, however important you think you might be, you always need to step back and take stock. If you live your life at a hundred miles an hour, as I have tended to do, sometimes you need to carve out the time to reflect in a calm, measured way on where you're going and how you're getting there, and to interrogate the strategy, confirm that the culture is right, and ask how things can be improved.

Although many people assume that the majority who serve in our Armed Forces are either small or large 'C' conservatives, politics itself had, in my experience, rarely been discussed in the military, with most preferring to talk about other less contentious issues. I'd been a Labour Party member and supporter nearly all my adult life, which might have come as a surprise to some people, who didn't think of the Army and Labour as being natural bedfellows. To me, though, there was a neat symmetry between the traditional values of the military and the traditional values of Labour. Ultimately, both are about the collective, not the individual, and premised by a fundamental truth: that you achieve much more together than you ever can alone.

This understanding was underpinned with a basic belief in the value and importance of public service. It may now seem old-fashioned to some, but I joined the Army because I wanted to make a contribution to society by doing something worthwhile. I always understood that joining the Paras placed me at the sharpest end of the public sector, but I relished the challenges I knew it would bring – albeit I had an admittedly naive and underdeveloped understanding of what that actually meant and the toll it might take.

My motivation for considering entering politics was entirely consistent with that – a simple desire to improve lives by working hard and getting things done that help other people. Unlike the veteran Conservative politician Michael Heseltine, I had no grand plan. No ambition to serve in high office. Just a basic desire to get up in the morning and go out to do something which I could believe in and which gave me the opportunity to add value to the lives of others.

Losing Caroline had only reinforced my understanding of how important it was to make the most out of life, and I had long before come to understand that what you do for a job really matters. It's where you spend much of your time – where I had spent nearly all of my time. If I was going to leave the Army, which had provided me with such a professionally challenging life (albeit admittedly perhaps sometimes a bit too challenging), it would have to be for something worthwhile that still gave me the opportunity to serve, to make a meaningful contribution, but in a different way.

The last few years had been unremittingly difficult, and although I missed Caroline enormously and felt that huge sense of loss, day by day, week by week, month by month, I had slowly started to work my way through the fog of grief to a point where I was able seriously to ask questions of myself about what I wanted to do in the future. I thought that serving in politics just might be the way to go, and I began to get excited at the prospect of this new challenge.

# 21

# A New Front

## *January 2011*

—

The MPs' expenses scandal had been rumbling on for some time, and it was still claiming casualties. By late 2010 it looked as though the latest one would be the sitting MP for Barnsley Central. It seemed all but certain that the Crown Prosecution Service would bring criminal charges against him for fraudulent expenses claims, and that at some point soon there would be a parliamentary by-election to elect a new MP.

I wondered if this might be the fresh start and new challenge I was looking for. Barnsley had been electing Labour MPs since 1922, so there was bound to be a lot of interest in the seat. Traditionally, the local constituency party had always adopted a local candidate, and to date it had always been a miner. The National Union of Mineworkers (NUM) had basically decided who the MP would be. They selected their Labour candidate, who was duly elected. Never before had an *outsider* been adopted. Although the world had moved on a bit, the prospect of being selected there seemed extremely remote. I asked a few knowledgeable people for their advice; was it worth considering? The overwhelming consensus was crystal clear: 'No – don't waste your time. You've got absolutely no chance. Whatsoever.' I listened carefully to all that advice, nodded sagely in response – and ignored it.

In January 2011, the Labour Party confirmed that it would be selecting a candidate for a by-election in the parliamentary constituency of Barnsley Central. At this point, the sitting MP had been suspended from the party but was still the incumbent MP. There was no absolute certainty that there would be a by-election as parliamentary rules state that MPs must only stand down from Parliament if given a twelve-month or more custodial sentence. Technically, therefore, the sitting MP could have been found guilty of fraud, sentenced to, say, nine months, and served time in prison, all without having to stand down as an MP. Consequently, there was the very peculiar situation of the party selecting a candidate for a by-election that no one knew for sure would be taking place.

Despite the uncertainty, the timeline for the Labour Party selection process was incredibly tight. Just as with any job opportunity, the vacancy was advertised and potential candidates were advised to submit a CV with covering letter by Friday, 21 January. A long-listing panel convened from the party's National Executive Committee (NEC) would meet to consider all applications and reduce to a long-list of twelve those who would be interviewed by a short-listing panel at the party's HQ in Victoria, central London, on Wednesday, 26 January.

This is where it then got a bit crazy. The successfully short-listed candidates would appear at a hustings event in

Barnsley the very next night, where the local constituency party members would vote to select a prospective parliamentary candidate for a by-election that had still not been triggered. This meant that there would only be just over twenty-four hours between finding out whether you had been short-listed to then appearing in front of the local party membership. This was an exceptionally short timeframe; normally this was a process that ran over many weeks.

I started to prepare an application, still not at all convinced that I would in fact submit it. The advice, after all, had been overwhelming – it's not going to happen – and still by far the most likely scenario was that if I applied I would not be either long-listed, short-listed or selected as the candidate, but worse, it would somehow get out that I had applied. It was something of a grey area as to whether serving military personnel were allowed to apply for such vacancies. The Queen's Regulations (the Army rule book) were not clear. You certainly were not allowed to participate overtly in political activity, but technically this wasn't that, though it was a pretty fine line. If my chain of command in the Army had got wind of it I have no doubt that a very dim view would have been taken, and it may well have brought to an end my service in the Army. I'd thought about the process by which at some point I would leave the Army and I was keen to do so on the best of terms. Eric Joyce, whom I'd met and who had generously given me lots of excellent advice, had also given me the perfect example of how not to do it. In 1998 he had nearly been court-martialled for contributing to a Fabian Society pamphlet while still serving in the Army. The Army had been good to me and I really did not want to go down that same road.

The decision to proceed therefore brought with it real risk, but I thought about it, weighed it up and carefully calculated that it was a risk worth taking. I am certain that Caroline would have agreed with me. Some may describe the decision as foolhardy. I understand that. It was certainly influenced by recent events. Caroline's death had taught me many things, not least among them that life was precious and sometimes shorter than you might expect, so seize the moment if a good opportunity presents itself. It had, so I submitted my application and started to make a plan for the admittedly very unlikely prospect that I was selected for an interview. I knew that these types of vacancies had tended to be filled by people who were either political insiders with close links to the national party leadership or the trade union movement, or by an outstanding local candidate behind whom a majority of people coalesced. I was neither of those things.

I knew that I wouldn't find out about a possible interview until the Monday so I had to start planning for a best-case scenario however remote that felt. As is often said in the Army, prior preparation and planning avoids a piss-poor performance. If I were successfully short-listed on the Wednesday there would be only twenty-four hours to try and contact local constituency party members ahead of the hustings meeting, so I needed to have a plan of action and enlist some support. I called a few friends to see if they might be able to help me out.

On the Monday night I received a call and was genuinely surprised to be told that I had been long-listed and was being invited for an interview on the Wednesday. I had already thought about how to respond on the off-chance that this happened, so having thanked the caller, I asked if it would be possible to be interviewed as early as possible on the Wednesday morning. I reckoned that the earlier it was done, the more time would be available for me to get up to

Barnsley to be meeting local members. If you don't ask, you don't get. On Tuesday, I was notified that I would be the first candidate to be interviewed, at 9.30 a.m.

On the Wednesday morning, having stitched together a childcare plan that involved grandparents, neighbours and our child-minder Liz, I jumped on an early train from Salisbury to London. The interview panel of NEC members asked a combination of local questions about Barnsley and national political issues. They were polite but businesslike. It was concluded in twenty minutes. I came out thinking it had gone OK and if nothing else I'd not embarrassed myself. It was now out of my hands.

I caught the train back to Salisbury. Scanning through some tweets on Twitter, I saw that an online LabourList political blog was speculating about who the potential candidates would be for the Barnsley Central seat. I'm not sure how my name had entered the frame, but I was mentioned. This was a bit concerning given that I'd always thought the most likely scenario was that I wouldn't be selected but would get exposed in the media as being a part of the process.

Oh well, I thought, you're committed now – just get on with it and see what happens.

Back at Salisbury station I got into my car and began the drive north to Barnsley. Halfway up the M1 in a motorway service station I picked up an answerphone message which confirmed that I had been short-listed along with three others.

Blimey, I thought, I'm going to get a run at it.

It all still seemed a bit surreal and I wondered what Caroline would have said to me at that point. I was sure it would have been: 'Go for it!'

Further up the M1, in another motorway service station, I

learned that alongside me, a local councillor from Barnsley, a councillor from Rotherham and a trade union lawyer from Leeds had also been short-listed. It felt to me (and I suspect to others) a bit like the Army Major living in Salisbury had been chucked in as the wild card entrant.

As arranged, my great friend from university and later the Army Jon Wheale was already in Barnsley waiting for me. He had found a hotel room and turned it into a mini campaign HQ, having printed off much relevant local information. We would soon be joined by another old friend, Stephen Carter, and together they would be my support team.

We ordered pizzas – none of us could decide what we wanted, which I didn't think boded well for the dynamic decision-making we would need over the next twenty-four hours – and tried to formulate a plan. By this stage I had been emailed a list of local party members, and between us, and with help from a few friends scattered around the country, we hit the phones and started to call and ask if people would be attending the hustings the following night. If they weren't able to make it a line went through their name, but if they were, a further question was asked: did they want to speak to me or meet me to discuss their voting intentions? Because the process was happening so quickly, not everyone was even aware there was a hustings event taking place. Some were surprised to be getting a call about it, others were keen to discuss it.

The next day saw me dashing around as many households as I possibly could. It was a weekday and most people were out but I had a series of useful conversations in person and on the phone. In between these I thought about what I was going to say in my speech that night and fed thoughts back to Jon and Stephen, who were making calls and jotting down notes for me to use as the basis of my speech.

We never paused for breath throughout the course of that manic day, and after several readthroughs of my speech and a discussion about likely questions that would follow it, and good responses, before we knew it, it was time to head off to the hustings event which was taking place at Oakwell – the home of Barnsley Football Club.

Jon, Stephen and I arrived and parked in the car park, from where you can see the old Barnsley Main Colliery pit head and engine house. We paused for a moment in the car. None of us really thought I was going to win, we all accepted that I was the rank outsider, but we were here now so we were determined to make the best of it. As I got out of the car I took my phone out of my pocket. It was no longer working; it felt like it had given up the ghost after so many calls. But there were no calls left to make now. I just needed to get inside and give it my best shot.

Before I could be met and directed to the candidate holding room, a member of the local party, Trevor Oldroyd, recognised me, grabbed my hand and thrust into it an old coin – for luck. 'Knock 'em dead, young man,' he said with a friendly smile. Some other locals had been supportive. John Parkinson and Mike Stokes both felt it was time for some 'new blood', but the prospect of being selected still felt remote. Very remote.

We were shown into a tiny room. All the other candidates – Linda, Emma and Richard – were already there. The hustings format gave us just five minutes to deliver our speech to the assembled members before taking fifteen minutes of questions. We would draw lots to determine the speaking order. The supposed logic was that it was best either to go first, and set the standard, or last, and leave the members with a strong impression just before they voted. I went second.

I was led from the holding room to a much bigger adjoining room – part of the hospitality suite overlooking the pitch. A lectern and a packed room waited expectantly.

I stood at the lectern, looked around the room and took a moment to compose myself. I began by talking about my background and then gave an assessment of the challenges I thought Barnsley was facing, and what I would do about them if I was elected as their local MP. I concluded my remarks by saying, 'If you choose to put your trust in me, I won't let you down. I can think of no greater honour than to serve as your local MP.'

I thought my speech went reasonably well. And then it came to the questions. Having given my speech from the lectern, somewhat to the consternation of the chair I walked forward to take the questions. There was now no physical barrier between the members and myself – I practically stood among them. I learned subsequently that the other three candidates had remained rooted behind the lectern throughout.

The questions came thick and fast, including a thoughtful one from local councillor Graham Kyte about how you get the best out of a team. It was a gift of a question for me. I spoke about my basic belief in the value of a team. That life and politics are team sports. That the ethos of working with others to get things done was what I had spent my whole working life doing. I assured the room that as their MP I would build the strongest team around me and that together we would make a real difference to people locally. I was able to say it with conviction because it is what I believe. The team works.

There were some tough questions, including a personal but not unreasonable one about how as a single parent I could manage as an MP. I gave assurances that I would be able to, and fielded the remainder of the questions as best I could. I was utterly straightforward in my responses, which seemed to flow reasonably smoothly, and I walked back to the holding room thinking it had gone fairly well.

I then sat and waited for the remaining candidates to take their turn. From the holding room you would hear a ripple of applause or a murmur of laughter and imagine the other candidates doing brilliantly, wowing the members. And then, finally, it was time for them to cast their vote, on what is called the Alternative Vote (AV) system. This is where voters rank the candidates in order of preference, in this case from one to four. In the event that one candidate fails to achieve a sufficient majority (50 per cent plus one), the candidate with the fewest number of first-preference votes is eliminated and their votes redistributed. The process is repeated until one candidate achieves the required majority. The votes are placed securely into a proper ballot box and the process is very carefully scrutinised by Labour Party officials to avoid any accusation of foul play.

Along with various party officials and the local party executive committee, the four candidates were invited into an adjacent room to witness the opening of the ballot box and the counting of the votes, ahead of the official announcement of the result. By now I just needed to know the outcome, one way or another. It had been a long few days and I craved the certainty of knowing what the result was. The other three candidates crowded around the table where the ballot box was about to be opened, understandably eager themselves to see the votes being counted and to get a feel for how it would play out. I am not entirely sure why I didn't join them, but I didn't. I stood back and adopted the old Brian Clough trick of playing it cool and feigning disinterest while making small talk with a cleaner – though inwardly my heart was pounding and I felt anything but cool at that moment.

After all the votes had been carefully counted and then recounted, just for good measure, they were placed in four distinct piles each marked with a candidate's name, so that the adjudicator could announce the first-round scores. Richard was out in front, Linda and I were tied in joint second place, and Emma was in fourth place.

This is when it started to get really interesting. Under the AV system, because no one candidate had achieved 50 per cent of the total votes cast, the candidate with the lowest number of votes, Emma, was eliminated from the process and her votes redistributed based on the second preferences of those who had voted for her. Remarkably, her votes split equally: half for Linda, half for me. Incredibly, this meant that Linda and I remained tied, but still with one fewer vote than Richard. Therefore, either Linda or I would have to be eliminated and the other would go into a final count-off with Richard.

My reading of the situation was that Richard had harvested a significant number of first preferences, and I sensed it was reasonably unlikely that there was much more support for him – therefore in my mind I was certain that whoever emerged from Linda and me would end up as the overall winner. This scenario of a tie was extremely unusual so at this point the rule book had to be consulted for guidance on how to proceed. This only added to the drama, and you could have cut the tension with a knife. Externally, I was trying my utmost to remain calm. Inside, I knew that the course of the rest of my life and that of my kids' lives would depend on the outcome of the next few moments.

The rule book was duly consulted, and after much discussion it was determined that Linda and I should draw lots to determine which candidate went forward to the final round. Neither Linda nor I thought this was a good plan or a sensible way to resolve the matter. I took her to one side to discuss it with her. We both thought drawing lots was a daft way to conclude matters, and wondered whether the members couldn't be asked which one of us they wanted to go forward into the final round.

Some of the members had already left so that was out of the question, and anyway rules, as they say, are rules. The drawing of lots it was. However, the rules didn't specify who was to draw the first lot – so we then entered into a farcical discussion about whether we should draw lots to see who got to draw the first lot. Nerves were starting to fray. Richard looked on impassively, waiting to see what happened and who his opponent would be in the final round.

The 'lots' consisted of two small identical white pieces of paper: one had the word 'win' written on it, the other simply said 'lose'. I decided I would grasp the nettle and I said to Linda firmly but politely, 'Linda, you choose whether you want to draw first or second.' She was happy to proceed and reached into the ballot box to pick one out.

Events seemed now to be moving in very slow motion. I thought some of the observers were going to pass out with the stress, never mind us candidates. Jon Wheale raised his eyebrows and shot me a look, which basically said 'Bloody hell . . .'

Linda took her piece of paper out. She paused. She unfolded it, slowly. She paused. She read it. She digested the information. She held up the small piece of paper for all to see. I could barely bring myself to look at it. It said 'lose'.

I was determined to retain my composure. This was an important process and I wanted to treat it with the dignity and respect I thought it deserved. But that was hard to do when all I really wanted to do was punch the air in celebration.

But it was not over yet. Given that Linda had drawn the 'lose' lot, I assumed we were then moving straight on to the final round, but I was still required to take out the other piece of paper, which I did. I unfolded it and held it up so it could be seen and read. It said 'win'. Linda very graciously shook my hand, said 'good luck', and with a dignified smile she withdrew to the corner of the room.

It still wasn't over, and at this stage my nerves were starting to fray. I was pretty confident that having jumped over that hurdle things would now be OK, but you never know for sure.

I attempted to present an air of calm. There was a more than reasonable chance that whoever emerged as the winner in the next few moments would become a Member of Parliament.

There was a pause, just to allow everyone a moment to regain their composure. All of Linda's votes were put back into the ballot box to be taken out again with third-preference votes being allocated either to Richard or me. As I had thought, nearly all of them came to me and the final official result showed that I had comfortably won by a significant margin. Those of us who were there knew that it had been anything but a comfortable win. It had been epic.

Once the result was re-checked – all of his votes and my votes were counted in order to satisfy the adjudicator that this was the correct result – I was taken back to meet those members who had stayed to hear the result. Richard left looking distraught, while I posed for photos with the many members who were still there. People were warm in their congratulations though many were no doubt surprised that someone who twenty-four hours ago they had not heard of was now their prospective parliamentary by-election candidate.

After a series of photos were taken including one of me drinking tea with members, some of which went straight to the printers so that a leaflet could be ready for the next morning, I was guided into a private room to sit down with the party's regional director, Paul Nicholson, who would be overseeing the campaign.

'Congratulations,' he said, 'I am sure you will be a great candidate and I am looking forward to working with you over the next ... well, however long it takes. But before we get to that, now is the awkward bit I'm afraid. I am required to ask you if there is anything about *you* that I need to know.' He continued, by way of explanation, 'With every by-election there is intense press scrutiny of the candidates. Given the circumstances of this one, that will certainly be the case. The press will dig into your life, so I need to know if there is anything about you, something in your background for instance, that might come out during the campaign. Is there anything I need to be aware of, Dan?'

I was tired and my mind was whirring from the drama and tension of the night. What had happened was only slowly starting to sink in: after many years I was now going to be leaving the Army; I was now a parliamentary candidate; I was going to be contesting a by-election (there was the small matter that there wasn't actually, as yet, a by-election to contest, but we could worry about that in the morning). My life had just dramatically changed. I needed to talk to the kids about all of this. Although clearly I had thought about it and what it would mean for us as a family, this moment had arrived much quicker than I had antici-pated, and it was taking me a while to process.

So I paused. I thought for a moment. I hadn't been expecting an interrogation like this.

'Paul,' I replied eventually, 'I have tried to live the best life I could. There have been tough times, some hard choices, but there is nothing that I am ashamed of.' I drew breath. Took another moment. Was there anything in my background that the press could dig up? Shenanigans from university, big nights out in the Army? Was there anything? 'Ah, there is one thing that I should probably make you aware of.'

I could see Paul tense at these words as he readied himself for me to reveal some unspeakable skeleton in my cupboard.

'The thing is, Paul ... well, you know I lost Caroline and it's been hard ... and just recently ... I hadn't planned for this to happen ... but I met someone. She is called Rachel. It's very early days and we're still getting to know each other ... but I like her. A lot.'

Paul took this in his stride. 'I'm really pleased for you, Dan, and to be honest a bit relieved that's all you have to admit. Don't forget, I have had quite a few of these conversations over the years!'

The local and regional press were gathered downstairs and I was told it would be very useful if I went and had a word with them. I thought I should probably inform the Army chain of command ASAP, so I asked Jon Wheale to call the MoD duty press officer, who was to say the least bemused by the news. I was keen to get back to the hotel with Jon and Stephen as there was now an awful lot I had to do, not least the sorting out of childcare, but I was already the candidate so I spoke to the press under the watchful eye of the party press officer. I managed not to say anything daft, but my brain was addled with tiredness and I was keen to get away for a cup of tea and to reflect on what had just happened.

'OK Paul, so when does the campaign start?' I asked before leaving, expecting to be told to go back home, have a rest, get myself sorted out ...

'Briefing at seven thirty in the morning,' Paul replied. 'Early campaign session straight after you've been live on BBC Radio Sheffield at ten past eight. Now, get yourself back to the hotel, we've got a busy time ahead.'

'OK ...' I said.

We went back to the hotel, exhausted but elated. Somehow we had pulled it off.

The next few weeks were a whirlwind of canvassing sessions overseen by Tom Watson, who was our political lead for the by-election. A week later, the sitting MP announced his intention to step down and we formally launched our campaign in a freezing-cold car park with Ed Balls and two mocked-up plastic petrol cans (as part of a national crusade about fuel duty). Who said politics was glamorous? Our industrious field coordinator, Gordon Patterson, named our campaign Operation Honeybadger. The honeybadger became our mascot: though it looks cute enough it is absolutely ferocious, and it demonstrated our resolve to fight for every single vote.

An old friend from the south-west, Kamella Hopkins, came to help us out. Nothing, and I mean nothing, fazed her. She organised my packed diary and many of the campaign events with a military precision. She made sure everything ran like clockwork. We had decided that because I wasn't a local, I needed to get out and meet as many people as I possibly could. Rather than wait for them to come to us, we would go to them. And we did. To their doorsteps. Each day we spent hours knocking on doors, meeting people locally and talking to them about the forthcoming by-election. We walked miles and miles each day, and I wore out two pairs of shoes.

A number of the conversations I had on those doorsteps

stuck in my mind, one in particular. As I walked up to one door a somewhat dishevelled man ambled out, unshaven, wearing braces and a vest. 'I want to speak with thee about the war,' he said in a broad Barnsley brogue. He talked me through his thoughts on the wars in Iraq and Afghanistan – it was brilliant, incisive analysis. We stood there and talked it through for twenty minutes. My young campaign aides were desperate to move me on, but he wanted to have his say and he wasn't going to be rushed. After a while he sat on a bench in his front garden, and based on the assumption that if you can't beat them, join them, I sat with him. We talked some more. His was wisdom you would perhaps more usually expect from a university professor.

His parting comment, after nearly half an hour, just before turning to wander back inside, was: 'I was going to vote for thee any road. I just wanted to be sure.' You couldn't argue with that.

Most people were friendly, but not everyone. I was doing an event in a library when someone approached me and started shouting at the top of his voice. The shouting seemed particularly unnerving in a library – as a society we have been conditioned that you can shout at a football match but not in a library. The shouted accusations were that I was a murderer. I initially assumed that this was a critique of my former service, but no, the individual in question held a grudge about the treatment of a close relative by the NHS. He believed the previous government, and me by association, was responsible for her death.

Out of the door of another house shot one man who told me, in a very aggressive and confrontational way, that he would not be voting for me because I was, as he put it, 'a scab' – a reference to me having been born in Nottingham. I think he thought his obnoxious tone would send me packing. He was wrong. I calmly pointed out that I was in short trousers when the miners' strike took place and that it might be more sensible to judge me on my values and views rather than on the place of my birth. He wasn't to be placated, and stormed back inside.

Most people, though, were a delight – straight-talking Yorkshire folk – and very quickly the place came to feel like home. My Army background was a massive help. People were interested in it; they wanted to talk about it, know more about it. Barnsley, a former coal mining town, is a close-knit community where people are extremely proud of the Armed Forces and proud of their family members who have served in it.

In such a community it quickly got round that I was a widower and a lot of people asked me about that, as well as sharing their own experiences of bereavement. I had countless conversations with older women in particular about their grief and sense of loss after forty, fifty, even sixty years of marriage. Some of those conversations were heartbreaking, as people poured out their hearts about losing their partner after so many years together.

Although Barnsley has a very strong Labour tradition, it wasn't an easy time to fight the by-election, not least because of the expenses scandal, which had gathered huge national attention. Politics and politicians were very unpopular, and I had that explained to me in no uncertain terms by many people. 'You're all the same. In it for what you can get out of it. What's the point of voting for any of you? Nothing ever changes.' I heard words like these many times. The fact that their local MP was heading to prison for his expenses claims gave people a focus to channel their anger, and to combat the prevailing mood of distrust we made sure that we ran a very strong, clear campaign, articulating a series of simple messages that spoke about the challenges people were facing in their everyday lives. We took nothing for granted.

We were besieged by visitors and supporters from right across the country, and though the snow and the rain came down we battled on through the elements. I remember one door-knocking session in driving sleet; it was pitch black and we were freezing and soaked to the skin, but we kept knocking on doors. None of the brilliant volunteers who were out with us suggested that we stop, so we just kept going, and people quickly saw that we meant business.

I kept in constant touch with the kids, who were being looked after by grandparents. They came up to visit a few times, and I went down to see them. There was little time to start planning for life on the other side of the election, and although I was obviously hopeful that we would win and I would be elected, I was careful to assume nothing. I knew that if I became the MP I wanted to relocate our family home to Barnsley and make an entirely fresh start, but I had to get elected first.

The night before polling day I was asked to say a few words to all the assembled volunteers who had turned up to help. After thanking them all from the bottom of my heart for their efforts, I couldn't resist a quip about how it was good to be able to give an eve-of-battle speech knowing that nobody would be firing at us the next day. While it got a good laugh on the night, it was comically undermined the next morning when, while out campaigning, we came under fire from a hail of eggs thrown from a passing car.

Polling day is the longest day. Volunteers were out before dawn delivering 'today is polling day' leaflets and we had lots of helpers out knocking on doors, reminding people to vote. When the polls closed at 10 p.m. I went for a shower, then Paul Nicholson drove me to the count, which was taking place at the Barnsley Metrodome leisure centre. There in a line-up to greet me were my family and many friends from the Army who had come to support me. Because of the unique set of circumstances surrounding my departure from the Army – nobody else in living memory had resigned a commission in order to contest a by-election – my discharge had been timed for midnight on polling day. I observed the moment, the transition from soldier to civilian. Also from employed to unemployed, though I hoped that would be rectified within an hour or two.

The piles of votes being stacked beside my name boded well, as did the number of reassuring comments about them weighing not counting the votes, and at about 1.45 a.m. I, Paul, the other candidates and their election agents were gathered together by the returning officer to be shown the provisional result. I had received 14,274 votes and had been elected with an increased majority of 11,771, despite the reduced turn-out you always get with a by-election. All the candidates were invited up on to a stage for the official declaration.

I stood on that stage looking out at the assembled crowds, wondering what Caroline would have made of it all. I knew she would have been proud. I could see the kids' faces beaming out at me – mostly because they were being allowed to stay up so late, but also because they too were proud. It had not dawned on them – maybe not even on me yet – that this was a very big moment for us: the end of the old era, the beginning of a new one. Life would never be the same again.

Having read out the results, the returning officer's speech ended with the words 'and I can now declare that the said Dan Jarvis has been duly elected to serve as the Member of Parliament for Barnsley Central'. The place erupted with cheers. I could see three friends from the Army clapping at the back of the hall. I made a short speech thanking all those who had helped, but above all the people of Barnsley for placing their faith and trust in me and for giving me the opportunity to serve them. The defeated British National Party (BNP) candidate insisted she be given the opportunity to speak and made some ill-judged remarks that were ignored by all other than the tiny clique of support she had brought with her.

As the proceedings were brought to an end, I was rushed straight off to do live TV interviews and spent the next hour talking to journalists. By about 3 a.m. I was able to join everyone at the end-of-campaign party and thank them all for their magnificent efforts. I spent the weekend with the kids, talking them through it all and getting them to understand that this wasn't just like another Army posting, I had actually now left the Army and had been elected to Parliament. After some urgent childcare organisation I found myself walking over Westminster Bridge on the Monday morning accompanied by Rachel. It was a wonderful spring morning and we took our time, enjoying the stunning views and savouring the moment.

It had been agreed that the British Forces Broadcasting Service (BFBS) would film my arrival at the House of Commons. I said goodbye to Rachel, and seeing the cameras, walked towards them so they could get the shots they wanted of me heading into Parliament. Before I got to them a great hulking man appeared from nowhere, leapt on top of me and gave me a massive bear hug. I was initially thinking 'What on earth is happening here?', but he just wanted to congratulate me on being elected. It gave BFBS a more interesting shot than had I just strolled in.

I walked up to Black Rod's entrance, where a policeman

was stood, and readied myself to explain who I was. I reached for some photo ID, but before I could get it out, the policeman gave me a cheery greeting and ushered me in with the words, 'Congratulations on your election, Mr Jarvis.' A small but rather grand-looking side door opened, and there on the other side was the Opposition Chief Whip, Rosie Winterton, with a beaming smile on her face.

'In you come,' she said.

I walked in, and the door closed behind me.

# The Other Side

## *June 2016*

—

Thursday, 16 June 2016 started off like a normal working day – albeit unusually for a weekday, and amid the ongoing European Union referendum campaign, I had grabbed half an hour to meet Rachel for a coffee at the Rob Royd farm shop in Barnsley. Sat there, I received a WhatsApp message informing me about press reports that Jo Cox MP had been attacked, twenty miles up the road in her West Yorkshire constituency. I'd known Jo from before she had been elected to Parliament and she had become a close friend, so I immediately messaged her to check she was OK. There was no reply. I was quickly filled with a terrible dread about what might have happened, and as the afternoon unfolded my worst fears were realised. At 6 p.m., West Yorkshire Police confirmed that Jo had been killed.

That night a vigil took place in St Peter's Church in Birstall. With sensitivity and compassion the Bishop of Leeds, Nick Baines, tried to comfort a packed congregation.

I sat and listened in stunned silence with Rachel and fellow MPs Yvette Cooper, Rachel Reeves, Mary Creagh, Caroline Flint, Naz Shah and Judith Cummings. As we walked out of the church in the late evening dusk we were confronted by a wall of photographers snapping pictures of us, their flash bulbs illuminating our tear-stained faces. In that moment the anger I had felt all those years before in Afghanistan returned, just like with Hama back in Helmand – anger at what had been done to wonderful Jo and to her family.

Ten months later I had just voted in Parliament and was about to walk back to my office when one of the door-keepers told me that Parliament was now in 'lockdown'. Four people had just been killed on Westminster Bridge and PC Keith Palmer had been stabbed to death defending Parliament. MPs were kettled in the chamber, not allowed to leave, and left wondering and worrying about what was happening. The spirit of the Blitz kicked in and I stood talking to Dennis Skinner, him reminiscing about his many years in Parliament. But while listening to Dennis I also thought about the life and the risks that I thought, and hoped, I had left behind.

It's now nine years since that door closed behind me and I first entered Parliament. Ten years since Caroline died. Thirteen years since our time in Helmand. I've learned and re-learned such a lot over that period, with much of what I'd known from serving in the Army being confirmed by service in politics, not least the importance of moral purpose. That as a leader you need to give a firm lead, give clarity to what you're trying to achieve and unite your team around a common purpose. Set your moral compass at the outset and march purposefully on that bearing. People will follow if there's a clear direction of travel. Get it right and you will be successful; get it wrong and you will be unsuccessful.

Over the years I have also often been reminded that culture beats strategy. Every time. You can have all the genius plans and flow charts you like, but in the end it is about what you actually do, not just what you say. People rightly judge by deeds, not words. Often it won't be easy. People, events, stuff will get in your way, there will be all sorts of frustrations and frictions, but show a clear lead and some courage and kindness and you'll at least be heading in the right direction. It is also crucial never to lose sight of the importance of good morale, having the will and determination to succeed and make things happen. Other factors are important, including ensuring that those around you enjoy good mental health, and if not that they get the support they need. Ultimately, if people believe in what they're doing, are inspired by good leadership and are committed to the cause, getting things done will be so much easier.

In different places and at different times, when I've been confronted by difficult challenges, whether that be in a military or civilian context, I've always found the best way through it is to take that moment to assess things – your Condor moment – and then break down what you want to achieve into smaller, manageable, bite-size chunks. Week by week. Day by day. Hour by hour if necessary. Sometimes step by step. Delegate where you can and take your time to work your way through it. It might be a professional challenge, it may be a personal one. Grief, for example, affects people in different ways. People find different ways around and through it. It's tough, but it can be done.

While the world is an increasingly complex place, some things remain simple, and I've also often been reminded about the basic importance of treating people decently and with respect. Being polite literally costs nothing. Take a moment to listen to what people have to say. Cooperate and compromise where necessary and then drive on and deliver. I've also learned about the importance of hope. Hope is the fuel that powered me through the tough times – hope that we would come through it together, and hope that we would get to a better place.

I said at the beginning of this book that there were two questions I was most frequently asked. What was it like at the sharp end of the Army? How did you cope with losing your wife? I think I've answered those questions, but people also often ask if I miss serving in the Army. My response is to say that I don't have much time to miss it and I'm lucky to be doing what I do now. That's true, but it's also true that there are aspects of the military life that I do miss. Above all, I miss being part of a team where people pull together, where they roll their sleeves up and get on with accomplishing challenging tasks. Yes, there was sometimes a bit of ego, a bit of thrusting, but never the wasteful and self-indulgent backbiting you too often find in our political culture.

I also said at the beginning that this book has been difficult to write. It has, partly because of the constraints of time, but mostly because it's meant that after all those years and all those different experiences I've finally stopped to open up the coping box. There was a lot in it! I am relieved to have got it off my chest, and I feel better for doing so. I wouldn't necessarily recommend the coping box as a strategy for others, but it somehow saw me through the toughest of times.

It feels as if a lot has happened over recent years. Of course I think about Caroline a lot. I will always remember what a wonderful person she was, and she lives on through our son and daughter. But after the tragedy of bereavement I was incredibly fortunate to meet Rachel. She is an amazing woman, and we married in 2013 and had a little girl, who is absolutely adored by her older brother and sister. I also think about the time I spent in Afghanistan; it's never far from my thoughts. I try to draw strength from it now and regularly remind myself that if I could get through that, I can get through whatever nonsense I'm contending with today.

A lot has also happened to others in the book. My old Colour Sergeant and mentor Frank Gargan has only just retired from the Army after serving for forty years. At a recent reunion of our platoon from Sandhurst he was rightly feted as someone who had set us out on the right course, who had invested in us so that we had the right skills and values to begin our service. You never forget a good teacher and I know that his advice and wisdom were instrumental in me being able to navigate the challenges I faced.

I'm proud that the SFSG unit at St Athan has gone from strength to strength. Despite the initial challenges of bedding-in the unit – those office politics – they are now firmly a part of the furniture and there to stay. It was a moment of real satisfaction when I recently heard someone who had previously been sceptical of the concept saying that the SFSG had been so successful that it needed to be expanded.

David Blakeley left the Army and has become a very successful international male model! He lives a glamorous life, has published a book about his service, and was briefly married to Jodie Kidd. As I work my way through my constituency surgery on a Friday evening, dealing with a diz-zying range of different subjects that often include parking and dog fouling, I will occasionally pause to look on social media to see what he's been up to. He's often at some glitzy party in an exotic location surrounded by super-trendy friends. I wouldn't swap places with him but sometimes when he asks me which one of us made the smartest choice when we left the Army, it takes me a few moments before I tell him it was me.

Andy Agombar, my hero who operated on Caroline and treated us with such sensitivity and compassion, continues to do extraordinary life-saving work as a surgeon.

Martin Hewitt, who was shot in Afghanistan, has long battled against the debilitating effects of serious injury, but despite that recently summited Mount Everest.

Corporal Kevin Mulligan, who served with such distinction on our 2007 deployment to Helmand, returned in 2009. He was tragically killed alongside two fellow paratroopers when the vehicle they were travelling in was hit by an explosion. He died as he had lived. Fearlessly.

Tom Tugendhat, who came down from the British HQ in Kabul to support us at Pluto, is now a Conservative MP and Chair of the House of Commons Foreign Affairs Committee.

Harry Parker, who lost his legs in Afghanistan and cheered me up in the aftermath of Caroline's death, is now a successful artist and author.

I don't know what happened to the Afghan soldiers and the terps I served alongside in Helmand, though I often wonder. I've never been back, but hope that one day I will.

So that is it, the end. I hope it's been useful and that it will focus your mind on what is really important in your life: what you want to do and who and what you care about. Times can and will be tough. Love, life and death, and all the stuff in between, will present challenges, and opportunities. But if you keep calm, keep going and, where you can, keep a smile on your face, it's remarkable what can be achieved. And if all else fails, put the kettle on and have a hot brew. It always helps.

# Acknowledgements

All the difficult things I've ever done have reinforced my belief in the importance of good teamwork. This book has been a team effort and I want to send my heartfelt thanks to all those who have supported me through what has at times felt like a long and torturous process!

I might not have started writing it in the first place had it not been for the encouragement of my long-suffering but always patient agent, Kate Barker. I am grateful for all her advice, reassurance and good sense. Alan Johnson and David Putnam both provided much-needed inspiration, and Richard Beswick, Nithya Rae, Daniel Balado, Grace Vincent, Linda Silverman and the team at Little, Brown have all been superb. I also want to thank those in the MoD and at the Regimental Headquarters of The Parachute Regiment who went through the text with a fine-tooth comb and made a number of very helpful suggestions.

I feel particularly indebted to those I had the privilege of serving with in the Army, especially the paratroopers in my Regiment who I soldiered alongside on operations. The Afghanistan tour of 2007 remains the toughest of tasks and I will forever be humbled by the stoicism, character, professionalism, loyalty and good humour shown by the officers and soldiers of the B Company group.

It is always invidious to pick out individuals, but my service was enriched by friendships with Giles Griffiths, Jon Wheale, Mark Thackstone, John Catto, Frank Gargan, David Blakeley, Nick Wight-Boycott, John Lorimer, Ed Sandry, Zac Stenning, Andy Redding, Matt Cansdale, James Everard, Mike and Sarah Jackson, James Cameron, Andy Wareing, Lee Elliot and many others, who all helped me through the tumultuous times.

I am also extremely grateful to those who have supported me on the other side. First and foremost, my brilliant constituents in Barnsley and South Yorkshire for giving me the opportunity to serve them. Friends in the House of Commons as well as the excellent Doorkeepers of the Houses of Parliament and the fabulous Chaplain, Rose Hudson-Wilkin. My local constituency party deserve my gratitude for their support, in particular my agent, Trevor Cave, local councillors led by Steve Houghton, and the volunteers who give up their precious time to get involved and turn out whatever the weather to knock on doors and deliver leaflets. They are heroes. As are the wonderful Mel Dyke, Rita Britton, Jenny Platts, Kathy Bostwick, Sharon Howard and Jim Andrews, Joe Hayward, Alice Cave, Margaret Bruff, Sarah Tattersall, Sarah Heaton, Margaret and Tom Sheard, Beryl Oldroyd, Dave Leech, Phil Watson and Caroline Makinson. All inspirational, and formidable!

I also want to acknowledge the incredible support I have had from those who have worked in my constituency, parliamentary and mayoral offices. There's a lot of drivel talked about what MPs actually do. The reality is that every day we are deluged with a dizzying range of urgent and important things to do. It's only made just about possible because of the dedication and service of those who don't occupy the limelight but do the lion's share of the work. I have been extremely fortunate to have been exceptionally well supported.

It is again invidious to pick out individuals, but there are a few friends in political service who deserve special thanks: Kamella Hudson (née Hopkins), Paul Nicholson, Eric Joyce, Stephen Carter, UNISON, Mollie Sheerien, Nikki Belfield, Rebecca Varley, Nick Button, Kellie Foster, James Higginbottom, Chris Stephenson, Laura Howard, Lucy Turner, Richard Mitchell, Trevor Chinn, Sug Sahadevan, Martin Taylor and many others who have all, in different ways and at different times, been sources of strength and wise counsel. Owen Pritchard and Peter Hearn have been outstanding friends. I also want to put on record how proud I am to be an honorary patron of the world-class Barnsley Youth Choir. Working with Mat Wright, Anne Wroe, Yvonne Worsley and the incredible team of volunteers has been a delight.

Finally, my family. My parents and step-parents, my grandparents, my brother, and wider family have always been a source of support and calm continuity. Caroline's parents and brothers are wonderful people. And of course Caroline, and Rachel and my three kids – their unstinting love and good humour has been the greatest pleasure of all.

# Index